MILWAUKEE STREETS:

THE STORIES BEHIND THEIR NAMES

MILWAUKEE STREETS:

THE *STORIES* BEHIND THEIR *NAMES*

CARL BAEHR

CREAM CITY PRESS

Milwaukee

MILWAUKEE STREETS:
THE STORIES BEHIND THEIR NAMES

Cataloging in Publication Data

Baehr, Carl
Milwaukee streets: the stories behind their names/Carl Baehr.

ISBN 0-9640204-4-0
1. Street names–Wisconsin–Milwaukee–History–Dictionaries. 2. Milwaukee (Wis.)--Street names–History–Dictionaries.
F589.M6 B3 1994 94-94149
917.77595

Editor: Ellen Baehr.
Cover designer: Molly Quirk, Montgomery Media, Inc.
Indexer: Darlene Waterstreet, Badger Infosearch.
Non-credited photos by Carl Baehr.

To Ellen,
who made it possible

To Patricia,
who would have enjoyed it

And to Joanne, Carl, and Daniel.

TABLE OF CONTENTS

Introduction

Scope

This book includes a listing for all public streets in the city of Milwaukee. It does not include private streets (except Water Tower Road, which is used by the public) and excludes two streets which are considered public right of ways but do not really exist; James Street (it's under Doyne Park) and Sterling Place (it's part of a parking lot). Many suburban street names are included by virtue of the fact that they have street names in common with Milwaukee.

Overview of the city's street naming

When the founders of the three competing villages that became Milwaukee named their streets in the mid-1830s, they intentionally used street names that differed from one another. And when new street names were added by land speculators and real estate developers, they often made no effort to integrate them with any of the three existing schemes.

During the 19th century, city officials made an occasional attempt to eliminate some duplicate street names, but by the 1900s Milwaukee's street name system was a mess. For the uninitiated, finding their way through the city was difficult at best. There were many duplications, and even triplications of names. And there was no system of house numbering or directional prefixes to help, as there are now.

Another problem was the lack of continuity in street names. Crossing a bridge could bring a name change. Sixth Street became First Avenue when traversing the Menomonee River Valley, and Wisconsin and Grand were names for the same street on either side of the Milwaukee River. A river wasn't a necessity for a name change, they occurred all over the city without rhyme or reason.

There were calls for a uniform naming system as early as 1868, and complaints by delivery people and visitors new to the city grew over the years. At the turn of century, postmasters throughout the country began demanding that cities eliminate street naming roadblocks to easy mail distribution. In 1913, Milwaukee made its first attempt when a commission was appointed to study the problem and offer solutions. They looked at three street naming systems.

The New York scheme calls for numbering of all streets. Those in one direction are called Avenues while those in the other direction are Streets. This was the naming plan used in the Northpoint neighborhood in the early 1870s. At that time, Farwell through Summit Avenues were known as First through Fifth Avenues, while Irving through Ivanhoe Places were called First through Sixth Streets.

The Boston system is just the opposite, using only names. Because there is no grid pattern to its streets, numbering them would only cause confusion. This is the system used in some of Milwaukee's newer neighborhoods, like Wedgewood and Pheasant Run. These developments have only curving streets which don't follow a geometric pattern.

The commission recommended using the Philadelphia scheme, which is a combination of the two systems. The streets are numbered in one direction and named in the other. This system was already in place on both the North and South Sides, but unfortunately the numbered streets didn't line up properly. Ideally, the named streets would follow an alphabetical sequence across town, a plan never considered in Milwaukee.

The commission also recommended street names to be eliminated and to be added, but in a city not known for hasty action, nothing was done, at least not right away. A lot of people thought changes were necessary but almost no one wanted their street name to change. And none did change.

In 1921 another commission was formed. This one came up with similar recommendations for a naming scheme. It was their plan to use 6th Street as the east/west dividing line and Wisconsin Avenue as the north/south dividing line. But the City Engineer wanted to use the Menomonee River Valley as the north/south border and the Milwaukee River downtown as the east/west baseline. He argued that his plan would be less expensive because the North Side numbered streets would remain the same, reducing the need for new street signs. Because of the impasse, Mayor Daniel Hoan disbanded the commission and ordered that the City Engineer draw up a plan for change.

The City Engineer's plan, using many of the name changes recommended by the second commission, was accepted in 1926. After years of threats, tears, complaints, petitions, discussions, and compromise, the changes began. By 1930, most duplicates had been eliminated, sound-alike names reduced, and street names carried through from one side of town to the other. A house numbering system was put in place, with Canal Street dividing north from south and 1st Street separating east from west.

To assure that there would be uniformity in the future, the City Engineer's Office assumed the street naming responsibilities that had been in the domain of real estate developers. As new areas were developed or annexed by the city, names were selected or changed as necessary. But the City Engineer's Department lost the right to name streets in the mid-1960s, when alderman took over the responsibility.

Since then enough deviations from the system have crept in to cause the people who worked for decades to assure uniformity in Milwaukee street naming to turn in their graves. Aldermen have named Park Place on the Northwest Side, a duplicate of Northpoint's Park Place. A portion of Mound Street has been renamed Marina Drive. And what should be known as Clybourn Street has been named McAuley Place.

Street names

Solomon Juneau and Morgan L. Martin named many of their streets using a practice begun fifty years earlier, as a result of the Revolutionary War. Prior to war with England, streets were rarely named for people, except for royalty. Most were named for features or occupations or destinations or trees, but not for individuals.

Because independence changed that, many Juneautown streets carried the names of people, many of them living. Cass, Mason, Jackson, and Van Buren were among the city's first street names. Across the river, Byron Kilbourn was following the time-honored tradition of using tree names for the streets, along with the names of his associates, Clybourn, Wells, and Vliet. In Walker's Point the streets were named for states and for George Walker and his associates. During the rest of the century, the majority of new street names were names of people, often developers and their families. Others were named for presidents, Civil War generals, and Milwaukee business leaders. Still more surnames were added as the city expanded and farms were broken up for subdivisions, with the resulting streets named for the former owners.

Most of the rest of the streets were named for places or features. The names of the Great Lakes were a common theme, as were the names of cities. Many roads were named for their destinations, such as Fond du Lac, Beloit, and Blue Mound. More exotic placenames, like Congo, Tripoli, and Klondike, were used toward the end of the century. Among the streets named for features were Pier, Ferry, Lake, Water, and Orchard.

In a unique move, the city renamed Northpoint's Fourth, Fifth, and Sixth Streets for the Walter Scott novels *Woodstock*, *Kenilworth*, and *Ivanhoe* in the 1870s. Developers gave some streets the names of literary and mythical figures like Columbia, Concordia, Achilles, and Uncas.

The late 1880s saw a trend toward using the more prestigious "Avenue" instead of "Street" in new names. In the same vein, this era also gave the first of the compound promotional names, like Fairmount, Fernwood, and Glendale. Many others of this sort were to be added in the 1900s, names like Woodlawn, Rosedale, Kenwood, Edgewood, Pinecrest, Elmhurst, Norwood, and Avondale.

The 1920s renaming program added many new surnames to the city's map, mostly those of men who had been prominent in civic affairs. There was little land development and few new streets named during the Depression and World War II, but the 1950s and 1960s saw a boom in new street names. While surnames were still used (city employees Edward Petersik and Donald Sleske, Archbishop Kiley, and Admiral Halsey were among those honored at the time), the trend was toward more pleasing sounding names like Harvest, Jewell, Villa, and Terra. Because Finley Fisler of the City Engineer's Office was interested in the West, many streets were named for cities of the western United States. Feminine names were given to other streets.

Aldermen assumed the responsibility for naming streets in the 1960s and they have continued to name streets for people. Streets bearing the names of their relatives, business associates, and community leaders have been added since then.

Street name research

Maps of subdivisions, called "plat maps" where they are located at the Register of Deeds Office in the Milwaukee County Courthouse, are the single most important resource in Milwaukee street name research. The maps include the names of those who developed the land, surveyed the plat, witnessed the transaction, and gave municipal approval to it.

So when Reichert Place shows up for the first time in a subdivision developed by Conrad and Joseph Reichert, or when Trowbridge Street initially appears in a development that was surveyed by William Trowbridge, or when Townsend Street originated in a land transaction witnessed by Hamilton Townsend, or when City Clerk George G. Dousman's name appears on the approval of the plat that includes Dousman Street, there is little doubt why the street carries the name that it does.

These maps also show the dates that the people involved signed the document. This date can misprove some commonly held assumptions regarding who a street was named for. For example, Benjamin Weil, a real estate dealer in the late 19th century, could not have been honored by having Weil Street named for him. The plat map shows that the street was named in 1857, when Benjamin was only seven years old and a resident of Baltimore. Wilson Street in Bay View has been said to memorialize Woodrow Wilson. But it was named in 1883, thirty years before Wilson was inaugurated as president.

After plat maps, street naming ordinances are the next most important resource. Municipalities rename streets, or sometimes give them their original names, and ordinances and related records tell when these streets were named. Although very few ordinances explain why a name was chosen, the date of the naming may provide a clue. For example, Logan Avenue, Everett Street, and Cleveland Avenue were all named within months of the deaths of national figures bearing those names.

The street naming policy of the City of Milwaukee helps solve the mystery of who some streets are named for. The policy states that streets can only be named for people involved in civic affairs. The policy prefers dead people, or at least those over seventy years old, to assure that no disgrace falls on a street name. This policy was apparently in effect, at least unofficially, throughout most of this century. When streets were given new names during the 1920s renaming program, many of the names that showed up on the new city map were those of Milwaukeeans of a previous generation, like Ely, Somers, and Peck.

The Legislative Reference Bureau at the Milwaukee City Hall retains all of the ordinances that named Milwaukee streets. But the ordinances of nearby communities need also be inspected because Milwaukee, as it expanded, assumed street names from neighboring communities like Cudahy and Whitefish Bay. The same is true of the records of annexed communities like Bay View and North Milwaukee, as well as the extinct towns (Lake, Granville, etc.) because they all named streets.

The Mapping and Drafting Section of the City Engineer's Department has kept a card file on street name origins and is a good source of information on streets named during the last forty years or so. A similar card file at the Legislative Reference Bureau was apparently instituted as a Depression era WPA project, but much of the information is suspect.

Land ownership maps, most of them from the 19th century, are useful tools. These maps show the names of the owners of farm land and can indicate for whom roads that became city streets are named. The best sources for these maps are the Milwaukee Public Library, the Milwaukee County Historical Society, and the American Geographic Society collection at Golda Meir Library.

The Milwaukee Sentinel Index from 1837 to 1890 at the Milwaukee Public Library provides access to a great deal of background information on the people who had streets named for them and sometimes indicates why a street has its name. Newspaper articles from a variety of local newspapers, and there have been many, also help to fill in the gaps. Generally, articles that present the news are useful, while those that give a reporter's ''historical'' overview of street name origins are less helpful.

City and county directories, census records, local histories, and biographies available at local libraries and historical societies are also valuable. For example, Ruby Avenue was platted by Charles Seefeld. Directories of the time show that Seefeld's daughter's name was Ruby. The biography of John Holt informs us that he is the J. Holt that Holt Avenue is named for.

A variety of other records can also be useful. The naturalization records at the Milwaukee County Historical Society Library show that the first name of B. Woelky, the owner of land where Bernhard Place was later developed, was Bernhard. The incorporation records in the Society's collection show that one of the directors of the Fond du Lac and Burleigh Land Company, which named Senator Avenue, was Christian Koenitzer. The *Wisconsin Blue Book* shows that Koenitzer was a state senator at the time. The personal papers of John Johnston, who platted Hilda, Dorothy, and Frederica Places, can be found at the Area Research Center in the Golda Meir Library. They show that Hilda was his daughter, Dorothy his niece, and Frederica, whom he called Freddie, was his sister-in-law.

Interviews with current and former city employees, officials, and developers shed light on other street names. There are no records that say that Renee Street was named for the daughter of former alderman Robert Ertl, or that Callahan Place was named for a friend of alderman William Drew.

Visiting the site where the street name was first used can be revealing. It is apparent to the observer that the Notre Dame tower at Mount Mary College was the inspiration for the naming of Tower View Boulevard, and that Hillcrest Avenue really does run over a hill.

For street names that remain a mystery, there may be information available which could de-mystify them. Perhaps there is a genealogy that would tell us why Hans Gosch named Christine Lane in 1856. Or maybe someone has personal knowledge as to why Gertrude Drive was named in 1954. If anyone knows of or has any information of this kind, I would be interested in hearing about it. Please contact Carl Baehr, 3011 E. Cudahy Avenue, St. Francis, WI 53235, (414) 483-4202.

Acknowledgments

Any thank you's for help with this book must begin with Ellen Baehr. I would not have had time for the research and writing of eight hundred street names had I been working full-time. Ellen provided the financial support for the project. Her job enabled me to work on the book while working part-time as a librarian at the St. Francis Public Library. For giving me this once-in-a-lifetime research opportunity, I am forever grateful.

Ellen also walked, bicycled, or drove over many of the city's streets with me in an attempt to understand their name origins. On many of her evenings and days off she helped me research at libraries and historical societies. She spent a lot of time listening to me give evidence for street name origins and then offered suggestions for more research.

Ellen edited the manuscript and proof-read it and then proof-read it again. She offered advice in all phases of the project, advice that I was happy to have. There would be no book without Ellen, not in this century anyway.

At Milwaukee City Hall I would like to thank: Bob Steege and Tom Staats of the City Engineer's Department; Pamela Booth, Eileen Bartness, Linda Elmer, and Mary Lohmeier of the Legislative Reference Bureau; Jack Goboury, Betty Becker, Lynn Bridger, Paul Yehle, and Janice Pittner of the City Records Center; and Nancy Torcivia and Roger Rick of the Department of City Development.

Also thanks to Judy Simonsen, Nick Neylon, and Steve Daily of the Milwaukee County Historical Society; and to the staffs of the Register of Deeds Office and the Reference and Law Library at the Milwaukee County Courthouse. Thanks to Virginia Schwartz and the staff of the Milwaukee Public Library Humanities Department.

Special thanks to Helen Hachmeister and the staff at the St. Francis Public Library. And to the employees at UWM's Golda Meir Library, particularly those in the Area Research Center and to Jovanka Ristic of the AGS Map Library. Thanks also to the Public Libraries in West Allis, Wauwatosa, Brown Deer, Franklin, Greenfield, Shorewood, and the North Shore.

Thanks also to Rebecca Roepke of the Cudahy Public Library and to Mimi Bird of the Whitefish Bay Public Library, libraries with excellent local history collections, and to the West Allis Historical Society. Also thanks to Jo Reitman and Rosemary Jensen of the News Information Center at the Milwaukee Journal. Thanks to the staffs in the Clerk's Departments of Oak Creek, Greenfield, Bayside, Brown Deer, Fox Point, and Shorewood.

And finally, thank you to the late Ted Samore, and to Pete Holzhauer, Joe Smetana, Ken Murray, George Olson, Daniel, Carl, and Ghennel Baehr, Joanne and Pete Goodman, Angie Laack, Tim Sharko, Clarence Miller, Linda Vincent, Don Empson, Dick Nelson, and Bill Drehfal.

Carl Baehr
August 1994

KEY TO USE

The neighbor-hood or suburb where the street name be-gan (see Neighborhood Maps). If there is no origin or if it is "Ordinance," no ——————one neighbor-hood was the source of the street name.

ALEXANDER STREET

500 South and 600 West

Origin: *Walker's Point*

Alexander Street was named for six month old Alexander *Nicholas* Sulkowski, the grandson of Robert Sulkowski, an alderman in 1967 when the street was named by ordinance. The one block long criss-crossing streets of Alexander and Nicholas route traffic to and from the south end of the Sixth Street Viaduct. They form one of two intersections in the city named for one person (see *Graham, Wilson*).

Names in italics have their own entries.

xvii

ABBOTT AVENUE

5200 South, between 600 and 2700 West
Origin: *City of Greenfield*

During the street renaming era of the 1920s and 1930s, many new names were chosen to honor prominent past Milwaukeeans, particularly those involved in civic causes. Only one Abbott, Edwin Hale Abbott (also spelled Abbot), fits this description. Abbott, real estate owner and railroad president, was an officer of Associated Charities and the Wisconsin Humane Society, among other benevolent organizations. He died in 1927 at the age of 93.

It is possible though, that the name Abbott, given to this street in 1934, may have been selected solely for its promotional quality. The street was previously called Underwood, a name eliminated because of duplication elsewhere.

ABERT COURT, PLACE

3900 North, between 100 East and 7300 West
Origin: *Arlington Heights*

George Abert, born in the Alsace region of France in 1817, came to Milwaukee when he was 19 years old. His first job was helping Byron *Kilbourn* with land surveys of the area. He eventually found a career in road

1

building and real estate. When Milwaukee moved from village to city status in 1846, Abert was among its first aldermen. During the 1860s and 1870s, he represented the city in the state legislature seven times. He died in 1890. This street was named by his grandson, Byron, in 1916, on land owned by the family.

Jones Island and environs on Increase Lapham's 1856 Map of Milwaukee. (Milwaukee Public Library)

Fifty years earlier there was another Abert Street, but it was named to scorn an Abert, not to memorialize one.

It was because of Lt. J. J. Abert, a government officer, that Great Lakes' vessels could not enter the city's rivers during the first twenty years of its development. Abert had recommended that the harbor entrance be located at the south end, rather than the north end, of the peninsula now known as Jones Island. His plan, which added two-thirds of a mile of marshy river to the journey downtown, made it nearly impossible for lake vessels to reach the city's docks. As a result, there was a need for either small boats to off-load the larger lake craft, or long piers, some extending over one-third of a mile into the lake. In 1857, years of frustration ended when the federal government reversed its decision and cut a channel through the north end of the peninsula, opening a way to the city.

The year before, in 1856, a city ordinance gave birth to the only Milwaukee street name chosen as an insult. The south end of the peninsula, which was really only a sandbar, was named Abert Street, "in perpetual remembrance of his ill-advised location of the harbor." It was a street on paper only, no thoroughfare was ever laid out there (see *Pier*).

ACACIA STREET

6500 North, between 6700 and 9100 West
Origin: *Village of Fox Point*

The Village of Fox Point named this street in 1930. The acacia is a small tree common in the southwestern United States.

ACHILLES STREET

100 East, between 3100 and 3300 North
Origin: *Harambee*

Achilles was a mythical Greek warrior. The naming of this short street may have been inspired by the street adjacent to it, *Concordia* Avenue. Concordia was the Roman goddess of peace and harmony. Achilles Street was platted by John T. Kelly and Edward Burns in 1892.

ADAMS AVENUE, COURT

500 East, between 2700 and 4500 South
Origin: *Bay View*

Adams Avenue was platted in 1909. It is apparently named after President John Adams since the other streets in the Humboldt Park Subdivision (*Quincy* and *Taylor*) allude to presidents.

John Adams, (1735-1826), was the second President of the United States, after having served as George Washington's vice-president. Adams, the father of John Quincy Adams, was a leader of the American Revolution and a signer of the Declaration of Independence. He served as president from 1797 to 1801.

John Adams. (Milwaukee Public Library)

ADLER STREET

400 South, between 5800 and 9500 West
Origin: *Johnson's Woods*

In 1854, at the age of 15, Frederick T. Adler walked from Chicago to Milwaukee, where he started a career in banking and real estate development. He served as alderman during the 1870s and platted this street in 1888. Adler died in 1929 at the age of 90.

3

AHMEDI AVENUE

1900 East, between 3400 and 3500 South
Origin: *City of St. Francis*

From the late 1870s to the early 1890s there were 16 streets named for states and provinces in the Bay View area. As land development extended southward, the place names used for streets became more exotic. In 1892 the St. Francis Heights Subdivision, platted by Henry Niedecken and George Ziegler, added Ahmedi, *Tripoli* and Bombay. Ahmedi is the name of places in Mauritania, Algeria, Turkey, Iran and Kuwait. It means "belonging to a man named Ahmed."

ALABAMA AVENUE

1700 East, between 3400 and 3900 South
Origin: *Bay View*

In 1926 the Savings and Investment Association added Alabama, *Iowa* and *Kansas* to the Bay View map, bringing the community's list of streets named for states to 19. The name Alabama comes from the Choctaw Indian language and means "plant reapers" (see *California, Delaware, Rhode Island*).

ALBANY PLACE

2800 North, between 1300 and 1400 West
Origin: *North Division*

Albany Place is one of the short North Side streets named for cities during the 1920s renaming project. The name was changed from Alten because of its similarity to Bay View's *Ellen* Street. Albany, the capital city of New York State, was named for James II of England, who was formerly James, Duke of York and Albany (see *Geneva*).

4

ALBION STREET

1500 North, between 1300 and 1400 East
Origin: *Lower East Side*

Hugh Ronalds gave the ancient name for England to this street in 1849. Albion is from Latin, meaning "white," for the white chalk cliffs of southeast England that greeted visitors from the continent who were crossing the English Channel at its narrowest point.

The chalk cliffs of southeast England. (Milwaukee Public Library)

ALDRICH STREET

800 East, between 1900 and 2300 South
Origin: *Bay View*

Arthur Aldrich operated an unreliable horse-drawn bus service between Bay View and Milwaukee in the early 1870s. His route, when he showed up, was from the Kinnickinnic River to downtown. His customers complained of being stranded downtown when Aldrich decided to go home before the appointed time. Aldrich said if his customers didn't like his service, they shouldn't use it. So they didn't, and before too long he was driven out of business by a punctual competitor and a new streetcar service.

Aldrich was born in Detroit in 1831 and came to Milwaukee as a five year old. As an adult he worked at quite a few jobs, none of them for very long. He was a fireman for a while, then ran a vegetable stand for a short time. He operated a saloon, where he made news for shooting a patron. After working as a postal agent, he opened another bar, where he was charged with assault. He was a gardener next, and after being fined for driving his wagon too fast, began his erratic bus service. Aldrich followed that with the running of a meat store for a year or two, then finished his career as a deputy sheriff.

Aldrich Street, near his home and the south end of his bus route, was named in 1876 as part of Aldrich's Division.

ALEXANDER STREET

500 South and 600 West
Origin: *Walker's Point*

Alexander Street was named for six month old Alexander *Nicholas* Sulkowski, the grandson of Robert Sulkowski, an alderman in 1967 when the street was named by ordinance. The one block long criss-crossing streets of Alexander and Nicholas route traffic to and from the south end of the Sixth Street Viaduct. They form one of two intersections in the city named for one person (see *Graham, Wilson*).

ALLERTON AVENUE

4500 South, between 100 East/West and 500 West
Origin: *City of Cudahy*

Samuel Waters Allerton, of English ancestry, was born in New York State in 1828. Like most of the men for whom the streets of *Cudahy* were named in 1892, Allerton's career was spent in the meat industry.

Allerton began by raising livestock, then moved on to cattle buying, and finally to the stockyard business, with interests in Chicago, Omaha, and St. Louis. A millionaire, he ran unsuccessfully for Chicago mayor in 1893 as the Republican candidate. He died in 1914. Besides the avenue that Patrick Cudahy called for him, the town of Allerton, Illinois carries his name.

ALLIS STREET

400 East, between 1900 and 2300 South
Origin: *Bay View*

When this street was named in 1870, Edward Phelps Allis' career as an iron manufacturer was in its infancy. Milwaukee's lack of a water system helped propel it to maturity. In 1871 Allis bid on the pumping engines for the system and on the contract to supply the pipe to carry the water, despite the fact that his company did not manufacture pipe. But that proved no problem to Allis, who, when he won the contracts, simply built a pipe producing facility.

Allis, born in New York State in 1824, came to Milwaukee in 1846. He tried both banking and the leather business before he found his niche in iron. Besides his Bay View facility on Allis Street, he had operations in Walker's Point that eventually moved west to the community that bears his name, West Allis. He died in 1889.

Edward Allis. (History of Milwaukee, 1881)

ALLYN STREET, COURT

9100 North, between 8400 and 9700 West
Origin: *North Meadows*

Clarence Miller, alderman on the city's Northwest Side from 1964 to 1978, named this street for his son in 1970. Allyn Miller was born in Milwaukee in 1946 and became the third member of the Miller family to have a street bear his name (see *Andrea*).

Clarence Miller, a native of Crookston, Minnesota, named five Milwaukee streets for members of his family. He was also responsible for honoring old town of Granville settlers by naming newly opened streets on the Northwest Side in their memory (see *Everts*).

ALMA STREET

2000 South, between 800 and 827 West
Origin: *Historic Mitchell Street*

Herman Wootsch, owner of the downtown Menomonee Hotel, named this short street in 1871. Alma was a popular name at the time. The Alma River in the Crimea had gained recognition because it was the site of a major Russian defeat during the Crimean War. Wootsch, born in Prussia in 1822, and probably no friend of Russia, died in 1894.

7

ALOIS STREET

4900 West, between 1000 and 1400 North
Origin: *Wick Field*

Alois Angermaier, who lived nearby, named this street for himself in 1887.

ALVINA AVENUE, COURT

6300 South, between 100 East/West and 2600 West
Origin: *Goldman Park*

Alvina Pfeiffer was the inspiration for this name. She and her husband, Charles H. Pfeiffer, named this street in 1941. Charles worked as an assembler at Galland-Henning Manufacturing Company during World War II and lived on the North Side.

AMY PLACE

From 1700 West and 1900 South to 1600 West and 1950 South
Origin: *Muskego Way*

This short street was known as 17th Street until 1930. The name was changed because the street ran into 16th Street, creating a confusing intersection of 16th and 17th Streets. The reason the name Amy was selected is a mystery.

ANDERSON AVENUE

1900 South, between 100 East/West and 200 East
Origin: *Clock Tower Acres*

A city ordinance changed Wine Street (which was too similar to *Vine* Street) to Anderson Avenue in 1926 as part of the city's street renaming program. It was probably named for William E. Anderson, who was the superintendent of schools and city clerk during the 1880s and 1890s. He was born in England in 1845 and died in Milwaukee in 1903.

ANDOVER ROAD

2600 South, between 5400 and 5700 West
Origin: *Jackson Park*

Andover, England is the source of this name. Andover Road was platted in 1953.

ANDREA STREET

8300 North and 10000 West
Origin: *Riverton Heights*

Andrea Miller, the granddaughter of Clarence Miller, was born in Milwaukee two years before this street was named for her in 1975. Her grandfather was an alderman on the Northwest Side from 1964 to 1978 (see *Angela*).

ANGELA AVENUE, DRIVE

From 9200 North and 8700 West to 9400 North and 7900 West
Origin: *Northridge*

Clarence Miller's granddaughter, Angela Ava Miller, was two years old when this street was named in 1978. Miller was a Northwest Side alderman from 1964 to 1978, a period of growth that included many street naming opportunities. He named streets after family members and old town of Granville settlers (see *Beatrice*).

ANN STREET

10000 West, between 8200 and 8400 North
Origin: *Pheasant Run*

Margaret Ann Wendler worked in the City Engineer's Office in 1963 when this street was named. There already was a street named *Margaret*, so this street was given her middle name.

APPLETON AVENUE, LANE, PLACE

From 2600 North and 5600 West to 6900 North and 12400 West
Origin: *Ordinance*

Before the city's street renaming program began in 1926, there were two parallel roads leading out of town toward the northwest, both called Fond du Lac. One was North *Fond du Lac* and the other was South Fond du

The city of Appleton about the time Appleton Avenue was named. (Milwaukee Public Library)

Lac. In 1926, because of the duplication, and because the new system would not allow a South designation on a North Side street, South Fond du Lac was changed to North Appleton.

The city of Appleton, 38 miles beyond the city of Fond du Lac, was named for Samuel Appleton, a Bostonian and benefactor of that community's institution of higher learning, Lawrence University.

ARCH AVENUE, COURT

8200 North, between 9300 and 10500 West
Origin: *Village of Brown Deer*

Arch was selected as the name for this curving street by developer Francis Schroedel in 1956.

ARCHER AVENUE

2200 South and 300 East
Origin: *Bay View*

Patrick H. Archer lived in Bay View and was the superintendent of the Illinois Leather Company located in the Menomonee Valley. He was a developer of the plat that named this short street in 1880.

10

ARDEN PLACE

4600 North, between 7800 and 8800 West
Origin: *Columbus Park*

The Forest of Arden, in central England, is often portrayed in English literature as a kind of paradise. Arden Place was named in 1927 as part of the Fondale Subdivision.

ARGONNE DRIVE

9600 West, between 3100 and 3334 North
Origin: *Mount Mary*

Argonne, a wooded plateau in northeast France, was the site of World War I battles involving American soldiers. In 1926 the American Legion, which was formed after the war, requested that *Capitol* Drive, then called Lake Road, be named Argonne in honor of the battles. Their request was denied, but they gained some satisfaction in 1933, when the old Town of Wauwatosa changed Harding, a much less significant street, to Argonne.

American artillery at Argonne. (Milwaukee Public Library)

ARIZONA STREET, COURT

2800 South, between 5300 and 6200 West
Origin: *White Manor*

Arizona Street was named in 1942 to fit in with the state name streets that extend into the area from Bay View. One interpretation of the name is that it is the Spanish word for "dry country" (see *California*).

ARLINGTON PLACE

1300 East, between 1600 and 1900 North
Origin: *Lower East Side*

Arlington was the name of the Virginia home of Robert E. Lee before it was made the Arlington National Cemetery toward the end of the Civil War in 1864. Arlington Place was named in 1875 by Henry and George Rogers, both Civil War veterans (see *Forest Home*).

ARMITAGE AVENUE

4600 North, between 6200 and 6300 West
Origin: *Lincoln Creek*

Frederick was the name of this short street, but because it was a duplicate of *Frederick* Avenue on the East Side, it was renamed Armitage Avenue in 1933 by an old Town of Wauwatosa ordinance. Armitage may have been selected simply as a promotional name, or, like many new street names of this era, it may have been named for a prominent past Milwaukeean. If so, William E. Armitage, Episcopal bishop of Wisconsin, would be the Armitage in question. Born in New York in 1830, he was instrumental in the building of All Saints Cathedral in Milwaukee and Kemper Hall in Kenosha before his death at the age of 43.

ARMOUR AVENUE

4500 South, between 300 East and 1600 West
Origin: *City of Cudahy*

Philip Danforth Armour, (1832-1901), most successful of the meatpackers and, in his time, one of America's wealthiest men, got his start in the meat industry in Milwaukee. Born in central New York State, he went to California during the 1849 Gold Rush while still a teenager. In a few years he accumulated over six thousand dollars, not by prospecting for gold, but by supplying miners with water for their gold mining operations.

In the 1850s Armour came to Milwaukee, where his brother Herman was in the grain business. Philip started a soap factory, but after it burned down he became involved in the meatpacking business with John *Plankinton* during the Civil War.

By 1875 Philip had moved on to Chicago, where he built the largest meatpacking and provision business in the world. It was claimed that he was the best known man in Chicago. The company slogan "Armour Feeds the World" was at least partially true as many of its products were exported around the globe.

Armour's success was not the result of learning the business from the bottom up. Armour claimed, "If you show me a piece of meat I could not tell you what part of the bullock it came from." One stockyard owner concurred when he said of Armour, "He don't know a hog from an umbrella."

It made no difference to Patrick *Cudahy*, a former plant superintendent of Armour's, who appreciated Armour's encouragement and advice. When Patrick founded his town of Cudahy in 1892, he honored his mentor with a street name. Because Armour was also a railroad executive, Armour, South Dakota was named for him in 1886.

Philip Danforth Armour. (Armour and His Times)

ARROW STREET

1600 South, between 1700 and 2000 West
Origin: *Muskego Way*

Bow and Arrow Streets were named by developers in 1855.

ARTHUR AVENUE, COURT

2500 South, between 300 and 4500 West
Origin: *Ordinance*

Chester Arthur, (1829-1886), our 21st President, succeeded Republican James *Garfield*, who was assassinated a few months after taking office. Arthur was president from 1881 to 1885. His administration is known

known for civil service reform that replaced the system of appointing new federal employees every time there was a change of political parties in the White House.

Located in a neighborhood of streets named for the country's early Republican presidents, Arthur Avenue was named by ordinance in 1884 while Arthur was still in office (see *Harrison*).

ASH STREET
2400 North and 2400 West
Origin: *Park West*

In 1889, a group of short streets in this neighborhood was named for trees native to Milwaukee. They included Ash, *Hickory, Oak,* and *Tamarack* Streets. Black, Blue, Green, and White Ash are all found in the area.

ASPEN STREET
6800 South, between 1700 and 1900 West
Origin: *City of South Milwaukee*

The Bucyrus Company platted the Forest Park Subdivision in 1925, naming the streets for trees. Both the Bigtooth and Quaking Aspen are native to the Milwaukee area. Aspen Street is one of only two South Milwaukee street names that show up on Milwaukee's map (see *Carrington*).

ASTOR STREET
1000 East, between 900 and 1900 North
Origin: *Juneautown*

John Jacob Astor, as head of the American Fur Company, was Solomon *Juneau's* boss when Juneau named this street in 1835. Astor was born in Germany in 1763 and immigrated to New York twenty years later, when he began his career in the fur trade. His company started in the Great Lakes area and then expanded to the Pacific Northwest where Astoria, Oregon is named for him. Later Astor extended operations around the globe, to the Hawaiian Islands, China and India. At his death in 1848 his wealth was estimated at $30 million.

14

ATHENS STREET

3700 South, between 8200 and 8400 West
Origin: *Rolling Green*

The naming of this street in 1963 may
have been inspired by nearby *Tripoli* Avenue,
which originated in a subdivision where the
streets were named for exotic foreign cities.
Athens, the classical Greek city, is a symbol of
learning and culture. Milwaukee during the latter
half of the 19th century was dubbed the
"German Athens" or "Deutsch-Athens" for the
music, plays, lectures, debates and other intellectual activities brought to the city by German
immigrants.

The Temple of Athena in Athens,
Greece. (Milwaukee Public Library)

ATKINSON AVENUE

From 600 West and 3500 North to 3200 West and 4600 North
Origin: *Arlington Heights*

Vickers T. Atkinson was a member of the County Board that
approved the Williamsburg Heights Subdivision in 1889. What had been
known as the County Road was renamed Atkinson Avenue in the newly
approved development. Besides being a county supervisor and city alderman,
Atkinson was the state veterinarian and president of the State Veterinary
Association. He died in 1891.

AUER AVENUE

3200 North, between 1300 East and 9800 West
Origin: *Riverwest*

Louis Auer Jr. was a unique landlord, especially for the late 1800s. A
prosperous real estate dealer and developer, Auer thought it unfair that many
landlords refused to rent to couples with children. So he built apartments

15

with courtyards, playgrounds and soundproof floors that he then rented to families. He even gave free rent during the month a baby was born in one of his flats, earning him the title "The Baby Flat Landlord."

Auer was born in Milwaukee in 1857 to immigrants from Baden, Germany. His father, Louis Sr., had been an alderman, a county supervisor, and school commissioner before his death in 1882. Louis Jr. was a general in the Wisconsin National Guard and a member of the Park Commission. He bought only Milwaukee-made products if there was a choice and he encouraged others to do the same. Auer, who died in 1910, named this street in 1888.

Louis Auer, "The Baby Flat Landlord." (Illustrated News Annual)

AUSTIN STREET

300 East, between 2200 and 4500 South
Origin: *Bay View*

John Clinton Austin, born in Rochester, Vermont in 1832, settled on a farm near Bay View in 1844 with his parents, Samuel and Sarah. Part of the farm, on the southwest corner of Chase and Oklahoma Avenues, was known as "Austin's Woods." In 1887, Bay View was annexed by Milwaukee. The city already had a *Center* Street, so Centre Street in Bay View was renamed Austin Street to avoid duplication. John Austin died in 1919.

There was another Austin Street in the area, an east-west street that was named for Isaac and Sarah Austin of New York. The Tippecanoe Austin was changed to *Warnimont* to avoid confusion with the Bay View Austin in 1929.

16

AVALON STREET

1400 West, between 6100 and 6300 South
Origin: *Maitland Park*

In Welsh mythology, Avalon was the kingdom of the dead, where King Arthur and other heroes found their final resting place. This street was named in 1959 as part of the Melody Acres Subdivision.

AVONDALE BOULEVARD

6500 West, between 2700 and 2800 North
Origin: *Enderis Field*

The name Avondale was popularized in the 1880s as the home of Charles Stewart Parnell, an Irish landowner who tried unsuccessfully to have an Irish Home Rule Bill passed in the English Parliament. The name is a combination of Avon, a river in England, and dale, a valley. This street was platted as part of the Avondale Park Subdivision in 1924.

BACK BAY

1900 North and 2300 East
Origin: *Northpoint*

Back Bay, one of the city's
shortest streets. (George Olson)

A swampy section along the Charles River in Boston was filled in the mid-1800s and the exclusive Back Bay section of the city was the result. The wealthiest families moved into the area and it soon became known for the finest restaurants and the most exclusive shops.

In 1916 Mrs. Walter Dake, a resident on the bluffs overlooking Lake Michigan, tried to bring a little of Boston to Milwaukee. She suggested that Terrace Place be renamed Back Bay. On January 2, 1917, the city granted her wish.

BALDWIN STREET

4500 North, between 6000 and 6200 West
Origin: *Lincoln Creek*

Baldwin Street was named by the old Town of Wauwatosa in 1933. The reason for the name is not known.

BARAGA STREET

500 West, between 1200 and 1300 South
Origin: *Walker's Point*

Frederic Baraga, who was born in Austria in 1797 of Slovenian parents, came to the United States in 1831 as a missionary priest. From then until his death in 1868, he spent most of his time and energy working among the Indians of the Lake Superior region. He was appointed as bishop of Upper Michigan in 1853. Michigan's Baraga County is named for him.

Baraga was a linguist; he spoke six languages when he left Europe and added at least two more in this country, Ottawa and Ojibwa. His dictionary and grammar of the Ojibwa language form a foundation for the study of that tongue today. Baraga Street was named by ordinance in 1968 (see *Milwaukee*).

Frederic Baraga is being considered for sainthood. Will it be called St. Baraga Street? (Milwaukee Public Library)

BARCLAY STREET

200 East, between 150 and 1600 South
Origin: *Walker's Point*

Barclay Street was named by George Walker in 1842, but for whom remains a mystery.

BARNARD AVENUE

4800 South, between 1300 and 2700 West
Origin: *City of Cudahy*

Henry C. Barnard was born in Missouri in 1837 and died in Milwaukee in 1923. His involvement in the meat industry was the reason for his name being included in Patrick *Cudahy's* new town in 1892. Most of the men that Patrick Cudahy named streets for either sold livestock to meatpackers, were meatpackers themselves, or sold the packers' products to the public. Barnard, as a livestock commissioner, bought pigs and cattle from farmers, then sold the animals to the packers for slaughter.

19

BARTLETT AVENUE

1700 East, between 1900 and 3500 North
Origin: *Riverside Park*

John Knowlton Bartlett was born in New Hampshire in 1816. He came to Milwaukee in 1841, one month after graduating from Yale Medical College. He was a founding member of the Milwaukee County Medical Society in 1846. Bartlett died in 1889 in California where he had moved a few years earlier for health reasons. This street was named for Bartlett, who was also a land speculator, in 1857 by Charles Larkin.

BAY STREET

From 2100 South and 300 East to 2700 South and 1300 East
Origin: *Bay View*

In 1882 the name of Bay View Street was shortened to Bay Street.

BEALE STREET

10100 West and 6500 North
Origin: *Royal Orleans*

Beale Street in Memphis, Tennessee is known as the "birthplace of the blues" and was made famous by the song "Beale Street Blues." The developers of the Royal Orleans Subdivision named this street in 1967, perhaps thinking they were giving their street a New Orleans street name (see *Bourbon*).

BEATRICE STREET, COURT

8900 North, between 6800 and 9700 West
Origin: *North Meadows*

Beatrice J. Prause, born in 1921, was the inspiration for this name in 1969. Her husband, Clarence Miller, was an alderman from 1964 to 1978. His ward, in the old town of Granville, experienced significant growth during his tenure, giving him more

Beatrice Miller hands her street sign to a city worker. (Clarence Miller)

street naming opportunities than other aldermen. Besides his wife, one of Miller's sons and three of his granddaughters have been memorialized on Milwaukee's street signs (see *Michele*).

BECHER STREET

2100 South, between 300 East and 3800 West
Origin: *Historic Mitchell Street*

John A. Becher, a Civil War veteran, was born in Germany in 1833 and came to Milwaukee when he was 24 years old. After a short stint in the grocery business, Becher began his long career in real estate. He served as state assemblyman, school board commissioner, and president of the State Board of Immigration before he died in 1915.

He was one of the developers of the *Burnham*, *Rogers* and Becher's Subdivision that included Becher Street in 1871. Although he pronounced his name "Becker," the street name is commonly pronounced "Beecher."

BECKETT AVENUE

From 3800 North and 7000 West to 5600 North and 9600 West
Origin: *Columbus Park*

Beckett Avenue was named as part of the Lake Boulevard Gardens Subdivision in 1926. The reason for the name is unknown.

BEECHWOOD AVENUE

6900 North, between 7700 and 10115 West
Origin: *Mack Acres*

This street was originally called Mack Avenue after the developer, Rudy Mack. In 1957 homeowners on the street petitioned to have the name changed because they said it reminded them of a Mack truck. Beechwood was selected as a more pleasant sounding name.

BEETHOVEN PLACE

4500 North, between 4200 and 4300 West

Origin: *Old North Milwaukee*

Ludwig van Beethoven. (Milwaukee Public Library)

Ludwig van Beethoven, (1770-1827), German composer, began a tradition of creating music solely for its own sake, rather than for religious, social, or teaching purposes. Milwaukee Germans formed the Beethoven Society in 1843 and were entertaining the city's citizens when Milwaukee was still a frontier town. Beethoven Place was named in 1926 by the Atlas Land Company.

BELLEVIEW PLACE

2600 North, between 1400 and 2600 East

Origin: *Murray Hill*

Frederick Johnson and Moses Brand chose a creative misspelling of the word "bellevue" when they platted this street in 1882. The French word means "beautiful view." The mixture of French and English in the same word so upset the sensibilities of some people that the "Milwaukee Sentinel," in 1890, unsuccessfully called on the mayor to correct the spelling. The view from the hilltop at Belleview Place and Maryland Avenue may have inspired the name.

BELOIT ROAD

From 3100 South and 9000 West to 3500 South and 10000 West

This road, named for the city that it led to, dates from the early 1850s. Beloit is said to be a combination name; the "bel," for beautiful, and "oit," for Detroit, the latter in an attempt to woo settlers from Detroit.

BENDER AVENUE, COURT, ROAD

6300 North, between 7700 and 12100 West

Origin: *City of Glendale*

Bender Road was officially named by ordinance by the old Town of Milwaukee in 1917, but it was known by the name Bender well before that. The Bender family emigrated from northeast France before the American Revolution.

Peter Bender, a tanner and shoemaker, came to Milwaukee at the fairly advanced age of 48 and, after a short time in the city, bought land on the Milwaukee River. He built a dam and a sawmill at what was then called Bender's Mill Road, now known as *Mill* Road, and a bridge over the river at Bender Road, earlier known as Bender's Bridge Road. Bender, who was born in New York State in 1798, died in 1876.

BENNETT AVENUE

3000 South, between 1700 East and 7200 West
Origin: *Bay View*

Russell Bennett, a native of New Jersey, settled in the area in 1840. His farm included the Gothic Revival home that still stands on a hill on Kinnickinnic Avenue a few blocks south of this street. In 1929, Northwestern Avenue (named for the Chicago and Northwestern Railroad) was changed to Bennett Avenue by ordinance.

The Bennett residence. (1876 Illustrated Atlas of Milwaukee, Wisconsin)

BERNHARD PLACE

3400 North, between 4200 and 4700 West
Origin: *Sherman Park*

Bernhard Woelky, born in Prussia in 1836, came to this country in 1852. After arriving in Milwaukee he settled on land along Fond du Lac Avenue. In 1922 his family subdivided the Woelky homestead and named this street in his honor.

Bernhard Woelky's land as shown on Epeneter's 1879 Map of Milwaukee.

BETTINGER COURT

1700 West, between 700 and 721 South
Origin: *Clarke Square*

In 1908 John G. Bettinger called the nine cottages and hotel he owned at this location "Bettinger Court." Over the years the name has become officially accepted for this short street. Bettinger also operated a saloon in the neighborhood, as had his father, Nicholas, before him.

Nicholas Bettinger emigrated from Prussia to Buffalo, New York, in 1840. A year later he and his five cousins walked to Milwaukee. Bettinger's first work in the city was as a trapper and hunter. As the area urbanized, he moved into the brick trade before starting his tavern business.

BIRCH AVENUE, COURT

5500 North, between 1000 and 10600 West
Origin: *Village of Whitefish Bay*

John H. Tweedy Jr., whose father, John Sr., lost to Solomon *Juneau* in the city's first mayoral election, platted this street in 1892. The white-barked trees are native to Milwaukee.

BIRCHWOOD AVENUE

5800 South, between 1300 and 3900 West
Origin: *City of Cudahy*

Henry and Lucille Swendsen dedicated land for this street through their property, which was then south of Cudahy, in 1925. Henry Swendsen manufactured horseless carriages before switching to the real estate business.

BLAINE PLACE

6200 West and 2700 North
Origin: *Enderis Park*

John J. Blaine, born in Wisconsin in 1875, was known as the "tightwad governor" for promoting government economy during his years in office. Blaine, who was the state's chief executive from 1921 to 1927, died in 1934. This street was named by ordinance in 1953.

BLUE MOUND ROAD, COURT

600 North, between 4400 and 11200 West

During the 1830s, Blue Mound Road was built following an Indian trail from Milwaukee to Blue Mounds in Dane County. The Blue Mounds are so called because of a bluish tint produced by copper in the soil.

Looking east on Blue Mound Road near Hawley Road. (Milwaukee County Historical Society)

25

BLUHMS PLACE

300 East, between 3100 and 3200 North
Origin: *Harambee*

Christian Bluhm, a masonry contractor, died in 1905. The next year his widow, Maria, subdivided their land and the one-block long Bluhm's Place was created.

BOBOLINK AVENUE, PLACE

5900 North, between 2700 and 12400 West
Origin: *Thurston Woods*

This bird name was added to the streetscape in 1925 by Erwin and Irma Wallschlaeger. Bobolinks are seen in fields around the city (see *Oriole*).

BODEN STREET, COURT

5900 South, between 100 East/West and 1300 West
Origin: *New Coeln*

Robert Boden and his family settled in the old town of Lake after emigrating from County Down, Ireland in 1842. The Boden farm remained in the family for over one hundred years. At the request of Robert F. Boden, dean of the Marquette Law School and great-grandson of Robert, *Bridge* Street was renamed Boden Street in 1981.

BOEHLKE AVENUE, COURT

6900 North, between 4200 and 6500 West
Origin: *Wyrick Park*

The Boehlke family settled in the old town of Granville during the 19th century. This street was named by the town when the Boehlke farm was subdivided in 1935.

BOLIVAR AVENUE

4300 South, between 1200 East and 1700 West
Origin: *Tippecanoe*

Simon Bolivar, known as "The Liberator" and the "George Washington of South America," helped several South American countries gain independence from Spain. Among them were Venezuela, where he was born in 1783, Bolivia, which was named for him, Colombia, Peru, and Ecuador. This street was named in 1892 by the Howell Avenue Land Company.

BONNY PLACE

3300 North, between 4200 and 4300 West
Origin: *Sherman Park*

Bonny Place was platted in 1913 as part of the Bonny Park Subdivision. Bonny is a Scottish term for beautiful or attractive.

BOOTH STREET

600 East, between 2000 and 3500 North
Origin: *Harambee*

In 1857, when this street was named for Sherman M. Booth, he was in the midst of a seven year legal battle for helping a former slave escape. The struggle began in 1854, when Booth led a group of Milwaukeeans who freed Joshua *Glover* from the local jail. Glover had been arrested as a fugitive slave from Missouri.

Glover continued on the Underground Railroad and reached safety in Canada. Booth, an abolitionist newspaper editor, was charged under the Fugitive Slave Law and was sued for $2,000 by the St. Louis slaveowner. The Wisconsin Supreme Court ruled the Fugitive Slave Law was illegal and set Booth free. The U.S. Supreme Court said the law was legal and ordered him imprisoned. After years of legal manipulations, he was pardoned by President Buchanan on the eve of the Civil War. After the war Booth, who had come to Milwaukee in 1847 from Connecticut, moved to Chicago. He died there in 1904.

BOTTSFORD AVENUE

4400 South, between 1000 East and 2500 West
Origin: *City of Cudahy*

Henry Botsford, born in Ann Arbor, Michigan in 1834, was a Chicago meatpacker and banker who died in 1919. It was as a meatpacker that Botsford's name was memorialized - although spelled incorrectly - as a *Cudahy* avenue name. Patrick Cudahy named this street during the founding of his meatpacking town in 1892.

BOURBON STREET

10100 West, between 6500 and 6700 North
Origin: *Royal Orleans*

Nightlife on New Orleans' Bourbon Street.
(Louisiana Tourist Center)

Bourbon Street, known for its jazz music and party atmosphere, is in the French Quarter of New Orleans. In 1968 the developers of the Royal Orleans Subdivision requested that this street in their development be changed from Joseph to Bourbon Street to fit in with the New Orleans theme.

The New Orleans Bourbon Street was named in honor of the House of Bourbon, the French royal family (see *Beale*).

BOW STREET

From 1400 South and 1800 West to 1600 South and 1600 West
Origin: *Muskego Way*

Bow and *Arrow* Streets were named by developers in 1855.

BOYLSTON STREET

2000 North, between 1200 and 1500 East
Origin: *Lower East Side*

28

Joel Parker, a Bostonian, platted Boylston Street as part of his *Cambridge* Subdivision in 1874. Boylston Street is a well-known Boston avenue named for a prominent family of Boston merchants and physicians.

BRADFORD AVENUE

2500 North, between 1500 and 2800 East
Origin: *Murray Hill*

In 1856 James *Murray* named this street for the Bradford brothers, John and Joseph, who had operated a dry goods business since arriving in Milwaukee in the mid-1840s. They were both born in New Hampshire, as was another brother, James, who came to the city and joined the firm in 1857. John, also involved in banking, was president of the Chamber of Commerce. Joseph later became a commission merchant while James sold pianos and organs.

BRADLEY AVENUE

3700 South, between 100 East/West and 1400 East
Origin: *Tippecanoe*

James, Michael, and Catherine Bradley, descendants of old town of Lake settlers, platted this street in 1891 as part of Bradley's Subdivision.

BRADLEY ROAD

8000 North, between 2900 and 12400 West
Origin: *Village of River Hills*

The Bradley brothers, from Bangor, Maine, came to Milwaukee after the Civil War, where they became wealthy lumbermen. William, Edward, and James Bradley had vast holdings of timberland in northern Wisconsin and Michigan. At the turn of the century, Edward bought a farm north of Bradley Road on the east side of the Milwaukee River. He built a home on the estate in 1903, although he didn't make it his permanent residence until 1909. He died three years later at the age of 70 years. The street name appears for the first time in 1926 in the Kirkwood Subdivision.

BRADY STREET

1700 North, between 600 and 1600 East
Origin: *Lower East Side*

Brady Street was named, so the story goes, after Abraham *Lincoln* was reelected president in 1864. James Topham Brady, a prominent New York lawyer, had been a strong supporter of Lincoln and so Milwaukeeans named the street in his honor.

The story has flaws. Brady Street was named in 1836, 28 years before Lincoln's reelection. The street was named by Chicago developers, not Milwaukeeans. And James Topham Brady was only 21 years old when the street was named. His parents had recently died and he was struggling to support his five orphaned sisters, leaving him little money for land speculation in the wilderness on the shores of Lake Michigan.

The subdivision that included Brady Street (it was spelled Braidy on the plat map), *Hubbard* and *Pearson*'s Addition, was platted by Christopher Hubbard and Hiram Pearson, both Chicagoans. Names of other Chicagoans like Hunter, Kinzie, and *Hamilton* appeared on the streets of their Addition. Brady Street may have been named for another Chicagoan of that era, George Brady.

30   The intersection of Brady Street and Farwell Avenue. (Milwaukee County Historical Society)

BRANTING LANE

1600 South, between 3200 and 3800 West

Origin: *Burnham Park*

Karl Hjalmar Branting, born in Stockholm, Sweden in 1860, won the Nobel Peace Prize in 1921. Socialism linked Branting and Milwaukee. Branting was the first Social Democratic Prime Minister of Sweden and Milwaukee was the first major American city to be controlled by the Social Democratic Party. Branting died in 1925 and Branting Lane, a street heavily inhabited by Scandinavians, was named by ordinance the next year (see *Brisbane*).

BREMEN STREET

900 East, between 2200 and 4000 North

Origin: *Riverwest*

Bremen, Germany, a seaport and the capital of the state of Bremen, was a point of departure for many Germans who immigrated to Milwaukee during the 19th century. The street was named in 1857 by Julius Franke.

In 1941, on the eve of World War II, the Polish residents along Bremen Street decided that they didn't want to live on a street with a German name. They hoped to accomplish what the South Side Poles did a half century earlier - have a German street name changed.

In the 1880s, Bismarck Street was a thorn in the side of the city's Polish community. It was the policies of Otto von Bismarck, Chancellor of Germany, for whom the street was named, that caused many Poles to leave Poland. He took land from the Polish and gave it to Germans. He suppressed the Polish language and tried to weaken the power of the Catholic Church. When Polish immigrants came to Milwaukee, the last thing they wanted was to live on a street honoring Bismarck. So they demanded that it be changed to Kosciusko, in memory of the Pole who gained fame during the American Revolution. The German aldermen would have nothing to do with that idea. A compromise was reached - the street was renamed American Avenue (although it was later changed to 15th Place).

The Bremen Street Poles wanted to rename their street (Bremen Street was nearly 100 percent Polish from North Avenue to Auer Avenue) to honor Woodrow Wilson. They were unsuccessful. There already was a *Wilson* Drive named for the former president and the city has a record of seldom agreeing to requests to change the names of its streets.

BRENTWOOD AVENUE, COURT

6500 North, between 4600 and 9400 West
Origin: *City of Glendale*

Brentwood is in Essex, England. Brentwood Avenue was platted as part of the Glen Mary Subdivision in 1947.

BRIDGE STREET

6100 South, between 2100 and 2600 West
Origin: *City of Greenfield*

Bridge Street was probably named because it led to a bridge crossing the Honey Creek at 28th Street. Today, the creek is channeled through a culvert that the road crosses. The name dates from the 1940s.

BRIGGS AVENUE

6800 North, between 6400 and 6700 West
Origin: *Menomonee River Hills East*

Briggs Avenue was named as part of the Green Tree Meadows Addition, platted in 1960. The reason the name was selected is not known.

BRISBANE AVENUE

400 East, between 2500 and 3200 South
Origin: *Bay View*

Albert Brisbane, (1809-1890), was a 19th century social reformer who honored manual labor and, as such, was a favorite of Milwaukee's socialists. In 1909, during an era when the Social Democratic Party was at the height of its power in city government, Robinson Street was renamed Brisbane Avenue. The socialists also named their headquarters Brisbane Hall in his memory (see *Branting*).

32

BROADWAY

300 East, between 100 North/South and 1500 North
Origin: *Juneautown*

Milwaukee's Broadway, like the famous New York street, is wide. The New York thoroughfare may have influenced the naming of Milwaukee's street, which was known as Main Street until 1870 when it was changed by ordinance. There was some criticism that the change was made only in hopes of increasing the value of property along the street. Broadway is one of only three streets in the city that have no suffix, such as street, avenue, lane, etc. (see *Back Bay, Tory Hill*).

Looking north on Broadway from Michigan Street.
(Milwaukee Public Library)

BROOKLYN PLACE

3300 North, between 5500 and 5800 West
Origin: *Grasslyn Manor*

Brooklyn Place was named for the New York City borough that took its name from the village of Breuckelyn in Holland. The street, formerly called Marion, was renamed by ordinance in 1929.

BROWN STREET

2000 North, between 500 East and 4100 West
Origin: *Triangle*

Samuel "Deacon" Brown, as one of the city's first white settlers, was involved in several Milwaukee "firsts." Brown, who was born in Massachusetts in 1804 and came to Milwaukee in late 1834, was the community's first carpenter, and built the first courthouse. He bought the

33

first lot sold by Byron *Kilbourn*. Brown's house was the site of the first recorded fire. His was the first white family to settle here. His son, Thomas, was the first Milwaukee native to be elected mayor. Brown was a promoter and director of the Milwaukee and LaCrosse Railroad.

He was the first "conductor" of another railroad, the "Underground Railroad," a network of antislavery people working to help slaves flee the country. During the summer of 1842, teenager Caroline Quarlles, a fugitive slave from St. Louis, arrived in Milwaukee. Brown transported her under cover from his farm to Pewaukee, surviving a close encounter with her pursuers. From there she continued her journey to freedom in Canada.

Samuel Brown platted Brown's Addition, which included Brown Street, in 1856.

BROWN DEER ROAD, PLACE

8800 North, between 6800 and 12400 West
Origin: *Village of Brown Deer*

Brown Deer Road was named for the community that it ran through. Legends abound about how the community received its name. One story is that the original name was White Deer, after an albino deer, but that the prevalence of brown deer forced a name change.

Most of the lore has to do with a deer (brown, in each case) entering a building. In one instance, the deer bursts through a tavern door and breaks up a card game. Other stories have the deer poking his head through a window of a house or a barn in the area. Given the timidness of deer, none of the stories seem probable. More likely, the railroad named its station here, dating from the 1850s, simply because of the presence of deer in the area.

BRUCE STREET

600 South, between 500 East and 1700 West
Origin: *Walker's Point*

William George Bruce, (1865-1949), was heavily involved in Milwaukee's seaport interests. He was the first president of the Harbor Commission and vice-president of the St. Lawrence Seaway Council. Besides

34

running his own publishing business, he was instrumental in the building of the Auditorium, whose Bruce Hall is named for him. Park Street was renamed Bruce Street by ordinance in 1929.

BRUNKS LANE

2200 South and 400 East
Origin: *Bay View*

Brunks Lane is one of the city's shortest streets. William Brunk, a carpenter, lived on it during the late 1870s when the name came into use.

BRUST AVENUE

1600 East, between 3400 and 4700 South
Origin: *Bay View*

Christian Brust came to Milwaukee from Prussia in 1843 at the age of five years. After growing up on a farm in the old town of Lake, he learned the trade of a pattern-maker, which provided him with work in Bay View factories. He saved money and was able to start a gardening business in 1880.

In 1891 Brust subdivided some of his land and named a street after himself. He was a Catholic who helped to organize both Immaculate Conception Church in Bay View and Sacred Heart Church in St. Francis.

BUFFALO STREET

300 North, between 100 and 700 East
Origin: *Historic Third Ward*

When this street was platted in 1837 by Solomon *Juneau* and Morgan *Martin*, the city of Buffalo, New York was the starting point for Great Lakes voyages to Milwaukee. Travelers from the Atlantic seaboard used the Hudson River and the recently opened Erie Canal to get to Buffalo, then completed the water route to Milwaukee (see *Chicago*).

The city's most decorative street sign (northeast corner of Broadway and Buffalo Street).

BUFFUM STREET

400 East, between 1900 and 3500 North
Origin: *Harambee*

David Hanson Buffum, (1833-1895), was a New Hampshire attorney for Milwaukee developer Jonathan L. Peirce. This street was platted in 1857 as part of the Otis B. Hopkins Subdivision (see *Burleigh, North Pierce*).

BURBANK AVENUE

6800 North, between 8300 and 8600 West
Origin: *Menomonee River Hills*

Located in a 1955 subdivision with streets named for western United States cities, this street was probably named for Burbank, California. The city was named for David Burbank, a Los Angeles dentist who was born in New Hampshire in 1821.

BURDICK AVENUE

3200 South, between 300 East and 9100 West
Origin: *Bay View*

When Morgan L. Burdick was twenty years old he assisted in the construction of the first frame house in Chicago and a year later, in 1834, he had the same distinction in Milwaukee. Morgan claimed land on the South Side for his potato farm that same year. An elementary school bearing his name is located near the site of his homestead.

Burdick, who was born in Jefferson County, New York in 1813 and died in 1886, was a county supervisor. He held a variety of posts in the old Town of Lake where he donated land for the town hall. This street was named for him in 1927.

BURLEIGH STREET

3100 North, between 1300 East and 10000 West
Origin: *Harambee*

Jonathan Peirce, an early Milwaukee land developer, named three

36

streets for his New Hampshire lawyers, this one in 1856. Nathaniel Wells (although this Wells Street was later renamed *Concordia*), David *Buffum*, and brothers George and John Burleigh were so honored. George William Burleigh, (1830-1878), and John Adams Burleigh, (1835-1872), were both graduates of Dartmouth Law School and lived in Somersworth, New Hampshire. The family name was pronounced (and sometimes spelled) Burley rather than the local pronunciation of Bur-lye (see *North Pierce*).

A wagon travels east on Burleigh from 6th Street in the 1890s. (Milwaukee County Historical Society)

BURNHAM STREET

1900 South, between 300 and 4200 West
Origin: *Historic Mitchell Street*

George Burnham, born in Plattsburg, New York in 1816, was in the brick making business from age 15 until his death at 72. He came to Milwaukee in 1843 after spending 11 years making bricks in Buffalo, New York. By 1880 Burnham employed two hundred men at his South Side yards and manufactured 15 million bricks annually.

Burnham had extensive real estate holdings throughout the county and in Iowa and Texas. He served on the waterworks commission and was a school board commissioner. He platted Burnham Street with John *Becher* and D.G. *Rogers* in 1871.

BURRELL STREET

200 East, between 2300 and 4500 South
Origin: *Bay View*

Samuel H. Burrell married Hannah W. Chase in 1868. In 1872 Hannah's father, Enoch *Chase*, platted this street.

BUSH LANE

1400 East and 2600 North
Origin: *Riverwest*

In 1926 this street suffered quite a comedown. It was reduced from a Forest to a Bush. There was concern that as Forest Place it might be confused with Forest Home Avenue, so it was changed to Bush Lane by ordinance.

BUTLER PLACE

4500 North, between 8900 and 9100 West
Origin: *Lindsay Park*

When Milwaukee was renaming streets in 1926, the suggestion was made that *Lisbon* Avenue be renamed Butler Road. Although the idea was rejected, when the old Town of Wauwatosa joined in the street uniformity plan in 1933, it changed a portion of 91st Street to Butler. The community of Butler was undoubtedly the inspiration for the name. As a post office, Butler received its name in the 1800s for a now unknown reason.

BYRON PLACE

4300 North and 9700 West
Origin: *Grantosa*

Byron Place was named in 1933 by the old Town of Wauwatosa. This could be a promotional name, a first name, or a surname. Or perhaps, like streets named for *Beethoven*, *Poe*, and *Paine* during this era, it was named for a famous person in the arts, the English poet Lord Byron.

CALDWELL AVENUE, COURT

5300 North, between 6800 and 7900 West
Origin: *Valhalla*

Caldwell Avenue was named as part of the Fondtosa Highlands Subdivision in 1929. After the city assumed street naming responsibilities about 1925, many of the new street names assigned were surnames of English background. Because they were easy for English-speakers to spell and pronounce, street names like *Abbott*, Caldwell, *Carter*, *Spencer*, and *Walton* were added to the city map. Caldwell may have been chosen for this reason alone.

CALHOUN PLACE

3000 North and 3000 West
Origin: *Park West*

John Tweedy named this street, really more of an alley, in 1889. Why he chose this name is a puzzle.

CALIFORNIA STREET

1300 East, between 2700 and 3500 South
Origin: *Bay View*

In the late 1870s, the *Herman* Mann family named eight streets in Bay View after states, territories, and provinces of western North America. This began a trend in Bay View of naming streets for American states that later culminated in more exotic place names, such as *Tripoli*, Bombay and *Ahmedi*. The name California comes from a 16th century Spanish story that referred to an island near paradise called California (see *Colorado*).

CALLAHAN PLACE

1500 West, between 1100 and 1200 North
Origin: *King Park*

The Callahan family of Merrill Park ran a tavern at 14th and Clybourn Streets for many years. At the time it was displaced by the freeway in the 1960s, Bob Callahan was the owner. A friend, William Ryan Drew, secretary of the City Redevelopment Authority, suggested the name for this new short street in 1978.

CALUMET ROAD

7600 North, between 3600 and 11400 West
Origin: *Village of Fox Point*

A calumet, or peace pipe. (Indian Art of the United States)

Calumet is the French word to describe the peace pipe used by North American Indians. It was considered almost sacred by Indians and would normally guarantee safe conduct to those who offered it. When the French explorer LaSalle offered a calumet to an armed group of Potowatomi Indians near Milwaukee in 1679, not only was his peace overture accepted, but the Potowatomis gave a feast in his honor and provided food for his journey.

The Calumet Land Company and the Calumet Cement Company owned large portions of the Fox Point area where this street was named in 1927.

CAMBRIDGE AVENUE

1500 East, between 1700 and 3400 North
Origin: *Lower East Side*

Joel Parker, born in New Hampshire in 1795, was Chief Justice of his native state's supreme court until he was appointed chairman of the Cambridge Law School at Harvard in 1847. Parker, who developed the Cambridge Subdivision that included Cambridge Avenue in 1874, died in 1875 (see *Boylston).

CAMERON AVENUE

5000 North, between 2800 and 11000 West
Origin: *Old North Milwaukee*

When North Milwaukee became part of the city in 1929, its Commerce Avenue became a duplicate of the downtown *Commerce* Street, so Commerce Avenue was renamed Cameron Avenue. It may have been named for John E. Cameron, who has been described as an early "first citizen." The jovial, well-liked Cameron ran the Plankinton House until his death in the cholera outbreak of 1852.

CANAL STREET

100 North/South, between 400 and 3500 West
Origin: *Menomonee River Valley*

The Menomonee River Valley separates the city's North and South Sides and, in 1926, the Valley's Canal Street was chosen as the north/south baseline for the city's house numbering system. The street, which dates back to at least 1870, was named for the canals that opened the Valley's businesses to Great Lakes' shipping. The canals have carried the names of influential Milwaukeeans like *Plankinton, Holton, Burnham,* and *Kneeland.*

CAPITOL DRIVE, PARKWAY, PLACE

4000 North, between 1100 East and 10800 West
Origin: *Ordinance*

Before 1926, Capitol Drive was known as Lake Street. Since the city had more than one street named Lake, and because it was attempting to eliminate duplicate names, Lake Street needed a new name. Among the suggestions was a proposal by W.J.C. Flieth that it be called Capitol Drive because the Capitol in Madison is due west of it.

76th Street and Capitol Drive at a quieter time. This view looks east on the westbound lane of Capitol Drive. (Milwaukee County Historical Society)

CARFERRY DRIVE

From 1100 South and 700 East to 2400 South and 1500 East
Origin: *Jones Island*

The name Carferry Drive refers not to automobiles, but to railroad cars. While autos were eventually shipped across Lake Michigan, railcars were being ferried before the 20th century. The freightcars were loaded with products destined for the East. Railroads could avoid the congested yards in

Chicago by being ferried to Michigan and then continuing the journey by rail. This street was named in 1957.

CARLTON PLACE

6400 West, between 2700 and 2800 North
Origin: *Enderis Park*

This short, curving street was called 64th Street until 1929. The problem was that because it curved, it was 64th on one end but 63rd on the other, so it was changed to Carlton. Why the name was selected is not known.

CARMEN AVENUE

5800 North, between 2700 and 12400 West
Origin: *Thurston Woods*

Carmen Gettelman named this street in 1927 as part of the Grantosa Heights Subdivision. Her husband, Sidney, worked for an investment securities firm.

CAROL STREET

3400 South, between 1600 and 2000 East
Origin: *Bay View*

Arthur Wenz named this street for a Christmas Carol. His daughter, Carol, was born on Christmas Day in 1907. Wenz, born in Milwaukee in 1880, was the developer of this 1926 subdivision. Wenz also named one of his businesses, the Carol Investment Company, for his daughter.

CARPENTER AVENUE

4900 South, between 600 and 2700 West
Origin: *City of Cudahy*

Carpenter was one of the few streets in Cudahy that Patrick *Cudahy* named in 1892 for someone outside the meat industry. Michael Carpenter, born in Milwaukee in 1847 of Irish immigrant parents, owned a large downtown baking business that he eventually sold to the National Biscuit Company.

Carpenter, an investor in the real estate boom of the era, speculated in land in the town of Cudahy. Any hopes he may have had for a quick profit were ended with the financial Panic of 1893. He died in 1926.

CARRINGTON AVENUE

6500 South, between 1800 and 2000 West
Origin: *City of South Milwaukee*

Carrington Avenue was named as part of the Carrington Heights Subdivision, platted in 1893. It may have been named for R.E. Carrington, a land speculator active in the Milwaukee area at the time.

CARTER PLACE

3200 North, between 4600 and 4700 West
Origin: *Sunset Heights*

This one-block long street was known as York Street until 1928. Then, probably because it was considered too similar to *New York* Avenue, it was changed. Carter Place may have been named for Charles Carter, a prominent lawyer who specialized in real estate law. Carter, who had come to Milwaukee in 1885 from Fond du Lac, died in 1923.

CASPER STREET

6700 North, between 5400 and 10600 West
Origin: *Menomonee River Hills*

Casper, Wyoming is among the western cities named in this 1955 subdivision. Casper W. Collins, a cavalry officer killed by Indians, was memorialized by the Wyoming city name.

CASS STREET

800 East, between 600 and 1800 North
Origin: *Juneautown*

Lewis Cass. (Milwaukee Public Library)

When Solomon *Juneau* and Morgan L. *Martin* named this street for him in 1835, Lewis Cass was serving as President Andrew *Jackson*'s secretary of war. Cass had been governor of the Michigan Territory, which included Milwaukee, for 18 years. In 1848, he lost his bid for the U.S. presidency to Zachary *Taylor*. Cass, who was born in New Hampshire in 1782, died in 1866.

CAWKER PLACE

2900 North and 3000 West
Origin: *Park West*

In 1836 Emanuel Cawker, a native of England, purchased the land that now includes Cawker Place, more a driveway than a street. Although he left Milwaukee the next year, the land remained in the family. When the property was subdivided in 1889, the street was named for him.

CEDARBURG ROAD

3900 West and 8000 North

In the 1860s this road was called New Fond du Lac Road. By the late 1870s it was more commonly known as the Cedarburg Plank Road for the community that it led to. Cedarburg, not surprisingly, was named for the many cedar trees in the area.

Downtown Cedarburg about 1930. (Milwaukee Public Library)

CELINA STREET

8100 North and 10100 West
Origin: *Pheasant Run*

In 1963 this street was named for Anita Celina Denemark, wife of the city's chief draftsman, Harold Denemark. Anita Celina was born in 1931 in Buenos Aires, Argentina.

CENTER STREET

2700 North, between 1300 and 9900 West
Origin: *Riverwest*

In 1832, Alexander Center and James *Doty* surveyed the first road in the state, from Green Bay to Prairie du Chien. Two years later, they did the survey for the second road, from Chicago to Green Bay, through Milwaukee. In 1837 Center surveyed Milwaukee Bay. He recommended that to improve water access to downtown, a channel be cut at the north end of the peninsula that separated Lake Michigan and the Milwaukee River. The federal government rejected the suggestion, but the city, strongly in favor of the idea, named the site of the proposed channel Center Street in his honor.

In 1857 the government relented and paid for the excavation of the channel that eliminated Center Street. But during that same year, when a new street opened on the north side of town, it was named Center Street. Alexander Center later became a railroad president.

CHAMBERS STREET, COURT

3000 North, between 1100 East and 9200 West
Origin: *Harambee*

Chambers Street was named in 1858 as part of John Tesch's Subdivision. It is not known why Tesch chose this name.

CHAPMAN PLACE

3900 North, between 7200 and 7400 West
Origin: *Dineen Park*

This short street was called *Melvina* Avenue until 1933 when it was changed to Chapman Place. Many city streets at this time were named for prominent people from the city's past who had contributed to the community's good. There were two Chapmans, Silas and Timothy, who may have been honored by this designation.

Silas Chapman, who was born in Massachusetts in 1813, was a mapmaker and publisher, as well as a dealer and publisher of books. He produced maps of Milwaukee from the 1850s until his death in 1899. Chapman served as a school commissioner and on the boards of other educational institutions.

Timothy Chapman, born in Maine in 1824, was the founder of the T. A. Chapman department store after coming to Milwaukee in 1857. Chapman was considered a progressive employer and was involved in many charitable activities. He died in 1892.

CHASE AVENUE

From 2300 South and 600 West to 3700 South and 100 East/West
Origin: *Bay View*

Enoch Chase is given credit for constructing the wagon trail leading to the Kinnickinnic River over what is now Chase Avenue. Chase was one of Milwaukee's early Yankee settlers. He was born in Vermont in 1809 and claimed land here in 1834. Because he served as a guard during the Sauk War, he was eligible for a soldier's entitlement of 160 acres of land.

The glassworks in Chase's Valley. (Milwaukee Public Library)

Chase, a physician, later bought the land that became known as Chase's Valley, where the Kinnickinnic River crosses Lincoln Avenue and where he established the Chase Valley Brickyards and the Chase Valley Glassworks. He was elected state legislator several times between 1848 and 1869 and state senator in 1881. He died in 1892.

When Chase subdivided some of his land, he named streets for his sons, *Clarence* and *Clifford,* and for his son-in-law Samuel *Burrell.* Chase Avenue was named for him by city ordinance in 1926.

CHERRY STREET

1500 North, between 100 East/West and 5800 West
Origin: *Kilbourntown*

Cherry Street was one of the city's earliest streets. It was named by Byron *Kilbourn* and Archibald *Clybourn* in 1835. Common Chokecherry, Black Cherry, and Pin Cherry are trees native to the area (see *Walnut*).

CHESTER STREET

300 South, between 8900 and 9400 West
Origin: *Johnson's Woods*

Thomas F. Chester, a real estate dealer, witnessed the platting of this street by Agnes Cuppel in 1918.

CHEYENNE STREET, COURT

6800 North, between 3700 and 9000 West
Origin: *Menomonee River Hills*

The Menomonee River Hills Subdivision, platted in 1955, has many streets named for cities of the American West. Cheyenne, Wyoming was named for a tribe of Indians known as "red talkers."

CHICAGO STREET

200 North, between 100 and 700 East
Origin: *Historic Third Ward*

When Chicago Street was platted in 1837, Chicago and Milwaukee were villages competing for eastern settlers. Many thought that Milwaukee had the advantage over Chicago because it was ninety miles closer to the East Coast via the Great Lakes water route. As railroads developed, the advantage passed to Chicago, which became ninety miles closer by rail. The Third Ward was platted by Solomon *Juneau* and Morgan *Martin*.

One of the Third Ward's unique street signs, this one is in the sidewalk.

CHRISTINE LANE

2700 North, between 300 and 500 West
Origin: *Harambee*

Hans Gosch, born in Denmark in 1807, platted this street in 1856. Why Gosch, who worked as a butcher and a barber in the city's early days, chose this name is not known.

CIRCLE COURT

7100 North, between 9400 and 9500 West
Origin: *Golden Gate*

Circle Court, named in 1962 as part of the Golden Gate Subdivision, is not a circle. But it does form a loop with *Orinda* Court, with both streets exiting on *Park Manor* Drive.

CLARENCE STREET

2500 South, between 400 East and 400 West
Origin: *Bay View*

Enoch *Chase* named this street for his 17 year old son Clarence in 1872. Clarence was later a partner with his father in the Chase Valley

Brickyards that manufactured six million bricks per year. In a short-lived attempt at politics, he lost his bid for an aldermanic seat in 1889.

CLARENDON PLACE

400 North and 4700 West
Origin: *Story Hill*

The source of this name is near Salisbury, England. Clarendon spawned the Clarendons, a family of nobility, for whom places in this country are named. In 1926, *Pinecrest* Court was changed to Clarendon Place because there were three other Pinecrests in the subdivision.

CLARKE STREET

2600 North, between 1300 East and 6100 West
Origin: *North Division*

Street name lore says that this avenue was named for William Clarke, who was variously described as a physician, a judge, an old resident, or the first white man to die in Milwaukee. There apparently was a physician named Clarke in early Milwaukee, but he didn't die until 1844, well after the city's first recorded death. Whatever William Clarke's claim to fame was, he didn't have this street named for him.

That distinction goes to Joseph Clarke, who surveyed for Ann Lee and G.W. Peckham the subdivision that included Clarke Street in 1856. Clarke was a civil engineer and assistant city surveyor in the 1850s.

CLAYTON CREST AVENUE

5300 South, between 1400 and 2700 West
Origin: *Clayton Crest*

The promotional name Clayton Crest was given to this street in 1955.

CLEMENT AVENUE

1200 East, between 2500 and 4300 South
Origin: *Bay View*

Stephen Clement, born of English stock in Pennsylvania in 1813, was a Great Lakes captain by the time he was 21 years old. He and Eber *Ward* founded a line of steamships on the Great Lakes and, later, a series of iron manufacturing businesses in Great Lakes' port cities. Clement was the first president of the Milwaukee Iron Works plant, which was founded in Bay View in the late 1860s. Clement Avenue was named by Eber Ward in 1870. Captain Clement, who named his only son Ward, died in 1894.

CLEVELAND AVENUE

2700 South, between 400 and 7100 West
Origin: *Ordinance*

Grover Cleveland, born in New Jersey in 1837, was both the 22nd and the 24th President of the United States. He served as president from 1885 to 1889, then lost to Benjamin *Harrison*. When Harrison ran for a second term, Cleveland defeated him and took over the White House again from 1893 to 1897. A portion of *Russell* Avenue was renamed for Cleveland in 1909, the year after his death.

Grover Cleveland.
(Milwaukee Public Library)

CLIFFORD STREET

2500 South, between 100 and 300 East
Origin: *Bay View*

Enoch *Chase* named this street for his 13 year old son Clifford in 1872. Clifford was one of ten children and the brother of *Clarence*, who also had a street named for him in Dr. E. Chase's Subdivision.

CLINTON AVENUE

7300 North, between 3700 and 8000 West
Origin: *Tripoli Park*

In 1947, some citizens of the old town of Granville petitioned to have Clinton Avenue laid out. It has been supposed that it, like many places of the same name, was named for De Witt Clinton. He was governor of New York and the man behind the Erie Canal, a project that opened the western Great Lakes area, including Milwaukee, to settlement.

CLOVERNOOK STREET, COURT

6500 North, between 6600 and 9400 West
Origin: *City of Glendale*

The pleasing name Clovernook dates back to 1902. That year the Clovernook Dairy Farm was established by the Hickox family. During the depression the Hickoxes began subdividing the farm. Clovernook Street was platted in 1946.

CLYBOURN STREET

500 North, between 900 East and 4200 West
Origin: *Kilbourntown*

In 1829, Archibald Clybourn built a twenty-room mansion next to Chicago's first stockyards. He built up the stockyards too, and is credited with beginning a tradition that would make Chicago the "hog butcher of the world." Clybourn, (1802-1872), speculated in Milwaukee real estate and was one of the founders of Kilbourntown in 1835. Although he remained a Chicagoan, Clybourn had a warehouse business in Milwaukee during its early days.

CODY STREET, CIRCLE

6600 North, between 7100 and 7300 West
Origin: *Menomonee River Hills East*

William Frederick "Buffalo Bill" Cody, (1846-1917), was an army

52

scout and a showman. During the 1870s Cody mixed these occupations, scouting when he wasn't performing on stage. He later dropped scouting for ranching and his "Wild West" exhibition, where he displayed his horse riding and shooting skills. Cody Street was named in 1958 for Cody, Wyoming, the western town named for Buffalo Bill.

Buffalo being shot by their namesake, "Buffalo Bill" Cody. (Illustrated London News)

COLD SPRING ROAD

4300 South, between 5000 and 6000 West
Origin: *City of Greenfield*

This road dates from the 1850s. Precisely where the spring that spawned the road's name was located has not been determined.

COLFAX PLACE, COURT

5000 North, between 2100 and 8200 West
Origin: *Whitefish Bay*

In the 1920s and 1930s Whitefish Bay changed the names of many of its streets. Local names like *Weil*, *Fratney*, and *Pierce* gave way to more

53

aristocratic sounding names like Marlborough, Sheffield, and *Lancaster*. Pabst Place, named for the Pabst Brewing Company that had operated Pabst's Whitefish Bay Resort until World War I, was changed to Colfax Place in 1926.

COLGATE CIRCLE

8600 West, between 4100 and 4200 North
Origin: *Lindsay Park*

Colgate Circle, which is not a circle or even an oval, was named in 1953 for the Washington County community. The town is believed to have been named for James B. Colgate of Colgate-Palmolive fame.

COLLEGE AVENUE

6300 South, between 1600 East and 2700 West
Origin: *City of South Milwaukee*

The name College Avenue originated with *Downer* College's plans to move to the north end of what is now Grant Park in 1893. A railway station was placed where the Chicago and Northwestern tracks crossed Town Line Road, the road that would take students to and from the college. But Downer College decided to build on the North Side, forming the core of the current UWM campus. The rail station, with no traffic, was turned into a private residence. But the name stuck, and Town Line Road, without the benefit of a college, became known as College Avenue.

COLONIAL DRIVE

9700 West, between 2700 and 3300 North
Origin: *Mount Mary*

E. H. Mushlmeir, president of the Burleigh Realty Company, was into colonial. In 1928 he platted the Colonial Highland Subdivision and named one of the streets Colonial Drive. The first house built on Colonial Drive was a Colonial Revival style home (now 3241 N. 97th, see photo next page).

54

COLORADO STREET

2700 South and 1300 East
Origin: *Bay View*

This is one of the streets named for western states by the *Herman Mann* family in 1879. Colorado is a Spanish word meaning "reddish-brown" and was first used to refer to the Colorado river (see *Dakota*).

COLUMBIA STREET

3000 North, between 1300 and 1600 West
Origin: *Upper East Side*

Columbia wrapped in the American flag. (The Columbia Story)

The term Columbia, used to honor Christopher Columbus, was first used during the Revolutionary War. The poets of the era began using it to describe the new nation that was emerging, much the way that Britannia was used as the symbol for England. Columbia became a popular U.S. place-name during the 1800s. In 1887, Milwaukee physicians C.D. Stanhope and Eugene Storke named this street as part of Stanhope's Subdivision.

COMMERCE STREET

From 1300 North and 200 West to 2100 North and 1100 East
Origin: *Riverside Park*

Commerce Street covers the short stub of a canal that missed its destination, the Rock River, by many miles. During Milwaukee's infancy, water was the primary mode of transportation. Much of the traffic coming into the city arrived via Lake Michigan. The Erie Canal, completed in 1825, gave many Easterners access to the Great Lakes and their shores. But travel west from the city was tedious and difficult at best. Byron *Kilbourn,* an Ohio canal builder, planned the Milwaukee and Rock River Canal, which would provide a waterway to the Mississippi River.

In 1839 the canal digging began at the Milwaukee River and North Avenue. However, a competing canal company, proposing a route from Green Bay to the Mississippi River, convinced the state legislature to withdraw its approval for the Milwaukee project. The Milwaukee canal had only made it to about Juneau Avenue. The miniature canal was used for water power for businesses along it, but, in 1885, the canal was filled in and dubbed Commerce Street.

COMSTOCK AVENUE

1900 West, between 1400 and 1600 South
Origin: *Muskego Way*

Ohio-born brothers Leander and Cicero Comstock settled in Milwaukee in 1844. They ran several businesses including saw and flour mills and both held elected political positions. But it was celery, grown by Leander and his nephew, Henry, that made the Comstock name well known in the area. Their celery was the best the region produced and was sold throughout the state and beyond. The celery farm was a few blocks west of the street named for them in 1926. The street had been known as Arthur, a duplicate name eliminated during the city's renaming program.

CONCORDIA AVENUE

3300 North, between 1300 East and 10100 West
Origin: *Franklin Heights*

Concordia was the Roman goddess of peace and harmony. The name, and its shorter form of Concord, were frequently used placenames in 19th century America. Horace Upham was the developer of the Concordia Heights Subdivision where this street was named in 1888.

CONGO AVENUE

1900 West and 2000 South
Origin: *Muskego Way*

The exploration of the Congo River by Henry *Stanley* and David Livingstone in the 1870s captured the imaginations of people around the world. The African river is one of the longest on the earth. Congo Avenue was named in 1887 by C.H. O'Neil and Anna M. Bergenthal.

CONGRESS STREET

4400 North, between 1300 and 10400 West
Origin: *Lincoln Creek*

This street was named in 1892 by the North Milwaukee Improvement Company. Congress Streets throughout the country are assumed to be named for the U.S. Congress. Attitudes toward Congress must have been different a century ago, for there can't be too many developers who would name a street for it today.

CONSTANCE AVENUE

4700 North, between 6500 and 6700 West
Origin: *Capitol Heights/Lincoln Creek*

Who the Constance was, if any, who inspired this street name is not known. It was named by the Realty Syndicate of America in 1928.

CONWAY STREET

2400 South, between 600 and 1400 East
Origin: *Bay View*

Joseph *Williams*, a Bay View farmer, subdivided his farm in 1870 and named Conway Street. It is not known why he selected the name, which is a surname of Welsh, Scots and Irishmen.

CORCORAN AVENUE

100 South, between 400 and 600 East
Origin: *Historic Third Ward*

Cornelius Joseph Corcoran, born in Limerick, Ireland about 1807, settled in the predominantly Irish Third Ward before the Civil War. Corcoran supported his family with a saloon and feed store in the ward. Juneau Street was renamed Corcoran Avenue in 1888, three years before he died. In 1892 his son, also named Cornelius, was elected Third Ward alderman, a position he held for 43 years. The younger Corcoran, known as "Connie da Cork," is remembered today for his philosophy that the lakefront belongs to all the people. He strongly influenced the development of *Lincoln Memorial* Drive and the parks and beaches along it.

CORNELL STREET

4500 North, between 1400 and 2700 West
Origin: *Rufus King*

This street was probably named for Cornell University, founded in Ithaca, New York in 1865 by Ezra Cornell. The street had been known as Southway until 1927 when it was renamed (see *Princeton).*

COTTAGE PLACE

2900 North, between 1300 and 1400 West
Origin: *North Division*

The small, wood-framed cottage was popular with Milwaukee's labor force in 1889, when this short street was named. While not evoking images

58

of grandeur like later *Manor* Court and *Villa* Avenue, Cottage Place appealed to the workers' dreams of owning their own homes.

COUNTY LINE ROAD

9600 North, between 6800 and 12400 West

This road, dating from the 1850s, marks the boundary between Ozaukee and Milwaukee Counties.

COURT STREET

1500 North, between 300 and 400 West
Origin: *Haymarket*

In 1835, Kilbourntown and Juneau-town, on opposite sides of the Milwaukee River, were both vying for the businesses and settlers that came to town. Milwaukee County needed to build a courthouse. A new county courthouse would attract significant traffic and give a certain legitimacy to the winning village. Both communities were willing to do whatever they could to have the building on their side of the river.

The first courthouse. (Buck's Pioneer History of Milwaukee)

Byron *Kilbourn* offered a plat of land on the west side for the new facility and named the street along it Court Street. But the land never held the courthouse. Solomon *Juneau* and Morgan *Martin* donated what is now known as Cathedral Square on the east side for the new building, which was erected in 1836. The second courthouse was also constructed on what was then called Court-house Square. It wasn't until 1930 that the county institution favored the west side. But Court Street was rebuffed again, this time for the current Kilbourn Avenue location.

COURTLAND AVENUE

4700 North, between 1600 and 9100 West
Origin: *Village of Whitefish Bay*

A portion of Cumberland Avenue was changed to Courtland Avenue in 1926 by the Village of Whitefish Bay.

CRAMER STREET

1900 East, between 2300 and 3500 North
Origin: *Murray Hill*

Eliphalet Cramer. (Buck's Pioneer History of Milwaukee)

Eliphalet Cramer settled in Milwaukee in 1836, the day after he became 23 years old. Cramer, born in Waterford, New York, was a lawyer, but his interests were in business. Like many of the city's early businessmen, he knew it was vital to improve the movement of goods between the city and outlying areas. Consequently, he invested first in plank roads, then railroads.

He was a founder, and later president, of the Milwaukee Gas Company and the State Bank of Wisconsin, and was especially interested in real estate. Cramer was a strong supporter of the anti-slavery movement and a benefactor of religious and educational institutions. This street was named for him in James *Murray*'s Addition in 1856. Cramer died in 1872.

CRAWFORD AVENUE

3800 South, between 1200 East and 9200 West
Origin: *Morgandale*

John Crawford, general, sailor, farmer, and county board supervisor, was born in Massachusetts in 1792 and died in Wauwatosa in 1881. After his

60

military career with the New York State Militia, where he was a Major-General, Crawford became a Great Lakes sea captain. His voyages brought him to the village of Milwaukee in 1836 where he was active in the affairs of Wauwatosa and Milwaukee County. Crawford was selected for the honor of laying the cornerstone of the county's second courthouse, built in 1870. This street was named by ordinance in 1927.

CROSSFIELD AVENUE

6300 North, between 8500 and 8700 West
Origin: *Menomonee River Hills*

Winfield Avenue started as an east-west street but then curved to a north-south direction. To eliminate confusion in house numbering, the north-south portion was changed to Crossfield Avenue in 1959.

CUDAHY AVENUE

4500 South, between 1000 East and 1600 West
Origin: *City of Cudahy*

Patrick Cudahy Jr., who founded the city of Cudahy, was born a few months before the family left Ireland in 1849 to escape the potato famine. His career in the packing business began at the age of 13 when he worked at a Milwaukee meatpacking firm for $3 a week as an unskilled laborer. He became a foreman, then a superintendent. By the time he was in his early thirties he earned $50,000 a year as plant manager for *Plankinton* and *Armour*, when the average annual income was less than $500.

When he was 39 he took over the Plankinton company, renamed it Cudahy Brothers (his brother John provided significant capital for the company), and a few years later moved the operation to its current Cudahy location. The company name was changed again in 1957

Patrick Cudahy. (Milwaukee Public Library)

to Patrick Cudahy, Inc. When Patrick died at the age of seventy in 1919, he was reported to "have paid the heaviest income tax" in Milwaukee and was termed one of its wealthiest citizens.

In 1892 Patrick, perhaps with help from John, named the streets of his company town after business associates. Most were in the meat trade. Some were in the raising of cattle or hogs, others in the slaughtering or packing of them. A few were brokers and others were retail butchers. Most were from the Midwest and many had their roots in Ireland. In later years, as the city of Milwaukee expanded southward, its new streets took on the already established Cudahy street names.

CURTIS PLACE

1500 North and 1300 East
Origin: *Lower East Side*

Because it was considered too much like *Keefe* Avenue, Keene Street was changed to Curtis Place in 1926. It may have been named for Milwaukeean Truman Curtis, described as a "progressive and public spirited citizen." Curtis, born in 1841, was a Civil War veteran who was elected to the state legislature.

CUSTER AVENUE

5400 North, between 2200 and 10600 West
Origin: *Old North Milwaukee*

George Armstrong Custer, Civil War cavalry general and Indian fighter, died at Little Big Horn in 1876. Custer (his grandfather, a Hessian soldier, spelled the family name Kuster), was born in Ohio in 1839. His popularity hit its peak right after the Civil War, earned by heroic leadership. From that time on his career went into decline and ended with his decision to attack a much larger force at Little Big Horn.

Tradition and recent histories say that the street, and Custer High School, which used to be on it, were named for Harvey Custer, an early settler in the old town of Granville. But a misspelling was the source of the error; the settler's name was really Harvey Carter.

Custer Avenue was named in 1892 by Henry Clay Payne. Payne,

rejected by the Union Army because he was too small, named at least two streets in his North Milwaukee subdivision for Civil War generals. Besides Custer, there was *Sheridan* Avenue, a block to the north. Sheridan and Custer were the two most popular Union cavalry generals of the war. Payne also named Wallace and Hammond Avenues, which may have been named for other generals who participated in the conflict. Both of these streets were subsequently renamed.

Custer's Last Stand. (Milwaukee Public Library)

CYPRESS STREET

2500 North and 2400 West
Origin: *Park West*

During the 1920s, Milwaukee street naming took on a strong promotional flavor. Naming streets for developers became less frequent and words that appealed to the ear or the imagination increased. The Roaring Twenties brought names like *Avondale, Lancaster, Clarendon,* and *Wellington.*

In 1926 even the tree names became more exotic. *Palmetto* Avenue was added to the streetscape and an ordinance was passed to replace the

63

common Pine with the exotic Cypress. This was during the street renaming program, when duplicate names were being eliminated, and this Pine Street lost to the South Side's *Pine* Avenue. Cypress trees are native to the warmer climates of the southern United States and Mexico.

DAKOTA STREET

2900 South, between 1300 East and 7100 West
Origin: *Bay View*

When the *Herman* Mann family named this street in 1879, the states of North and South Dakota had not yet been formed from the Dakota Territory. To the Dakota Indians, also known as the Sioux, the word means "friend." North and South Dakota entered the Union in 1889.

DALLAS STREET

6800 North, between 8600 and 9100 West
Origin: *Menomonee River Hills*

Western American cities are well represented in this 1957 subdivision. Dallas, Texas was named for George Dallas, a United States senator and vice-president under James Polk.

DANA STREET, COURT

100 South, between 5800 and 8400 West
Origin: *Story Hill*

Charles L. Dana, born in Illinois, came to Milwaukee to farm in 1865. In 1889, he was the director of the Advancement Association of North

Greenfield (now West Allis). Dana was one of the developers of the Maple Wood Subdivision that included this street in 1892.

DAPHNE STREET

6700 North, between 5700 and 11400 West
Origin: *Village of Fox Point*

Formerly called Kronshage (after Fox Point's first village president), this street name was changed to Daphne in the early 1930s.

DARIEN STREET

3600 West, between 6800 and 7000 North
Origin: *Town and Country Manor*

Darien Street was named in 1957 for the Walworth County community that was settled by pioneers from Darien, New York.

DARNEL AVENUE

8300 North, between 9300 and 10500 West
Origin: *Village of Brown Deer*

The developers, the Francis Schroedel family, chose the name for Darnel Avenue in 1956. It has no particular significance.

DAVIDSON STREET

Thomas Davidson. (Conard's History of Milwaukee County)

200 East, between 300 and 400 South
Origin: *Harbor View*

Thomas Davidson was born in Scotland in 1828. He immigrated to Milwaukee in 1855 and worked for shipbuilder Captain J. Jones. Davidson later joined with William H. Wolf in forming Wolf and Davidson, Milwaukee's largest shipbuilders. Their shipyards were at the junction of the Milwaukee and Kinnickinnic Rivers. Davidson, a founder of the St. Andrew's Society and a Templar of Temperance, was voted the

66

most popular shipyard executive in 1883. He died in 1895. This short street was named by ordinance in 1875.

DAYFIELD AVENUE

2100 East, between 3200 and 3400 South
Origin: *Fernwood*

In 1927, Walter Bennett subdivided part of the farm that had been in the *Bennett* family for nearly a century. The Bennett Hill Subdivision included Dayfield and *Springfield* Avenues.

DEAN ROAD

8400 North, between 6800 and 10600 West
Origin: *Ordinance*

James H. Dean ran a tavern and feed store in Milwaukee during the 1880s. In 1891 he moved north and farmed on land that would become part of River Hills. The land had been owned by his grandfather, James C. *Howard*. The old Town of Milwaukee officially named this road in 1917.

DEBBIE LANE

7000 North, between 9500 and 9800 West
Origin: *Golden Gate*

This street was named for Debbie Schroedel in 1962. Debbie, the granddaughter of developer Francis Schroedel, was born in Milwaukee in 1959.

DEER PLACE

2600 South, between 200 and 400 East
Origin: *Bay View*

Deer Creek, which began in the St. Francis area, flowed north into Bay View where it formed a small lake between what are now Russell and Lincoln Avenues. In 1870 Eber *Ward* platted Deer Street, near Deer Lake. In later years the street was extended westward and the lake was drained.

When the original section of Deer Place was renamed *Otjen* Street, it left this short section blocks west of where the small lake had been. Consequently, Deer Place remains as a reminder of Deer Creek, something that wouldn't have happened if the 1913 Street Renaming Commission's suggestion had been accepted. The commission wanted to rename it Fawn Place.

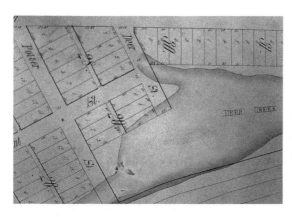

The plat map naming Deer Place in 1870. Logan Avenue (formerly Mitchell Street) runs along the top of the picture. (Milwaukee County Register of Deeds)

DELAWARE AVENUE

From 1300 East and 2400 South to 2600 East and 3500 South
Origin: *Fernwood*

In 1888 Thomas Kennan and his associates continued the Bay View tradition, started by the *Herman* Mann family, of naming streets for states. While the Manns favored western states, Kennan's group preferred eastern and midwestern states. Delaware took its name from Delaware Bay, which was named for Thomas West De La Warr, the first governor of Virginia, in 1610. Thomas Kennan was the grandfather of noted Milwaukeean, George F. Kennan (see *Illinois*).

DELTA PLACE

5300 West, between 7600 and 7800 North
Origin: *Bradley Estates*

Delta Place is not at the mouth of a river, in spite of its name. It was platted in 1955 by developer Francis Schroedel.

DENIS AVENUE

5600 South, between 1400 and 4000 West
Origin: *Mitchell Field*

Jacob and Tillie *Klein* named Denis Avenue as part of Klein's Subdivision in 1937. The subdivision is now part of Mitchell International Airport. It is not known for which Denis, if any, the street was named.

DENMARK STREET

9900 West, between 6000 and 6400 North
Origin: *Little Menomonee Parkway*

This street was named not for the country of Denmark, but for Harold Denemark. Denemark was an employee in the City Engineer's Office when the name was chosen for this street in 1958. Because of a concern that the name would be misspelled, the second "e" was dropped. Denemark, who was later chief draftsman in the department, was born in Trenton, New Jersey in 1926 (see *Celina*).

DENVER AVENUE

6700 North, between 7600 and 9100 West
Origin: *Menomonee River Hills*

Another of the western cities named in this 1955 subdivision, Denver, Colorado was named by Kansas settlers for James Denver, the governor of the Kansas Territory.

DERBY PLACE

4700 North, between 4200 and 8400 West
Origin: *Old North Milwaukee*

The Earl of Derby established the tradition that gave the name "derby" to any important horse race. His race drew spectators who wore stiff, felt hats called "derbies." The North Milwaukee Heights Company named Derby Place in 1893.

DEWEY PLACE

3000 South, between 100 West and 400 East
Origin: *Bay View*

Nelson Dewey. (History of Wisconsin from Prehistoric to Present Periods)

Nelson Dewey, (1813-1889), was the first governor elected in the state of Wisconsin. There were earlier governors of Wisconsin, but they were appointed, rather than elected, when Wisconsin was still a territory. Dewey, a lawyer who served as the state's chief executive from 1848 to 1852, was born in Connecticut. He died penniless and obscure in Cassville, Wisconsin in 1889. Elliott Place, because it was a duplicate of *Elliott* Circle, was renamed Dewey Place by ordinance in 1929.

DEXTER AVENUE

2400 West, between 5300 and 5400 North
Origin: *City of Glendale*

Dexter Avenue was named as part of the Crestwood Subdivision in 1926. The reason the name was selected is not known.

DICKINSON STREET

700 South, between 6000 and 7000 West
Origin: *Johnson's Woods*

James Wilson Dickinson, born in New Hampshire in 1846, arrived in Milwaukee as a Civil War veteran in 1869. He was a deputy sheriff and a real estate developer. This street was named for him in 1888 as part of the Euclid Park Subdivision. Dickinson died in 1902.

DIXON STREET

200 South, between 5900 and 9400 West
Origin: *Johnson's Woods*

In the 1870s, Samuel M. Dixon was a newspaperman turned politician. The story goes that people were so thankful that Dixon gave up writing that they elected him to the Common Council. He was also an attorney for the Chicago and Northwestern Railroad and was responsible for naming the community of North Greenfield, now known as West Allis. In 1927 the Common Council renamed Cross Street for Dixon.

DODGE PLACE

3700 South, between 6400 and 6700 West
Origin: *Wedgewood*

Henry Dodge was the first governor of the Wisconsin Territory. He was born into a frontier family in what became the state of Indiana in 1782. Dodge spent his youth in the territory included in the Louisiana Purchase. After sixteen years as sheriff and marshall in the Missouri Territory, he moved to the lead mining region of Wisconsin in 1827, settling in the Dodgeville area.

Henry Dodge. (History of Wisconsin from Prehistoric to Present Periods)

Dodge, who fought the English in the War of 1812, also served during the Winnebago War of 1827 and the Black Hawk War of 1832. In 1836, when Wisconsin was made a territory, he was appointed governor, a position he held for eight of the next 12 years. In 1848 he was elected the state's first senator. Dodge died in 1867. This street was named for him in 1954 (see *Doty*).

DOGWOOD STREET

7400 North, between 8700 and 9100 West
Origin: *Melody View*

Dogwood Street was named in 1964 in the Melody View Subdivision. The name was chosen to fit in with the other flora-named streets in the area, *Juniper*, *Tupelo*, and *Hemlock* (see *Magnolia*).

71

DONGES COURT

9500 North, between 10400 and 10700 West
Origin: *Village of Bayside*

Jacob Donges Jr. started working as a janitor at age 11, established a business when he was 24, and owned three miles of Lake Michigan shoreline property before he was thirty. His father, Jacob Donges Sr., had immigrated to Milwaukee from Germany in 1842. Jacob Jr., born in Milwaukee in 1860, was 11 years old when his father, the city hall janitor, died. Jacob took over his father's job to support his mother and six brothers and sisters.

When he was 24, he started a hat business downtown that is still in operation. A few years later he bought three miles of lakefront property on the bay near the Milwaukee-Ozaukee county line which became a resort area known as Donges Bay. Two resorts, Donges Bay and *Fairy Chasm*, were established in 1890, providing Milwaukeeans with a clean, quiet spot to get away from the city's fumes and noise.

In 1940 Alpine Lane, on the southern portion of the Donges land, was changed to Donges Court by the old Town of Milwaukee.

DONNA DRIVE, COURT

8500 North, between 7600 and 10900 West
Origin: *Village of Brown Deer*

Harry Forman platted the Rosedale Subdivision in 1954. He named the streets in it for his wife, Rose, and his daughters, Donna and Terry. Donna was born in Milwaukee in 1938.

DOROTHY PLACE

1300 South, between 3700 and 3800 West
Origin: *Silver City*

Street name lore has it that Dorothy Place and nearby *Frederica, Hilda,* and *Margaret* Places were named for sisters. These one-block long, parallel streets, between 37th and 38th Streets south of National Avenue, are often said to be named for the daughters of one man. Some say his name was Trowbridge, some say Shinner. In fact, the man who named the streets was

John Johnston and only Hilda Place was named for his daughter.

Dorothy Place was named for Johnston's niece. She was one year old and lived in London with her parents, Emma and John Purchas, when Johnston platted the streets in 1893. The others memorialized, besides his daughter, were Johnston's sister-in-law and mother (see *Frederica*).

DOTY PLACE

4100 South, between 800 and 1000 East
Origin: *Tippecanoe*

James Doty. (Milwaukee Public Library)

James Duane Doty, governor of the Wisconsin Territory from 1841 to 1844, was an early investor in Milwaukee and other Wisconsin communities, especially Madison. Doty lobbied for the state capital's location on lands that he owned. To assure their votes, he gave preferred lots to the legislators who made the decision. Actions like these, as well as his use of public money for personal land speculation, led to criticism that he used political positions for his own profit rather than the common good.

Doty, a lawyer of English ancestry, was born in Salem, New York in 1799. He explored Wisconsin in the 1820s while serving as judge for the territory and was later its delegate and representative in Congress. Doty was subsequently governor of the Utah Territory and died in Salt Lake City in 1865. This street was named for him in 1954.

DOUGLAS AVENUE

6300 North, between 3200 and 12300 West
Origin: *Fairfield*

Douglas Avenue was platted by Arthur Wenz as part of his Northern Heights Subdivision in 1926. Why he chose the name is not known (see *Carol*).

DOUSMAN STREET

100 East, between 2400 and 3500 North
Origin: *Riverwest*

George G. Dousman was the city clerk who registered this plat in 1867. Dousman, who was city clerk throughout the 1860s, died in 1879.

DOVER STREET

2700 South, between 200 and 700 East
Origin: *Bay View*

Sanford J. *Williams*, a Bay View settler, named Dover Street in 1879. The Cliffs of Dover in Kent, England are the source of the Dover name in the United States. The 1913 Street Renaming Commission tried unsuccessfully to change the name to London Street.

DOWNER AVENUE

2600 East, between 2400 and 3500 North
Origin: *Ordinance*

Jason Downer, justice of the Wisconsin Supreme Court, was born in Vermont in 1813. After a law education at Dartmouth College, Downer arrived in Milwaukee in 1844, where he worked as editor of the "Milwaukee Sentinel" for a short time. After serving as circuit judge he was appointed, and later elected, to the state supreme court. Downer died in 1883. Glen Avenue was renamed Downer Avenue in 1898, shortly after Downer College (named for Downer, one of its founders) was established on this street (see *College*).

Downer College at the turn of the century.
(Milwaukee Public Library)

74

DRURY LANE

3300 South, between 3100 and 3300 West
Origin: *Jackson Park*

Like the other streets in the Concord Hill Subdivision, this one alludes to the fine arts. London's Drury Lane was the home of theaters that presented plays as far back as the 16th century. Milwaukee's Drury Lane was named in 1929 (see *Lakefield*).

DULUTH AVENUE

3800 South, between 7300 and 7400 West
Origin: *Wedgewood*

Duluth, Minnesota is the namesake of the French explorer Daniel Greysolan, Du Luth. This street was named for the Lake Superior port in 1959.

EDEN PLACE, COURT

3600 South, between 1700 East and 9900 West
Origin: *City of St. Francis*

During the late 1800s, many new South Side streets were given the names of places. First came state names, followed by more exotic names like *Tripoli*, Bombay, and Arctic. This one, platted by John *Stowell* in 1892, may have been called for the earthly paradise, the Garden of Eden.

EDGERTON AVENUE

5100 South, between 100 East/West and 2700 West
Origin: *City of Cudahy*

Elisha W. Edgerton, as a 19 year old, worked as a clerk for Solomon *Juneau* during Milwaukee's founding year of 1835. As a 76 year old, he had a street named in his honor by Patrick *Cudahy* when he founded the town of Cudahy in 1892.

In between, Edgerton, who was born in Connecticut in 1816, had a varied career. After working for Juneau, he began a very successful farming career that culminated in his farm being proclaimed the best in the state. Edgerton was elected president of the State Agriculture Society three times and also served on the county board. At the age of 54 he ran stockyards in the Menomonee Valley and began a livestock commission business. As with most of the men named in Cudahy streets, it was the meat connection that gave him this honor. Edgerton died in 1904.

EDGEWOOD AVENUE

3500 North, between 1800 and 3000 East
Origin: *Downer Woods*

This street borders the village of Shorewood and runs along Downer Woods. It was changed from *Keefe* Avenue by ordinance in 1909.

EDGEWORTH DRIVE

5200 West, between 7600 and 8000 North
Origin: *Bradley Estates*

This street was given the promotional name Edgeworth in 1955.

EDISON STREET

100 East, between 1000 and 1300 North
Origin: *Juneautown*

In 1912, River Street was renamed Edison Street to wipe out a reminder of the city's former red light district. Houses of ill repute in the River Street area had been Milwaukee's largest tourist attraction for decades. The city's socialists had been against the "white slave traffic," and when they assumed power in 1910 one of their first orders of business was to close these houses. The electricity-generating power plant at the south end of River Street was the inspiration for the new name.

EGGERT PLACE

5200 North, between 1900 and 8800 West
Origin: *Old North Milwaukee*

Peter Eggert was born in Mecklenberg, Germany in the 1820s. He came to Milwaukee in 1852 and started a farm on 140 acres of land that became part of the city of North Milwaukee in the 1890s. As the area urbanized, Eggert sold his land and began a building supply business. He and his son, Charles, each served as North Milwaukee village treasurer.

Peter Eggert died in 1905, and the City of North Milwaukee reached its end in 1928, when it was annexed by Milwaukee. A few months later, in 1929, this street was changed from Payne to Eggert Place because it was too much like *Paine* Street on the South Side.

ELGIN LANE

1200 South, between 1200 and 1500 West
Origin: *Walker's Point*

In 1926 Union Avenue was changed to Elgin Lane because of nearby *Union* Street. Elgin Lane, which is really an alley, may have been named for a city or a ship. Since the city was naming other streets during its renaming program for cities like *Albany*, *Scranton*, and *Medford*, this street may be named for Elgin, Illinois.

However, the sinking of the "Lady Elgin," one of the city's major disasters, may be memorialized in this street name. In 1860 the "Lady Elgin" was returning from an excursion to Chicago. In a fog, it was rammed by a schooner and sunk. Two hundred and twenty-five people, mostly Third Ward Irish, died in the largest loss of life disaster in Milwaukee's history.

ELLEN STREET

From 1800 East and 2800 South to 2200 East and 3500 South
Origin: *Bay View*

Zebiah *Wentworth Estes* named this street in 1871 for her daughter Ellen. Ellen Estes, who was born in 1837, was among the first children born to white settlers in the area. She married clergyman Isaac *Linebarger* and died in Bay View in 1910.

ELLIOTT CIRCLE

2200 North, between 5800 and 5900 West
Origin: *Washington Heights*

Eugene Elliott's family moved to Milwaukee from Illinois in 1852,

Eugene Elliott. (Illustrated News Annual)

when he was ten years old. After serving in the Civil War, he became a lawyer in 1876, city attorney in 1885, and judge in 1900. Even with this distinguished career, Elliott is best known for the games he played.

Elliott, a founder of the Milwaukee Chess Club in 1875, was a frequent winner of chess tournaments held during the 1880s and finished the decade as city champion. The club's interest in whist, the forerunner of bridge, led to it reorganizing as the Milwaukee Whist Club. Elliott became a charter member and ''Father of the American Whist League'' in 1891. In 1902 he died at the Milwaukee Whist Club while playing his favorite game.

Elliott left his real estate investments to his wife, Catherine E. Dousman Elliott, whom he married in 1865. She named this street in 1918. It is the only truly circular street in the city.

ELM STREET

6700 North, between 3400 and 3900 West
Origin: *Fairfield*

In 1929 the old Town of Granville laid out Elm Street. Although there have been others with this classic American street name in Milwaukee's past, this is the only survivor. The American Elm, Rock Elm, and Slippery Elm are all Milwaukee natives.

ELMHURST ROAD

3700 West, between 400 and 4200 North
Origin: *Lincoln Creek*

The word Elmhurst refers to a wooded hill covered with elms. Elmhurst Road was named by Nicholas Ewins and John H. Wiersum in 1923.

ELMORE AVENUE, COURT

From 3600 North and 8700 West to 3900 North and 9700 West
Origin: *Golden Valley*

This avenue was named in 1928, during an era when the city was naming many streets for prominent Milwaukeeans. Riverious Elmore, who came to the city from New York State in 1851, began the first coal company in Wisconsin. His son, Eltinge, expanded the family business with Alabama coal mines. Eltinge Elmore was active in local organizations, including one that operated a farm in Waukesha County that took care of homeless boys.

Elmore's coal business. (Illustrated Description of Milwaukee)

ELY PLACE

4300 North and 5500 West
Origin: *Lincoln Creek*

Lydia Ely. (Illustrated News Annual)

Ely Place, named by the city in 1929, honors Lydia Ely, an artist who organized the first art exhibition in Wisconsin in 1865. It ran in conjunction with a fair to raise money for a home for Civil War veterans. Ely also served as the fair's president. During the 1890s, Ely almost single-handedly raised money for the Civil War monument on 9th and Wisconsin Avenue. She died in 1914 at the age of 79 (see *National*).

EMERY AVENUE

6600 West and 2800 North
Origin: *Enderis Park*

Emery Galineau, president of the Wisconsin Land and Realty Exchange, platted this street in 1924.

EMMBER LANE

1300 West, between 100 North/South and 700 South
Origin: *Menomonee River Valley*

Emmber is a contraction of the names EMMett and BERnard Peck, brothers who owned Peck Foods Corporation. Emmber is also the brand name of a line of the company's products. The brothers, born around 1930, are the grandsons of the company's founder, Bernhard Peck. Bernhard, who was born in Bohemia, came to Milwaukee in 1889 and established a butcher shop.

This street name was changed from *Muskego* Avenue in 1982 at the brothers' request. Visitors had a hard time finding this section of Muskego, as it was nearly a mile from the main portion of the street. In 1913 the Street Renaming Commission had recommended calling this thoroughfare through the city's meatpacking area Packers Avenue.

ERIE STREET

From 100 North and 100 East to 500 South and 900 East
Origin: *Historic Third Ward*

Erie Street was named in 1856 for Lake Erie, joining other Third Ward streets named for the Great Lakes and Great Lake ports. The word Erie comes from an Indian term meaning "long tail," which referred to a tribe of Indians along the south shore of Lake Erie (see *Michigan*).

81

ESTES STREET

2900 South, between 1700 and 2200 East
Origin: *Bay View*

Elijah Estes, born in North Carolina in 1814, came to Milwaukee in 1835. Estes claimed a sizable portion of the lakefront property that was to become part of Bay View, where he built a log cabin for his wife, Zebiah *Wentworth*. As the area became urbanized with the founding of the rolling mills, the Estes' began subdividing their land, naming some streets for family members. This street was named by Zebiah Estes in 1871.

EUCLID AVENUE

3200 South, between 2400 East and 9800 West
Origin: *Bay View*

Cleveland's Euclid Avenue was known as the "Showplace of America," and was called the world's most beautiful street during the latter half of the 19th century. Beginning in Cleveland's downtown, the tree-lined street of elaborate residences extended four miles into the suburbs. Country-style homes on "Millionaires' Row" were set on large, manicured grounds, giving the avenue a park-like appearance. The street was named for Euclid Township, to the east of the city. The name honors Euclid, the Greek father of geometry.

Euclid Avenue became a popular street name throughout the country and in Milwaukee. This Euclid Avenue, platted in 1888, was one of three Euclid Avenues in the city. The others were changed to eliminate duplication (see *State*).

EVANS STREET

7900 West, between 4800 and 4900 North
Origin: *Long View*

Evans Street was named in 1954. It may have been named for Harris K. Evans, a real estate developer active at the time. Evans made many contributions to the community, including serving on the board of the Rescue Mission.

82

EVERETT STREET

600 North, between 200 and 400 West
Origin: *Kilbourntown*

Edward Everett, one of the country's great orators, spent the last ten years of his life inspiring Americans. In the five years leading to the Civil War, Everett spoke to groups in both the North and South. He appealed to their nationalism with tales of George *Washington* and the union tradition started in the revolutionary period.

After the war began, Everett continued his talks to Northerners, encouraging them to preserve the *Union*. Everett's only scheduled Milwaukee appearance was canceled due to illness. He died during the closing days of the war, and a few weeks later, in March of 1865, a city ordinance named Everett Street in his honor.

EVERGREEN LANE

600 South, between 2700 and 2800 West
Origin: *National Park*

This street was changed from Mitchell Park Drive to Evergreen Lane in 1926. Duplicate street names were being eliminated during this period and there already was a *Mitchell* Street on the South Side.

EVERTS STREET

7500 North, between 9400 and 9900 West
Origin: *Calumet Farms*

Brothers Truman and Charles Everts settled in the northwest part of Milwaukee County in the mid-1830s. They, along with others, named their new township Granville, after their home in New York. Truman, born about 1790, farmed until his death in 1855. Charles, who was born in 1799 and died in 1871, was a farmer who was active in the municipal affairs of the town, as was the next generation of Everts. Alderman Clarence Miller suggested the name for this new street in 1977.

FAIRFIELD COURT

6300 North, between 3800 and 3900 West
Origin: *Fairfield*

Fairfield, which describes a pleasant, open place, is a common city and street name in the United States. Fairfield Court was named as part of Zingan and Braun's Fairfield Subdivision in 1928.

FAIRLANE AVENUE, COURT

8300 North, between 8000 and 11000 West
Origin: *Village of Brown Deer*

Fairlane Avenue, while a little redundant, is one of the pleasant sounding street names in the Bradley Estates Subdivision that was platted in 1956.

FAIRMOUNT AVENUE

5000 North, between 1600 and 11000 West
Origin: *Village of Whitefish Bay*

Fairmount Avenue was platted in 1888 as part of the Fairmount Heights Subdivision. The name was chosen for its sound rather than its meaning. There is no mountain, not even a small hill, in this subdivision.

FAIRVIEW AVENUE

100 North/South, between 5900 and 8000 West
Origin: *Johnson's Woods*

When the name of this street was changed from Johnson to Canal in the 1920s, the residents were irate. The city's program to standardize street names required that all streets along a line have the same name. If a street was called *Canal* Street in the eastern part of the city where it ran along a canal, then it had to be called Canal Street in the western highlands.

The inhabitants of the new Canal Street petitioned the city for a change. They did not want the name because "as everybody knows throughout the United States the streets having the name 'Canal' have a very poor reputation." Milwaukee's Canal Street had been no exception. Decades before, the stench from the canal area had driven away local homeowners and the foul air given off by industries along the canals was blamed for epidemics on the near South Side.

The petitioners argued that the new Canal Street was not contiguous with the old Canal Street and that it would never be near a canal. Residents wanted it changed and they weren't going to be fussy. "Fairview or any other suitable name" would be acceptable. On March 1, 1927 their wish became law and Canal Street between 60th and 68th Streets became Fairview Avenue. The whole issue would have been avoided if the recommendation of the 1913 Street Renaming Commission had been followed. It had suggested changing Canal Street to Valley Street.

FAIRWAY PLACE

5200 West, between 7700 and 8000 North
Origin: *Bradley Estates*

There can be little doubt what the namers of this street had in mind when they platted it in 1955. Fairway Place is a few blocks from both the Brynwood and Tripoli golf courses (see *Link*).

FAIRY CHASM DRIVE

9200 North, between 8500 and 9100 West
Origin: *Bayside*

Before being used as a street name, Fairy Chasm was the name of a Lake Michigan resort. According to legend, the name was inspired by Jacob *Donges'* daughters, Irma and Elsie. They were frolicking on the beach as Donges stood above on the deeply chasmed bluff. Their chasing and laughter, with their dresses billowing in the wind, made their father think of a painting he had seen of dancing fairies. Fairy Chasm became the name of the resort, and then of nearby Fish Creek. In 1927, it became the name of this street.

"Gardens and Chasm's in Donges Bay," (at the gate to Donges Bay).

FALLING HEATH PLACE

3300 South, between 2300 and 2400 East
Origin: *Fernwood*

John T. *Meredith*'s sons named this short street in 1923. Fallings Heath was a village outside Wolverhampton, England which Meredith listed as his place of birth. His sons dropped the "s" from Fallings when they

86

named the street. Meredith, and his Bay View-born sons, ran a general contracting business in Bay View (see *Malvern, Meredith, Swain*).

FARDALE AVENUE

3800 South, between 3000 and 3300 West
Origin: *Southpoint*

Fardale Avenue was named as part of the Forest View Subdivision in 1959. Dale means valley and the name may have been chosen for the view of the low land to the east of this street.

FARWELL AVENUE

From 1200 East and 1400 North to 2300 East and 3100 North
Origin: *Lower East Side*

Leonard James Farwell, born in New York State in 1819, came to Milwaukee in the 1840s and started the largest wholesale hardware business in the Midwest. In 1849 he moved to Madison where he owned almost half the village and, at 32 years of age, was the youngest man ever elected governor of Wisconsin. But he had reversals. In the depression of 1857 he lost all his wealth. Then, while in an appointed position in Washington, D.C., he witnessed the assassination of Abraham *Lincoln*. When his wife died three years later, Farwell and his children moved to Chicago, where his law office was destroyed in the Great Fire of 1871. Farwell finally settled in Missouri where he died in 1889. This street was named for him by David Hull in 1854.

FAULKNER ROAD

8800 West, between 7800 and 8400 North
Origin: *Land Bank*

Thomas Faulkner, born in Ireland in 1811, settled in the old town of Granville in 1837. Faulkner, a farmer and justice of the peace, was honored with a street named for him in 1974 by alderman Clarence Miller.

FERNWOOD AVENUE, CIRCLE

3200 South, between 3000 East and 7500 West
Origin: *Fernwood*

This street was platted as part of the Fernwood Subdivision in 1888. In the 1890s, in the "Milwaukee Sentinel's News from the Suburbs" column, Fernwood was treated as a suburb along with Wauwatosa, Whitefish Bay, and St. Francis, although it is now considered part of Bay View.

FERRY STREET

200 East, between 100 and 200 South
Origin: *Walker's Point*

This short street led to the ferry crossing of the Milwaukee River when it was named in 1842. Two years later there were complaints from farmers trying to get into the city that "the ferry at Walker's Point is sunk." In August of 1844 a float bridge was opened and the need for ferrying was eliminated. During the 1860s this half-block long street was known for its gambling and drinking, with at least 14 taverns and gambling houses jammed on it.

FIEBRANTZ AVENUE, COURT

4100 North, between 300 East and 10300 West
Origin: *Rufus King*

William J. Fiebrantz, real estate developer, local Republican politician, and bicycle racer, was born in Milwaukee of German parents in 1858. He platted this street in 1892.

William J. Fiebrantz. (Men of Progress, 1897)

88

FILLMORE DRIVE

2400 South, between 4400 and 5100 West
Origin: *Jackson Park*

Millard Fillmore, (1800-1874), became president when Zachary *Taylor* died in office in 1850. Fillmore's primary action as president was approving the Compromise of 1850, which delayed the Civil War. He lost the support of most Northerners by enforcing the compromise's provision to return runaway slaves and was not nominated for another term. This street, in the presidents' section of town, was named in 1948.

FINGER PLACE

2500 South, between 6700 and 6800 West
Origin: *Fairview*

Emanuel Finger, born in Germany in 1841, immigrated to the U.S. in 1860 and to the old town of Greenfield in 1866. He started a dairy farm that was continued by his sons until it was subdivided in the 1920s, when this short street was platted.

FINN PLACE

3600 North, between 900 and 2400 West
Origin: *Arlington Heights*

Richard J. Finn, born in Milwaukee in 1853, began his apprenticeship as a plumber and gas fitter when he was 15 years old. By the time he was 24 he had his own business. During the next ten years his trade grew, much of it due to city contracts for water and sewer work. At 34 he married and cashed in on the real estate boom with a land sale that propelled him up the earnings ladder.

A few months after turning 36, he joined two other Irish Americans, Michael *Carpenter* and Edward *Hackett*, in the development of the Williamsburg Heights Subdivision. Each had a street named for himself, although Carpenter and Hackett Places were later replaced as duplicates. Only Finn's Place, as it was called in the fall of 1889, endured. But Finn didn't; he died the next spring.

FLAGG AVENUE

5800 North, between 8800 and 11900 West
Origin: *Silver Swan*

Before 1959 Flagg Avenue was known as Douglas Road. After the Post Office complained that Douglas Road and *Douglas* Avenue caused confusion in mail deliveries, the city changed the name to Flagg Avenue. There is no record of why the name was chosen.

FLORIDA STREET

400 South, between 200 East and 600 West
Origin: *Walker's Point*

Florida wasn't a state when this street was named in 1842. It may have been named because one of the developers, Daniel *Wells*, had surveyed parts of the Florida Territory just before settling in Milwaukee. Florida is a Spanish word that means "flowering." The name was given by Juan Ponce de Leon when he first saw Florida on Easter Sunday in 1512.

FLORIST AVENUE

6000 North, between 2700 and 12400 West
Origin: *Thurston Woods*

Early in the 20th century, August Manke conducted his florist business at the corner of what are now Teutonia and Florist Avenues. At that time, Teutonia was known as Cedarburg Road and Florist was unnamed. When real estate man Arthur Wenz began development along the unnamed road in 1926, he called it Florist Avenue.

FOND DU LAC AVENUE

From 1700 North and 1300 West to 7800 North and 12400 West
Origin: *Kilbourntown*

This early 1850s plank road led to the city of Fond du Lac. The French name means "bottom of the lake," a reference to that city's location at the south end of Lake Winnebago. The French took the name from the Indian village there known as Wanikamiu, "the farthest point of the lake."

FOREST HOME AVENUE

From 1800 South and 1400 West to 4300 South and 6900 West
Origin: *Ordinance*

Forest Home Avenue and *Arlington* Place are two streets in the city named after cemeteries. In 1850 St. Paul's Episcopal Church established the Forest Home Cemetery at Janesville Plank Road and Kilbourn Road. In 1872 Janesville Plank Road was renamed Forest Home Avenue (Kilbourn Road was later changed to South 27th Street).

Forest Home Avenue. (Milwaukee County Historical Society)

FOSTER AVENUE

4700 South, between 1400 and 1600 West
Origin: *Mitchell West*

Foster Avenue was named in 1958 as part of the Layton Acres Subdivision. The reason this name was selected is not known.

FOUNTAIN AVENUE

7700 North, between 5600 and 10700 West
Origin: *Village of Brown Deer*

Fountain Avenue is part of the Fountain Acres Subdivision that was developed in the 1920s. The name was probably chosen for the natural springs prevalent in the area.

FRANKLIN PLACE

1100 East, between 1200 and 1800 North
Origin: *Ordinance*

In 1856, Elizabeth Street was renamed Franklin Place. Julia Alcott Lapham, daughter of Increase *Lapham*, claimed the street was named for Franklin Peirce, son of real estate developer Jonathan Peirce (see *North Pierce*). Milwaukee historian John G. Gregory thought it may have been named for Benjamin Franklin, (1706-1790), diplomat, printer, scientist, author, and American revolutionary. Who was right? The evidence supports Gregory's theory.

Prospect and Franklin Avenues. (Milwaukee's Great Industries, 1892)

Jonathan Peirce named other city streets for family members and friends during this time (*Buffum, Burleigh, Julia,* and *Ring*). But Peirce didn't name this street, it was changed by city ordinance. And aldermen generally selected names with broader appeal, like those of presidents, national figures, local leaders, or others of local significance. It's more likely that they would name a street for Benjamin Franklin than for the son of a real estate developer.

Also, 1856 was Franklin's sesquicentennial and celebrations marking the event were conducted throughout the country. Milwaukee was no exception. The city's printers observed the occasion as did its firemen. And presumably so did the city fathers when they named Franklin Place on May 26th of that year.

FRATNEY STREET

800 East, between 2400 and 4000 North
Origin: *Riverwest*

Frederick Fratney, who was born in Poland, fled Austria as a political refugee and later edited a German-language newspaper in Milwaukee. Fratney was associated with the "Forty-eighters," a German revolutionary group that advocated freedom of speech, trial by jury, and a representative form of government in a united Germany. Their unsuccessful revolution was supported by freedom-loving Milwaukeeans of all nationalities, as city residents were led by Byron *Kilbourn* in a public demonstration in the spring of 1848.

The Forty-eighters preached independence of thought, the need for education, and opposed both official dishonesty and priests. Besides hating priests, Fratney hated Catholics and Irish. Just what part his Irish wife, Bridget, played in this dislike is unknown. Fratney Street was named by Julius Franke in 1857, two years after Fratney's death.

FREDERICA PLACE

1100 South, between 3700 and 3800 West
Origin: *Silver City*

Freddie, as the family called her, was Frederica Thorsen Seaman, sister-in-law of Milwaukeean John Johnston. Freddie was 41 years old and the wife of furniture maker and lumberman Alonzo D. Seaman when Johnston named this street for her in 1893.

Johnston, the wealthy immigrant Scotsman who developed this subdivision, was proud of his sporting skills. He was part of the city's four-man curling team that won the national championship in 1881. A rifleman and president of the rifle club, he won shooting events in Milwaukee, Scotland, and England. He died in 1904 at age 68 (see *Hilda*).

FREDERICK AVENUE

2100 East, between 2400 and 3500 North
Origin: *Murray Hill*

James *Murray* platted Murray Hill in 1856. Why he chose the name Frederick for this street is not known.

FREMONT PLACE

2700 South, between 500 East and 6700 West
Origin: *Bay View*

This street, platted in 1911 by Burnham Realty, was probably named for John Fremont, considering the Burnhams' tendency to use the names of American political figures for the streets of this neighborhood (*Quincy*, *Adams*, and *Taylor)*.

John Charles Fremont, (1813-1890), was an explorer, a soldier, the first Republican candidate for president - he lost to James Buchanan in 1856 - and governor of the Arizona Territory. Fremont, who led California in its revolt against Mexico, later became wealthy but lost his money in railroad speculation.

94

FRESNO STREET

8800 West, between 6400 and 6500 North
Origin: *Menomonee River Hills*

Fresno, California was named for the Spanish word for the "ash trees" which were prevalent in the area. In 1955, Fresno was one of the western cities named in this subdivision.

FRONT STREET

100 East and 800 North
Origin: *Juneautown*

Front Street, 1994.

In June of 1855 some downtown businessmen wanted to add some class to the short, unnamed alley near the Milwaukee River where they conducted their trade. The American tradition was to name streets near water either Water Street or Front Street. Since *Water Street* was already in use, Front Street was proposed to the Common Council, which approved the name that September.

FULTON STREET

1500 East, between 2600 and 2800 South
Origin: *Bay View*

Fulton is one of the country's most common street names. Most of them are the namesakes of Robert Fulton, the American who designed the first successful steamship. His invention changed the transportation industry by providing shipping that could meet service schedules, something that sailing ships could not do well. The Pennsylvania-born Fulton, (1756-1815), was a landscape and portrait painter besides being an engineer and inventor. Milwaukee has had at least four streets named Fulton; this Fulton Street is the lone survivor. It was named in 1926, during the street renaming project, and replaced Davelaar, a street named on paper only. At the time, the street was the site of a brick yard.

GALENA STREET, PLACE

1000 North, between 200 and 6000 West
Origin: *Kilbourntown*

Galena, Illinois, on the Rock River, was the commercial center of the lead mining region when this street was named in 1835 by Byron *Kilbourn*. Galena, then larger than Chicago, was the distribution center for lead taken from galena, a lead sulfide ore (see *Mineral*).

GARFIELD AVENUE

2200 North, between 1100 East and 6000 West
Origin: *Ordinance*

James Garfield, (1831-1881), was the 20th President and the second to be assassinated. He was shot a few months after taking office by an unsuccessful job seeker, and after lingering for two months, died in September 1881. Within weeks, talk of naming a Milwaukee street in his honor surfaced but bogged down in politics. Finally, in the fall of 1883, Beaubian Street was named for Garfield.

Garfield was a Civil War general, member of Congress, college president, and professor. He composed poetry and could write Latin with one hand while simultaneously writing Greek with the other. He was followed as president by Chester *Arthur*.

GAUER CIRCLE

2800 South, between 100 and 400 East
Origin: *Bay View*

Paul Gauer, the son of a French immigrant, was born in Bay View in 1881. A socialist, Gauer represented the South Side community as its alderman from 1920 through 1936, including terms as president of the Common Council. Henry Otjen was the owner of the land that includes Gauer Circle. Although Otjen named the street in 1928, the city called it Bennett Street until 1939, when it made Gauer Circle the official name. The Circle suffix isn't quite accurate; the street is an oval (see *Elliott*).

Paul Gauer. (The Gauer Story)

GENEVA PLACE

2900 North, between 1700 and 1800 East
Origin: *Riverside Park*

Because North Park Front could be confused with *Park* Place, two blocks to the south, it was changed to Geneva Place during the 1920s renaming program. Several North Side streets were given names of cities at this time. Geneva, the city, lies on Lake Geneva in Switzerland (see *Montreal*).

GEORGIA AVENUE, COURT

3700 South, between 7200 and 7400 West
Origin: *Wedgewood*

In 1956 this street was named for the state of Georgia. George Augustus of Hanover, (1683-1760), crowned George II of England, was the inspiration for the state's name.

GERTRUDE DRIVE

4900 North, between 7700 and 8100 West
Origin: *Long View*

Gertrude Drive was named in 1954 as part of the Longwood Parksites Subdivision. Who the street was named for, if anyone, is a mystery.

GIRARD AVENUE

2900 North, between 6100 and 6700 West
Origin: *Enderis Park*

Paul *Hartung* subdivided the family farm in 1916 and named Girard Avenue for a now unknown reason.

GLADSTONE PLACE

200 East, between 2700 and 2800 South
Origin: *Bay View*

William Ewart Gladstone.
(The Two Mr. Gladstones)

In a rare display of ethnic benevolence, Gladstone Place was named for an English prime minister by three Irishmen in 1887. Milwaukeeans John Somers, William Jordan, and Humphrey Desmond were strong supporters of Irish independence. They named their street in the Orchard Park Subdivision for William Ewart Gladstone. Gladstone was instrumental in the passage of the Irish Land Act which gave Irishmen the opportunity to own their own land. And he favored Irish Home Rule, an issue important to Milwaukee's Irish.

Gladstone, born in 1809, was noted for his reforms at home, too. In England he lowered taxes, instituted the vote by secret ballot, abolished import duties, expanded education, reformed parliament, and abolished the sale of army commissions. He was hated by Queen Victoria but very popular with the English people.

GLEN AVENUE

5500 North, between 8100 and 8300 West
Origin: *Village of Whitefish Bay*

Glen Avenue was named in 1922 by Whitefish Bay ordinance. The original section of the street, which is named for the Scottish word for valley, runs through a low-lying area.

GLENBROOK ROAD, COURT

9400 North, between 6900 and 10700 West
Origin: *Village of Bayside*

The original section of this aptly named road runs parallel to a stream in an area known for its chasms and ravines. Originally called Staunton Avenue, the street name was changed to Glenbrook about 1950.

GLENDALE AVENUE, COURT

4600 North, between 1200 and 9200 West
Origin: *Village of Whitefish Bay*

Glendale Avenue was named in 1890, making it a grandfather of promotional street names formed by combining terms for natural features. It wasn't until the 1920s that it became fashionable to combine words like hill, lake, dale, lawn, wood, crest, pine, spring, and rose to create pleasant sounding names. Glendale is a peculiar combination in that both terms mean the same thing. Glen is a Scottish term for valley and dale is the English version, so the name means valleyvalley, a feature that does not abound in the area.

The street was named by the Glendale Investment Association. The city of Glendale, which grew around it, was incorporated in the 1950s.

GLENVIEW AVENUE

8400 West, between 100 North/South and 500 North
Origin: *City of Wauwatosa*

The glen viewed is the one that Honey Creek runs through to the east. Glenview Avenue, which led south to the old town of Greenfield, was known as Greenfield Avenue until it was renamed about 1930.

GLOVER STREET

2000 North and 500 East
Origin: *Riverwest*

Glover Street was named in 1994 as the result of efforts by students of Chuck Cooney, a history teacher at Riverside High School. The students encouraged residents on a portion of *Reservoir* Avenue to sign a petition to rename it for Joshua Glover, a runaway St. Louis slave who was arrested in Milwaukee in 1852. This street was chosen as the one to honor Glover because it intersects with *Booth* Street, named for Sherman Booth, the man who helped Glover to freedom in Canada by aiding in his escape from the city jail.

GOLDCREST AVENUE

5800 South, between 1300 and 2700 West
Origin: *Goldman Park*

Leo and L.O. Goldman of Goldman Realty liked gold in their street names. They dedicated this street in 1931 (see *Goldleaf*).

GOLDLEAF AVENUE

6000 South, between 100 East/West and 200 West
Origin: *New Coeln*

The name of this short street was inspired by the gold theme started by Goldman Realty in the 1930s. It was platted in 1978 (see *Mangold*).

GOOD HOPE ROAD, PLACE

7200 North, between 2700 and 12400 West
Origin: *City of Glendale*

The community of Good Hope, at the intersection of Good Hope Road and Green Bay Avenue, dates back to at least 1848. There was an inn called the Good Hope House there then. The next year the Good Hope Post Office, a stopping point for the mail stage between Milwaukee and Green Bay, was established. One researcher believes the name may be traced to the mid-1830s and that it was bestowed by Jefferson Davis, later President of the Confederacy. Davis was a government surveyor of the Green Bay Road from Chicago to Green Bay.

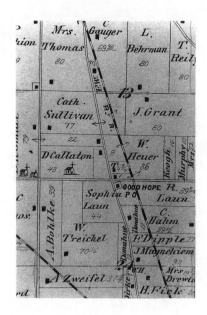

The Good Hope Post Office at Good Hope Road and Green Bay Avenue. (Illustrated Atlas of Milwaukee, Wisconsin, 1876)

GOODRICH AVENUE, COURT

8100 North, between 9300 and 10500 West
Origin: *Village of Fox Point*

William Osborn Goodrich was born in Milwaukee in 1862. As a young man he took over his father's linseed oil business. He was appointed a director of the Pabst Brewing Company after marrying Marie Pabst, daughter of Captain Fred *Pabst*. Goodrich, who was blinded in an accident when he was 12, was well known for his singing ability. At the age of 85 he amazed professional singers with his ability to sing well, and with a powerful voice, for extended periods of time. Goodrich died in 1956. Goodrich Lane, the street on which he lived, was named by Fox Point ordinance about 1930.

GORDON CIRCLE, COURT, PLACE

1300 East, between 2400 and 3400 North
Origin: *Riverwest*

Gordon Place was named in 1901 by Charles B. *Whitnall* and his wife, Annie Davis Gordon, as part of what is now called Gordon Park. Whitnall and Annie Gordon, who grew up on the banks of the river north of the park, were neighbors as children and married in 1883. They were later divorced.

101

GRAHAM STREET

500 East, between 2400 and 2700 South
Origin: *Bay View*

Wilson Graham was born in Ireland in 1815. He received his legal education in Ohio and became one of Milwaukee's first lawyers when he arrived here at age 23 in 1838. Graham served as town clerk when Milwaukee was still a town and, after it reached city status, he was elected an alderman. Later he represented the city on the county board and as state assemblyman.

The intersection of Wilson and Graham Streets is one of two intersections in the city that have the names of one person (the other was named for six month old *Alexander Nicholas* Sulkowski). Graham served as attorney for Sanford *Williams*, who named Graham Street in 1879, and for his mother, Catherine Williams, who named Wilson Street in 1883.

GRANADA STREET

6100 South, between 1300 and 1500 West
Origin: *Maitland Park*

Granada, the Spanish word for pomegranate, is the capital of the province of Granada in southern Spain. The street was named in 1959.

GRANGE AVENUE

5500 South, between 100 East/West and 3800 West
Origin: *City of Cudahy*

Patrick *Cudahy* named this street in 1892 for William Grange, who, like many of the men whose names appear on Cudahy street signs, was involved in the meat industry. Grange's parents emigrated from England in 1841 and set up a business near the harbor supplying meat to Great Lakes' vessels.

Grange, born in the Third Ward in 1848, worked with his father but later developed a real estate business and speculated in Cudahy property. Grange Avenue in Racine is also named for Grange, who died in 1932.

GRANT BOULEVARD

4200 West, between 2300 and 2900 North
Origin: *Sherman Park*

Ulysses S. Grant and William T. *Sherman* were the best known Union generals to serve in the Civil War. Both were honored with boulevards named for them in the Boulevard Park Subdivision in 1909. Grant was president from 1869 to 1877. His administration was infamous for its corruption, although Grant's reputation was unmarred.

GRANT STREET

2200 South, between 500 and 3800 West
Origin: *Lincoln Village*

When this street was named in 1871, Ulysses S. Grant, (1822-1885), was in his first term as president and was the most popular man in the country. Grant had accepted Lee's surrender to end the Civil War and became the first U.S. citizen since George *Washington* to be made a full general.

GRANTOSA DRIVE, COURT

From 4000 North and 10500 West to 4900 North and 8400 West
Origin: *Grantosa*

This street name is a combination of the names of the two towns it runs through, GRANville and WauwaTOSA. Granville is the name of an Englishman and Wauwatosa comes from an Indian word for firefly. The street name was taken from the Grantosa Heights Subdivision which was named by *Carmen* Gettelman in 1927.

GRANVILLE ROAD

From 9100 West and 7200 North to 10700 West and 8800 North
Origin: *Granville Station*

Granville, an area that extended from 27th Street to Waukesha County and from Hampton Avenue to Ozaukee County, was one of the townships that formed Milwaukee County. A group of the town's settlers named it for their former home, Granville, New York. The New York Granville was named for an English statesman, John Carteret, Earl of Granville, (1690-1763), who had large land holdings in America.

This 19th century road took its name from the town, most of which became part of Milwaukee through annexation in the mid-1900s.

GRANVILLE WOODS ROAD

7000 West, between 8000 and 8400 North
Origin: *Granville Woods*

Granville Woods Road, located in the old town of Granville, was platted in the Granville Woods Subdivision in 1990.

GREELEY STREET

200 East, between 2500 and 2900 South
Origin: *Bay View*

Horace Greeley, a newspaper editor best known for popularizing the slogan "Go west young man," ran for president against U.S. *Grant* in 1872.

104

He was popular with Milwaukee's German and Irish communities, and Greeley Clubs sprang up in support of him. The strenuous campaign, his election loss, and the death of his wife led to his physical and mental breakdown, resulting in his own death in November of that year, the same year that Enoch *Chase* named this street for him.

Greeley visited Milwaukee in 1854 and was impressed with the productivity of the city, which he judged by the smoke pouring from the chimneys of its factories. He did have some reservations about the personal habits of Milwaukeeans though. He warned that they should stop "using tobacco and other hurtful superfluities." Milwaukee's beer production and Greeley's support for total abstinence from alcohol give clues to what the "hurtful superfluities" were.

Horace Greeley didn't approve of Milwaukee's smoking and drinking habits. (Milwaukee Public Library)

Greeley was born in New Hampshire in 1811. Perhaps because of Greeley's "Go west young man" phrase, Chase designated the street next to Greeley Street as West Street, a road that no longer exits.

GREEN AVENUE

5800 South, between 3000 and 3400 West
Origin: *Gra-Ram*

This street, platted by Harold and B.J. Sampson in 1957, was probably named for the green space provided by the park it leads to.

GREEN BAY AVENUE, ROAD

From 900 West and 4000 North to 1900 West and 5600 North
Origin: *Kilbourntown*

Green Bay was the most important city in Wisconsin when the road from Chicago to Green Bay was laid out during the 1830s. It is the oldest

105

road in Milwaukee; the northern portion was known as Green Bay Road while the road south was called Chicago Road (now *Whitnall* Avenue). The city of Green Bay was named for its location on the bay of green-tinted water.

Green Bay Road leads north from the city.
(Milwaukee County Historical Society)

GREENBROOK DRIVE, COURT

8900 North, between 6900 and 8800 West
Origin: *Village of Brown Deer*

Between Greenbrook and Silverbrook Drives is a creek that apparently inspired the naming of both streets. They were named in 1962 as part of the Green Brook Estates.

GREENFIELD AVENUE

1400 South, between 500 East and 4300 West
Origin: *Ordinance*

Greenfield Avenue, which divides Milwaukee County in half, was named in 1885. Formerly called Railroad Avenue, it was the northern border of the old town of Greenfield, which covered an area from Greenfield to College Avenues and from 27th Street to Waukesha County. In its early days, the town was covered with forests, but did have some open prairie and marshy areas. Perhaps the dream of green farm fields inspired the town's name in 1841.

GREEN TREE ROAD

6800 North, between 3100 and 11800 West
Origin: *Fox Point*

Maps of the 1870s show the Green Tree Tavern where this road now intersects Port Washington Road. Germans in the area claimed that a large "grunerbaum" in front of the tavern gave it its name. By the 1880s the neighborhood was known as Green Tree and, eventually, so was the road.

GREENWICH AVENUE

2400 North, between 1800 and 2200 East
Origin: *Murray Hill*

Greenwich, a borough of London, England, is best known for its observatory, which established the system of geographic longitude and time keeping. The prime meridian, or zero longitude, passes through Greenwich. Greenwich means "green village," making New York's Greenwich Village a redundant name. The street was named by James *Murray* in 1856.

GREENWOOD TERRACE

7400 North, between 5200 and 10700 West
Origin: *Calumet Farms*

In 1947, J. Arthur Ehn asked the old Town of Granville to take over the responsibility for a road that he called Greenwood Terrace.

GREVES STREET

From 100 North/South and 3000 West to 300 North and 2300 West
Origin: *Merrill Park*

James Porter Greves, a physician, came to Milwaukee from Michigan in 1845. Before he left the city for health reasons in 1857, he had given up medicine for real estate speculation. Just before leaving, the New York native named this street for himself.

Greves moved to the West Coast where he was a founder of

Riverside, California. The climate apparently was good for his health, as he lived for another 32 years, dying in September 1889.

GRIFFIN AVENUE

400 East, between 3100 and 4500 South
Origin: *Bay View*

John Griffin farmed this land before it was subdivided by William Jordan and John Toohey in 1889.

John Griffin's farm is shown at the corner of Oklahoma and Howell Avenues. (1876 Illustrated Atlas of Milwaukee, Wisconsin)

GROELING AVENUE

2900 North, between 1300 and 1600 West
Origin: *North Division*

August Groeling subdivided his land in 1889 and named this street. Groeling, who was a gardener, died in 1895.

HACKETT AVENUE

2700 East, between 2600 and 3500 North

Origin: *Upper East Side*

Edward Hackett was born in Milwaukee in 1858 of Irish immigrant parents. Hackett made his mark in real estate and later branched out into mining and railroads. It was as a developer that Hackett had this street named for him, but not without controversy.

Among Hackett's subdivisions was a former farm he called Prospect Hill, on the Upper East Side. Anticipating that the diagonal *Prospect* Avenue would continue north to his subdivision, he named the street in line with it Prospect Avenue. Two years later, in 1895, the Common Council passed an ordinance to change the name of the Prospect Hill portion of Prospect Avenue to Hackett Avenue. That is when the controversy began.

Edward Hackett. (Milwaukee County Historical Society)

To some, Prospect had a better sound for this upscale neighborhood than Hackett did. They agitated to have the old name restored. But Judge Joseph Donnelly jumped to Hackett's defense with these lines:

Peace, Prospect Hill! It seemeth ill
To raise this clamorous racket,
As if your street were too elite
To bear the name of Hackett.

'Tis true the name's unknown to fame;
No storied knight doth back it;
But we can cite full many a night
Made glorious by Hackett.

Not his renown to take a town
And ruthless raze and sack it.
He takes a farm and by his charm
Creates a town, does Hackett.

When Prospect Hill had prospects nil,
Who flashed the scheme to track it
With rich stone curb - this mere suburb -
And costly asphalt? Hackett!

Ah, Prospect Hill, it seemeth ill!
Let other tongues attack it.
Your tongue should wag and never flag
In grateful praise of Hackett.

Hackett refused to be drawn into the argument, which ended with his name remaining on the street signs. Prospect Avenue eventually aligned with a street a few blocks to the west. Hackett died in 1910.

HADLEY STREET

2800 North, between 1100 East and 9800 West
Origin: *Riverwest*

Before coming to Milwaukee in 1849, Jackson Hadley taught school in New York State, where he was born in 1815. Hadley was primarily a politician during his stay in this city. By the time he died 18 years later, he had been president of the Common Council, chairman of the county board, president of the school board, and had served as both state assemblyman and senator.

Hadley's business pursuits included railroads, produce, and real estate. He was frequently accused of taking advantage of his political positions. In 1856 he and Byron *Kilbourn* were implicated in the bribing of the governor and members of the Wisconsin Legislature to gain land grants for their railroads. In 1857 Hadley was accused of planning municipal projects to increase the value of Otis B. Hopkins' real estate. That same year, Hopkins named this street for Hadley.

HALE PLACE

3200 North, between 4600 and 4700 West
Origin: *Sunset Heights*

James Street was changed to Hale Place in 1928 because there was another James Street in town. During the late 1920s, when the city was renaming many streets, its practice was to use names of past Milwaukeeans who had made a contribution to the city. Ozro Judson Hale served as alderman, was president of the Chamber of Commerce, and was involved in many charitable activities. He was born in New York in 1828 and came to Milwaukee in 1852. Hale was in the grain commission and shipping business. He died in 1886.

HALSEY AVENUE

5000 South, between 1400 and 2600 West
Origin: *Castle Manor*

William F. Halsey, born in New Jersey in 1882, was made a five-star admiral after his success in directing U.S. naval operations in the Pacific Ocean during World War II. Halsey died in 1959, two months before this street was named for him.

William Halsey. (Milwaukee Public Library)

111

HALYARD STREET

700 West, between 2000 and 2200 North
Origin: *Halyard Park*

Wilbur Halyard, born in South Carolina, came to Milwaukee in 1923 from Beloit, where he had worked to help African Americans find housing. At the time he arrived in this city it was nearly impossible for people of his race to get loans to buy homes. Halyard started the Columbia Savings and Loan Association to remedy the problem. Halyard's wife, Ardie, was president of both the Milwaukee and the Wisconsin chapters of the National Association for the Advancement of Colored People during the early 1950s. This street, created by the construction of the freeway system, was named in 1965.

Wilbur and Ardie Halyard.
(Milwaukee Sentinel Photo)

HAMILTON COURT

6200 West, between 3500 and 3600 South
Origin: *Root Creek*

This court was named in 1962 for Alexander Hamilton High School. Alexander Hamilton, born in the West Indies in 1755, was George *Washington's* secretary during the Revolutionary War. He was a delegate to the Constitutional Convention and the first secretary of the treasury. Hamilton was killed in a duel with Aaron Burr in 1804.

Hamilton High School as viewed from Hamilton Court.

HAMILTON STREET

1800 North, between 800 and 1200 East
Origin: *Lower East Side*

112

Richard J. Hamilton was an early Chicago lawyer, clerk of courts, alderman, and real estate developer. Hamilton Street was platted by Chicago speculators Christopher *Hubbard* and Hiram *Pearson* in 1836.

HAMPSHIRE STREET

3200 North, between 1500 and 3300 East
Origin: *Ordinance*

This street was formerly known as Concord Avenue, one of the streets named for East Coast cities by John *Stowell* in 1887. In 1926, because Concord was too much like the nearby *Concordia*, it was changed to Hampshire. Hampshire is a county in England (see *Hartford*).

HAMPTON AVENUE

4800 North, between 300 East and 12400 West
Origin: *Village of Whitefish Bay*

Festus Stone named this street as part of the Fairmount Heights Subdivision in 1888. The name, apparently chosen for its marketing value, can ultimately be traced to Hampton, Middlesex, England.

HANSON AVENUE

1500 East, between 3000 and 4000 South
Origin: *Bay View*

Like so many other Bay View streets, this one was named for someone associated with the rolling mills. But Thomas A. Hanson quit his job at the mills in 1885 to enter the real estate business. In 1891 Hanson Avenue was named in the subdivision that he platted.

Thomas Hanson was born in Birmingham, England in 1842 and moved to Bay View in 1868. Hanson was active in village politics and in 1884 he was nominated for village trustee. The next year he lost his bid for the village presidency to Frank *Seeley*, but was elected village assessor a short time later.

HARBOR DRIVE, PLACE

From 2100 South and 700 East to 500 North and 1100 East
Origin: *Historic Third Ward*

This street along the city's harbor was named in 1856.

HARRISON AVENUE

2600 South, between 200 and 7100 West
Origin: *Layton Park*

In 1888, Benjamin Harrison joined the other Republican presidents named in this part of town; *Lincoln, Grant, Hayes,* and *Arthur.* The only Republican missing was *Garfield* and that was because a city ordinance had already named a North Side street for the assassinated president.

Strangely though, Harrison wasn't yet president at the time of the street naming, which occurred several months before the election. Perhaps reflecting the wild, speculative period they were in, the developers were betting that he could beat *Grover Cleveland.* Of course, if he lost, they could say the avenue was named for Harrison's grandfather, William, the country's ninth President.

Benjamin Harrison.
(Milwaukee Public Library)

William Henry Harrison, (1773-1841), a hero in the War of 1812, lived in the White House for only one month before he died. His grandson, Benjamin Harrison, (1833-1901), a Civil War officer and 23rd President, was more fortunate. After winning what was called the most corrupt campaign ever, he served all four years of his term from 1889 to 1893.

HARTFORD AVENUE

3300 North, between 1500 and 3100 East
Origin: *Cambridge Heights*

John Maxwell *Stowell* named the four streets in this subdivision for East Coast cities in 1887. Only three remain because one of them, Concord, was renamed due to its similarity to *Concordia*. Hartford, Connecticut was named for Hertford, England, whose pronunciation accounts for the difference in spelling (see *Newport*).

HARTUNG AVENUE

6600 West, between 2700 and 2900 North
Origin: *Enderis Park*

Paul Hartung subdivided family land, creating the Lenox Heights Subdivision in 1916. The Hartung family had farmed the land since the 1850s. Paul Hartung was born about 1853 and had died by 1930.

HARVEST LANE

4900 North, between 10300 and 11000 West
Origin: *Timmerman West*

Harvest Lane was platted as part of the Harvest Estates by Harry E. Sampson and Harold Nash in 1956.

HASSEL LANE

6700 North, between 5100 and 5400 West
Origin: *Graceland*

Henry Hassel, born in Hanover, Germany in 1819, came to the Milwaukee area in 1844. He settled in the old town of Granville where he farmed until his death in 1891. This street was named in 1938.

HASTINGS STREET

8600 West, between 6500 and 6700 North
Origin: *Menomonee River Hills*

This street, in a 1955 subdivision of streets named for western United States cities, was probably named for Hastings, Nebraska. The city was named for Thomas Hastings, a railroad official (see *Kearney*).

HAUSER AVENUE

4300 North, between 1300 and 1500 West
Origin: *Lincoln Creek*

Henry Hauser was a real estate dealer in the old town of Wauwatosa when this street was named there in 1893.

HAWLEY ROAD, COURT

5800 West, between 700 South and 1700 North
Origin: *Johnson's Woods*

Cyrus Hawley had some harsh things said about him in 1837 when he ran for Register of Deeds. But he won and, like the rest of the victors, didn't waste time gloating. Instead, the newly elected officials popped for a barrel of whisky that was consumed in the street at Wisconsin Avenue and Water Street. It was a party to remember and lasted until the next morning. Many stayed the night, some for the good time and some for "having forgotten where they lived."

Hawley was 33 when he came to Milwaukee in 1835 from Hampton, Connecticut. Most of his career after serving his elected term was in appointed positions at the courthouse. His wealth was acquired through his land holdings in the area. Hawley died in 1871. The street name appears on subdivision maps beginning in 1885.

HAWTHORNE AVENUE

200 North, between 8700 and 9200 West
Origin: *City of Wauwatosa*

Despite the spelling, this street was probably named with the hawthorn tree, not author Nathaniel Hawthorne, in mind. These thorny trees, with their red haws, are common in the Milwaukee area. The street was named in 1925 as part of the Ravenswood Subdivision in Wauwatosa.

The name was the center of a controversy in the early 1940s. A person traveling west on Hawthorne Avenue through Ravenswood would, in mid-block, enter Milwaukee and be on *Fairview* Avenue. This caused no end of confusion for delivery people and visitors looking for a Fairview address on Hawthorne and vice versa. The Milwaukee portion of the street was called Fairview because that was what the street was called east of Ravenswood, and a Milwaukee ordinance required that city streets in line with one another carry the same name. But the residents of this section of Fairview petitioned the city to solve the problem and, in 1943, Hawthorne Avenue became their new address.

HAYES AVENUE

2400 South, between 200 East and 3700 West
Origin: *Layton Park*

Rutherford B. Hayes, (1822-1893), was our 19th President. His election was disputed and he was declared the winner by an Electoral Commission. Hayes, a Civil War general, was president from 1877 to 1881. This street, in a neighborhood of streets honoring presidents, was named in 1887.

Rutherford B. Hayes.
(Milwaukee Public Library)

HAZELTON COURT

800 North, between 2600 and 2700 West
Origin: *Avenues West*

Gerry Whiting Hazelton, United States congressman, Wisconsin lieutenant governor, state senator, and U. S. Attorney for the Milwaukee area, was born in New Hampshire in 1829. An orator, he delivered the welcoming address to President Grover *Cleveland* when he visited Milwaukee in 1887. As a lawmaker, Hazelton supported such diverse legislation as a ban on polygamy and support of the eight-hour workday.

Hazelton, who died in 1920 at the age of 91, was honored by an ordinance changing the name of the one-block long Washington Place to Hazelton Court in 1926.

117

HEATHER AVENUE

8600 North, between 7600 and 11000 West
Origin: *Servite Woods*

Heather is a low evergreen shrub found in Ireland and Britain. This street was named in 1959.

HELENA STREET, COURT

7100 North, between 3700 and 9100 West
Origin: *Menomonee River Hills*

Helena was added to a subdivision of streets named for western United States cities in 1957 and was probably named for Helena, Montana. The city was named for the community of Helena in Minnesota.

HEMLOCK ROAD, STREET

7400 North, between 3700 and 8700 West
Origin: *Village of Fox Point*

The Village of Fox Point named this street in 1930. Presumably it was named for the tree rather than the herb. The hemlock tree is an ornamental evergreen native to North America. The herb provided the poisonous drink used for the execution of Greek criminals of antiquity.

HENRY AVENUE

6000 South, between 1800 and 2600 West
Origin: *Goldman Park*

Henry Avenue is among a group of streets dedicated by Leo and Leopold Goldman and local land owners in 1931. The reason for the name is not known.

HERBERT AVENUE, COURT

From 4600 North and 9200 West to 5500 North and 6900 West
Origin: *Lindsay Park*

118

Herbert Avenue was named in 1928 as part of the Hampton Gardens Subdivision. The reason for the name is a mystery.

HERMAN STREET

1100 East, between 2700 and 4200 South
Origin: *Bay View*

Herman Mann, born in Prague in 1817, owned a Milwaukee wholesale grocery business with his brothers. The Manns had other investments, including an unlucky pail and tub factory located in Peshtigo, Wisconsin, with a branch in Chicago. In 1871, the famous Chicago and Peshtigo fires destroyed both these cities, including both the Manns' facilities.

Herman Mann died the next year. When his children platted Mann's Subdivision in 1879, they commemorated their father with this street name (see *Idaho*).

HIBERNIA STREET

400 North, between 1000 and 1200 West
Origin: *Marquette*

Hibernia was the Latin name for Ireland. This street was originally platted by James *Kneeland* in 1871. The neighborhood, which was heavily Irish, was known as *Tory Hill*. Freeway construction in the 1960s eliminated the street but the name was reestablished nearby under the resolution of Robert Dwyer in 1966.

A Celtic cross in Hibernia, now called Ireland.

HICKORY STREET

2700 North and 2500 West
Origin: *Park West*

In 1889 a group of short streets in this neighborhood was named for trees native to Milwaukee. They included *Ash*, Hickory, *Oak*, and *Tamarack* Streets. Bitternut, Pignut, and Shagbark Hickory trees are found locally.

HIGHLAND AVENUE, BOULEVARD

From 1100 North and 300 East to 1400 North and 4000 West
Origin: *Cold Spring Park*

Highland Boulevard was created from Edward *Holton*'s farm, "Highland Home." It was subdivided by the Highland Home Land Company in 1887 (see *Hillcrest, Land*).

HIGHVIEW DRIVE

5400 West, between 7600 and 8000 North
Origin: *Bradley Estates*

Highview Drive climbs up a low hill in the Bradley Estates Subdivision that was developed in 1955.

HIGHWOOD AVENUE

3500 North and 10000 West
Origin: *Golden Valley*

The aptly named Highwood Avenue was platted in 1927 by Boulevard Lane Realty. The wooded street climbs a hill from the Menomonee River Parkway.

A view up Highwood Avenue.

HILBERT STREET

300 East, between 1900 and 2100 South
Origin: *Bay View*

Heliodore J. Hilbert, born in Germany in 1829, came to Milwaukee in 1849 and built a distillery on the Kinnickinnic River near this street. He was an alderman in 1870 when this street was platted.

HILDA PLACE

1000 South, between 3700 and 3800 West
Origin: *Silver City*

120

Lady Hilda Johnston Butterfield was not quite ten years old when her father named this street for her in 1893. Scottish-born John Johnston came to Milwaukee in 1856 at age 20. He married Ethelinda Thorsen, the daughter of Norwegian immigrants, in 1881. Their daughter Hilda, who married an English lord, died in 1957.

John Johnston, a nephew of Alexander *Mitchell*, was a wealthy man. His business career was spent in his uncle's bank; the public library and humane society were his public service interests; and his social life included curling, shooting, and frequent visits to Scotland and the rest of Europe (see *Margaret*).

HILLCREST AVENUE

3200 South, between 1800 and 2100 East
Origin: *Fernwood*

This street, named Highland when it was platted in 1886, runs over a little hill. It was renamed Hillcrest to eliminate duplication in 1926 (see *Highland, Land*).

HI-MOUNT BOULEVARD

5000 West, between 1700 and 2300 North
Origin: *Washington Heights*

Hi-Mount Boulevard was platted in 1910 by August Richter, Jr. as part of the Hi-Mount Subdivision. Aptly named, the subdivision is on high land in the Washington Highlands.

HINMAN STREET

400 North, between 500 and 600 West
Origin: *Kilbourntown*

Samuel Hinman came to Milwaukee in October of 1836 and two months later Byron *Kilbourn* named this street for him. Hinman was active in the early politics of the community and in the temperance movement. Within ten years he had moved to Waukesha.

HOLMES AVENUE, COURT

5000 South, between 1300 and 2000 West
Origin: *City of Cudahy*

Jerome W. Holmes was a Milwaukee livestock commissioner during the time that the city of *Cudahy* was founded. Like most of the new community's avenues, this one, platted in 1893, was named for someone in the meat industry.

HOLT AVENUE, COURT

3400 South, between 2900 East and 9200 West
Origin: *Fernwood*

John A. Holt, Sr., born in Canada in 1838, came to Milwaukee in 1858. After serving in the Civil War, he started a business grading and laying streets. Holt named this street for himself in 1889.

HOLTON STREET

500 East, between 1900 and 4200 North
Origin: *Riverwest*

Edward Holton was against slavery. He ran for Wisconsin governor for the Free Soil Party in 1853 under the motto, "Free soil, free speech, free labor, and free men." In 1856 he sponsored a resettlement of Milwaukeeans to Kansas, hoping the settlers' numbers would help shift the balance of power to the abolitionists of that state. The settlers named their community Holton.

Besides the town, Holton has a building at UW-Milwaukee and a canal in the Menomonee Valley called for him. Born in New Hampshire, Holton was 25 when he came to Milwaukee in 1840 from Buffalo, New York. He was a railroad promoter, bank president, merchant, and baking soda producer. Holton died in 1892. This street was platted in 1857 by Otis B. Hopkins (see *Highland*).

HOMER STREET

2500 South, between 400 and 1000 East
Origin: *Bay View*

Joseph *Williams* named Homer Street when he subdivided his farm in 1870. The Greek poet is the source of the name Homer, though who Williams had in mind when naming this street is not known.

HONEY CREEK DRIVE, PARKWAY, CT

From 8400 West and 400 North to 3500 West and 5900 South
Origin: *City of West Allis*

Tradition says that the Honey Creek got its name because of the many beehives in the fruit trees along the creek where it crosses National Avenue. In 1836 the area was surveyed by Increase *Lapham*, and the hamlet near that point was called Honey Creek. The name began to be used for the roadway along the creek in the 1930s.

Honey Creek Historical Marker at 84th Street and National Avenue.

HOPE AVENUE

4200 North, between 500 East and 9100 West
Origin: *Garden Homes*

Charles Kiewert and Adolph Segnitz named Hope Avenue in 1899. Whether it was named for a woman, or in the hope that their real estate venture would be a success, or for some other reason is not known.

HOPKINS STREET

From 1300 West and 2700 North to 4300 West and 5600 North

Several men have been credited with being honored by the naming of this street. Ed and B.B. Hopkins, druggists, and Otis B. Hopkins, an early settler, are among them. It is more likely, however, that it was named for Sherman Hopkins, also an early settler, who was a commissioner in charge of laying out this road in 1847.

HOUSTON AVENUE

8100 West, between 4400 and 4700 North
Origin: *Arlington Gardens*

Many city streets were named for U.S. cities during the 1950s. Houston Avenue was named in 1956. Houston, Texas was named for Samuel Houston, (1793-1863), the President of the Republic of Texas who was elected governor after Texas became a state.

HOWARD AVENUE

3900 South, between 1800 East and 10000 West
Origin: *Saveland Park*

In 1836, land in Milwaukee County was inexpensive. That year, James Corydon Howard got his 160-acre farm in the old town of Lake for nothing from his father-in-law, Israel Porter. It was no great loss for Porter, who had traded an old rifle for the wooded land.

James Howard's farm near Howard and Howell Avenues. (Illustrated Atlas of Milwaukee, Wisconsin, 1876)

124

Howard, born in Vermont in 1804, was active in the affairs of the town of Lake and farmed there until his death in 1880. He is remembered as a rigid and temperate man with 15 children. Howard Avenue was named in 1884. Howard also owned land in the River Hills area, where a street was named for his grandson, James H. *Dean*.

HOWELL AVENUE

From 100 East/West and 6300 South to 400 East and 2200 South
Origin: *City of Oak Creek*

In the 1830s the Howells owned a large section of land in the old town of Oak Creek. Josephus, Cyrus, Enoch, John, and Emily Howell's holdings stretched along a six-mile route, from College Avenue south to Racine County. When a road was cut through their land in the 1840s, it became known as the Howell Road.

HOWIE PLACE

3800 North, between 4400 and 4500 West
Origin: *Roosevelt Grove*

Janet Lenz, president of Lenz Development Company, platted this street in 1923. Why the name was chosen is unknown.

HOYT PLACE

3700 North, between 4600 and 5000 West
Origin: *Grasslyn Manor/Roosevelt Grove*

Emerson D. Hoyt, (1847-1924), was a farmer until he was nearly forty. Then he turned to politics, transportation, banking, and real estate. Hoyt, whose grandfather settled in Milwaukee in 1835, was a state assemblyman, Wauwatosa's first mayor, president of the Bank of Wauwatosa, and a member of the park commission for 12 years. This street was platted by the Finance and Investment Company in 1922.

HUBBARD STREET

300 East, between 1800 and 3900 North
Origin: *Brewers Hill*

Several Milwaukee Hubbards have been credited with being the source of this street name, but it was more likely named for Chicago Hubbards. In 1836 and 1837 Chicago speculators platted the Brewers Hill area and the land across the Milwaukee River on the Lower East Side, and named the streets for themselves. Some names like *Hamilton*, *Pearson*, and *Lloyd* remain, while others, like Beaubian, Harmon, Hunter, and Kinzie have been changed.

One of the speculators was Christopher Hubbard whose brother, Gurdon, was one of the largest land owners in Wisconsin. Gurdon Hubbard, fur trader and meat packer, owned large tracts of land in Milwaukee and Ozaukee Counties. He lost most of his Chicago holdings in the Great Fire of 1871 and died in 1886.

HUMBOLDT BOULEVARD, AVENUE

1100 East, between 1400 and 4300 North
Origin: *Riverwest*

Aside from Napoleon Bonaparte, Alexander Humboldt was the most famous man in Europe during the first half of the 19th century. Humboldt, a German, made important observations in botany, geology, geography, and meteorology as he explored the globe. In 1850, when a little community was being organized around a paper mill on the Milwaukee River, near what was later called Capitol Drive, it was named for Humboldt. The road to Humboldt carried both its traffic and its name. Alexander Humboldt, who was born in 1769 in Berlin, died in 1859.

HUMBOLDT PARK COURT

500 East, between 2700 and 2800 South
Origin: *Bay View*

Humboldt Park was named in 1900 for the German explorer,

naturalist, and scientist, Alexander Humboldt. This short street north of the park was named in 1911 by Burnham Realty.

HUSTIS STREET, COURT

7000 North, between 4700 and 9000 West
Origin: *Menomonee River Hills*

John Hustis, born in the state of New York in 1810, arrived in Milwaukee ready to practice law in 1836. The study of law had been more interesting than the practice however, so he soon branched out into real estate. In 1837 Hustis built grist and saw mills on the Rock River at what became known as Hustis Rapids, and later, as Hustisford.

In 1955, Hustis' grandson recommended that the city name a street for his grandfather, who had entertained Milwaukee pioneers with stories and songs at the ''Shanty'' in the early days of settlement. This street was named in 1957.

John Hustis. (Gregory's History of Milwaukee)

IDAHO STREET

2900 South, between 1400 East and 6300 West

Origin: *Bay View*

Idaho was a territory when the *Herman* Mann family named this street in 1879. Idaho is a Shoshone Indian word that has been interpreted as meaning something akin to "sunlight on the mountain." Idaho achieved statehood in 1890 (see *Manitoba).*

ILLINOIS AVENUE

2800 East, between 3100 and 3500 South

Origin: *Fernwood*

This is one of Thomas Kennan's streets named for midwestern states in 1889. The Illinois were an Indian tribe whose name means "perfect and accomplished men" (see *Indiana).*

INDIANA AVENUE

2700 East, between 3100 and 3500 South

Origin: *Fernwood*

Indiana, Latin for "land of the Indians," is another of the Bay View state streets named by Thomas Kennan in 1889 (see *New York*).

INDUSTRIAL ROAD

From 6400 North and 6400 West to 6800 North and 7100 West
Origin: *Menomonee River Hills East*

Industrial Road, which parallels a railroad track and runs through an industrial park, was named in 1955.

IONA TERRACE

5800 South, between 1400 and 3900 West
Origin: *City of Cudahy*

Maple Terrace was changed to Iona Terrace in 1930. The old Town of Lake was part of the county-wide program to eliminate duplicate street names and there were too many "Maples" around. Why the name Iona was chosen is not known.

IOWA AVENUE

2000 East, between 3400 and 3600 South
Origin: *Bay View*

Iowa is the French version of the name of a Sioux Indian tribe and is thought to mean "the sleepy ones." Iowa Avenue was platted in 1926 by the Savings and Investment Association (see *Kansas*).

IRON STREET

2700 South, between 1600 and 2000 East
Origin: *Bay View*

Iron production was the reason for the founding of Bay View, which was originally known as the "Village of the Milwaukee Iron Company." In 1887 Bay View, along with its Lake Street, was annexed by Milwaukee. Since the city already had a Lake Street, this one was renamed Iron Street.

The rolling mills were the inspiration for the naming of Iron Street.
(Milwaukee's Great Industries)

129

IROQUOIS AVENUE

300 West and 4800 North
Origin: *Village of Fox Point*

The Bay Shore Manor Subdivision in the old town of Milwaukee named streets for Indian tribes in 1927. The Iroquois were a confederation of the *Mohawk*, Cayuga, Onondaga, Oneida, and Seneca tribes of New York State.

IRVING PLACE

2000 North, between 1500 and 1800 East
Origin: *Northpoint*

In 1875 the city changed First through Sixth Streets in this East Side neighborhood to named streets. Milwaukee already had two other sets of streets with the same numbers; one in Kilbourntown and another in Walker's Point. Three of the new names were of Walter Scott novels, one of a Revolutionary War hero, another for English royalty, and this one, Irving. There were no prominent Irvings living in the city at the time, and the city usually names streets for the well-known. This, plus the literary bent of the other new names, makes it seem quite possible that this street was named for Washington Irving, the first American author to gain international fame. Irving, (1783-1859), a friend of Walter Scott, is best remembered for his stories "The Legend of Sleepy Hollow" and "Rip Van Winkle" (see *Waverly*).

IVANHOE PLACE

2300 North, between 2000 and 2200 East
Origin: *Northpoint*

Walter Scott's "Ivanhoe," a popular romantic novel published in 1819, was the source of this street name. Previously called Sixth Street, it was renamed by ordinance in 1875 (see *Kenilworth*).

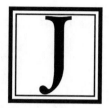

JACKSON STREET

600 East, between 400 South and 1700 North
Origin: *Juneautown*

Andrew Jackson, (1767-1845), was President of the United States when Morgan *Martin* and Solomon *Juneau* platted Jackson Street in 1835. A few months earlier, Jackson had appointed Juneau as Milwaukee's first postmaster. Old Hickory, as Jackson was called, gained fame for defeating the British at New Orleans during the War of 1812. He was president from 1829 to 1837.

"Old Hickory." (Milwaukee Public Library)

JACKSON PARK DRIVE

2700 South, between 4700 and 5800 West
Origin: *Jackson Park*

Jackson Park Drive does not run through Jackson Park, as might be expected, but lies several blocks west of it. The street runs along the Kinnickinnic River and was officially named in 1953 by the Park Commission. The park is named for Andrew *Jackson*, seventh President of the United States.

131

JACKSON PARK OVERPASS

3500 West, between 2400 and 2800 South
Origin: *Jackson Park*

This overpass, part of 35th Street along the east edge of Jackson Park, was named in 1960.

JASPER AVENUE

300 East, between 4200 and 4600 South
Origin: *Town of Lake*

The reason for the name of this street is unknown. It had been called Burdick, but during the renaming program it was changed to Jasper to avoid duplication with Bay View's *Burdick* Avenue. It was named in 1930 by the old Town of Lake.

JEFFERSON STREET

500 East, between 300 South and 1600 North
Origin: *Juneautown*

Thomas Jefferson, (1743-1826), Revolutionary War patriot, drafted the Declaration of Independence and became the third President of the United States. Jefferson drew up the Northwest Ordinance of 1787, which covered an area that included Wisconsin. Solomon *Juneau* and Morgan *Martin* named this street in 1835.

Thomas Jefferson. (Milwaukee Public Library)

JEFFREY COURT, LANE

4900 North, between 10800 and 11100 West
Origin: *Timmerman West*

132

Jeffrey Lane was platted by Gerald and Margaret Wichman in 1955. It may have been named for someone associated with the City Engineer's Department, which had street naming responsibility at the time.

JERELYN PLACE

2600 South, between 4900 and 5600 West
Origin: *Jackson Park*

Jerelyn Ganser was two years old when her grandfather, Roman, named this street for her in 1947. Jerelyn was named for her uncle Gerald.

JEWELL AVENUE

6500 South, between 1700 and 2000 West
Origin: *College Heights*

Jewell Avenue was platted in 1956. It was part of the Harmony Homesites Subdivision developed by Rudolph, Paul, and Winona Povlich.

JOLENO LANE

9000 North, between 9100 and 9400 West
Origin: *Village of Brown Deer*

The name Joleno comes from JOseph SiLENO, the developer who platted the Green Brook Subdivision in 1962. Sileno was fond of forming new words from his name. Gesil Corporation, the company that developed Green Brook, was named for Henry GEpfert and Joseph SILeno.

JONEN STREET

6400 North, between 10100 and 10700 West
Origin: *Royal Orleans*

The Jonen family, which had settled in this area by the 1860s, had a farm nearby. Alderman Clarence Miller suggested the name in 1978.

JOSEPH AVENUE

10200 West, between 8100 and 8400 North

Origin: *Pheasant Run*

Joseph Eckmann, a city planner, was memorialized by Joseph Avenue in 1963.

JOYCE AVENUE

8500 West, between 6100 and 9400 North

Origin: *Northridge*

Joyce T. Schmidt, the city engineer's secretary, was the inspiration for this street name in 1956.

JULIA STREET

400 West, between 3100 and 3300 North

Origin: *Harambee*

Jonathan Peirce named this street for his daughter, Julia, in 1870. Julia had married Oliver C. Ely in 1865 and moved to Chicago (see *N. Pierce*).

JUNEAU AVENUE

1200 North, between 1300 East and 5300 West

Origin: *Juneautown*

Solomon Juneau, (1793-1856), came to Milwaukee from Canada about 1818 as an agent for John Jacob *Astor*'s American Fur Company. In 1820 Juneau married Josette *Vieau*, the daughter of a Menominee Indian woman and a Frenchman who traded in Milwaukee. In the mid-1830s Juneau formed a partnership with Morgan L. *Martin* in developing Milwaukee Village. Juneau, considered the founder of the city, was its first postmaster and its first mayor. In later years he moved to Theresa, Wisconsin, which he named for his mother.

There have been several streets named for Juneau; this one, which he called Division Street in 1835, was renamed Juneau Avenue in 1885. Juneau Park and Juneau County are also his namesakes (see *Kilbourn*, *Walker*).

134

The statue of Solomon Juneau in Juneau Park was erected by Charles Bradley and William Metcalfe in 1887.

JUNIPER STREET, COURT

7300 North, between 8600 and 10500 West

Origin: *Village of Fox Point*

The Common Juniper is a low, mat-forming shrub prevalent in cold climates, including Wisconsin's. This street was platted in 1930 in the Glenbrook Subdivision in the old town of Milwaukee.

KANE PLACE

1900 North, between 1000 and 1800 East
Origin: *Lower East Side*

Alonzo Kane, born in Waterloo, New York in 1823, was the most prominent member of the Kane family that settled in Milwaukee in 1846. The family owned a hotel at the site of the Grand Avenue Mall and land that included this street. They also owned a spring near North and Oakland Avenues.

Alonzo and his brother Sanford became wealthy selling the spring water, claiming it was especially beneficial to the health. Alonzo was also a real estate developer, an alderman, a county board supervisor, and an owner of a newspaper, "The Milwaukee News." Dane Place was renamed Kane Place in 1890. Alonzo Kane died in 1899.

Alonso Kane's residence on Prospect Avenue. (Milwaukee Illustrated)

136

KANSAS AVENUE

1800 East, between 3400 and 4000 South
Origin: *Bay View*

August H. Vogel, the Milwaukee-born son of Frederick *Vogel,* was an officer of his father's tannery, a banker, and president of the investment association that platted Kansas Avenue in 1926. Kansas Avenue kept alive a tradition in Bay View of naming streets after states and territories. The word Kansas means "people of the south wind" in a Sioux Indian language (see *Alabama*).

KATHRYN AVENUE, COURT

From 8200 West and 5000 North to 7000 West and 5500 North
Origin: *Silver Spring*

Kathryn Avenue was named in 1953 as part of the Chevi-Park Subdivision. Neither the developers nor the City Engineer's Department know why the name was selected.

KAUL AVENUE

6100 North, between 3500 and 12200 West
Origin: *Village of Whitefish Bay*

William J. Kaul, president of the North Lawndale Company, platted this street in 1892. Kaul, the son of a German immigrant who settled in Milwaukee, later moved to Salt Lake City, Utah.

KEARNEY STREET

500 South, between 5900 and 8400 West
Origin: *Fair Park/Johnson's Woods*

Finley Fisler, the chief draftsman in the City Engineer's Department, had primary responsibility for street naming at the time Kearney Street was named in 1963. During this era, Fisler, an avid traveler throughout the western United States, named many Milwaukee streets for cities west of the Mississippi River. This one was named for Kearney, Nebraska, which

137

honored Stephen Kearny, a general in the War of 1812 and the Mexican-American War. Not surprisingly, when Fisler retired, he moved to the West.

KEEFE AVENUE, PARKWAY

3500 North, between 1100 East and 10000 West
Origin: *Riverwest*

John C. Keefe. (Conard's History of Milwaukee County)

John C. Keefe, born in Massachusetts in 1846, was a teacher at age 17. His teaching skills were such that "even little dullards" in his classes liked to learn. After a six-year journalism career, Keefe spent the next 12 years pursuing his "desire to accumulate wealth" in manufacturing. In 1892, at age 46, Keefe's success in business and real estate enabled him to quit working and enter law school, a lifelong ambition. He was admitted to the bar two years later. Keefe Avenue was named for him in 1891.

KENILWORTH PLACE

2300 North, between 1800 and 2300 East
Origin: *Northpoint*

Kenilworth Place was named for one of Walter Scott's "Waverley" novels; this one, "Kenilworth," was published in 1821. This street, which had been Fifth Street, was renamed in 1875 (see *Waverly*).

KENTUCKY AVENUE

2200 West, between 4300 and 4500 South
Origin: *Wilson Park*

Kentucky Avenue, along with *Louisiana* and *Tennessee*, was named in 1955 in the Villa Mann Subdivision by the City Engineer's Office. Kentucky is an Iroquois term meaning "plain" (see *Alabama*).

138

KENWOOD BOULEVARD

3100 North, between 1500 and 3300 East
Origin: *Downer Woods*

Burleigh Street, between the Milwaukee River and Lake Michigan, was given the promotional name Kenwood Boulevard in 1906. The name was taken from the Kenwood Park Subdivision, which was platted on Burleigh Street between Downer Avenue and Lake Drive by Clarence *Shepard* in 1891.

KERNEY PLACE

2400 South, between 1800 and 1900 West
Origin: *Forest Home Hills*

Walter Hull, with his mother Ellen and sister Clara, named Kerney Place in 1902 as part of their subdivision. The reason for their choice is not known.

KEWAUNEE STREET

1600 North, between 800 and 1100 East
Origin: *Lower East Side*

Kewaunee, Wisconsin was founded as a trading post on the Kewaunee River in 1836 by John Jacob *Astor*. Its streets, with names like *Kilbourn, Juneau, Vliet* and *Center*, reflect the names of Milwaukee men who speculated on its future. A year later, in 1837, a Milwaukee street was named for Kewaunee. The name means "prairie chicken" in Potawatomi.

KIEHNAU AVENUE

6600 North, between 3300 and 10500 West
Origin: *Graceland*

Heinrich and Mary Kiehnau emigrated from Germany and settled in the old town of Granville during the 19th century. This street, on Keihnau land, was named in the 1930s.

KILBOURN AVENUE

900 North, between 1000 East and 6000 West
Origin: *Ordinance*

Byron Kilbourn. (Gregory's History of Milwaukee)

Byron Kilbourn, one of the founders of Milwaukee, was born in Connecticut in 1801. In 1834 Kilbourn, a civil engineer searching for a site for a port city on the western shores of Lake Michigan, came to Milwaukee. After buying land downtown west of the Milwaukee River, Kilbourn set about turning it into a city. He replaced trees and marshes with streets and sidewalks. Over the years he helped improve access to the city with bridges, roads, railroads, and enhanced harbor facilities. For 34 years Kilbourn promoted the city and grew wealthy. In 1868 he moved south for his health and died in Florida two years later.

The streets of Kilbourntown were intentionally laid out to not align with the streets of Solomon Juneau's competing village on the east side of the river, and they were given names different from those in Juneautown. By the time the two communities united to form the city of Milwaukee in 1848, the streets were joined by bridges, somewhat askew, over the river. But the street names, much to the confusion of the uninitiated, remained different for many decades.

In the 1920s the city-wide street renaming program limited each street to only one name. The Juneautown street names of Oneida, Huron, and Martin gave way to the Kilbourntown names of *Wells*, *Clybourn*, and *State* Streets. The West Side gave up the names of Sycamore, Grand, and Chestnut for the East Side's *Michigan*, *Wisconsin*, and *Juneau*. Kilbourn Avenue, though, was a new name on both sides of the river.

A contest was run in the "Milwaukee Sentinel" to give one name to Kilbourntown's Cedar Street and Juneautown's Biddle Street. Kilbourn Avenue was the popular choice, and in 1929 Byron Kilbourn, one of Milwaukee's three founders, was honored with a downtown street bearing his name (see *Juneau, Walker*).

140

KILEY AVENUE, COURT

7000 North, between 3500 and 5900 West
Origin: *Town & Country Manor*

Moses Elias Kiley was born in Nova Scotia. After serving as a bishop in New Jersey, he came to Milwaukee in 1940, at the age of 63, having been appointed the sixth Roman Catholic archbishop of the city. Kiley, six and a half feet tall, died in the spring of 1953. A few weeks later this street memorialized his name.

KILLIAN PLACE

400 East, between 1900 and 2300 North
Origin: *Brewers Hill*

Killian Place was known as Lawton Place until 1926, when it was changed because it was too similar to *Layton* Boulevard on the South Side. Why Killian was chosen as a replacement is not known. There was a nearby Killian family, but to name the street for them would have been a significant departure from the city's practice of naming streets for prominent past individuals.

KIMBERLY AVENUE

6100 South, between 1800 and 2700 West
Origin: *Goldman Park*

Both the land for and the name of Kimberly Avenue were given to the old Town of Lake by Leo and Leopold Goldman in 1931. Why they chose the name is not recorded.

DR MARTIN LUTHER KING JR DRIVE

From 300 West and 1700 North to 900 West and 4000 North
Origin: *Ordinance*

In 1984 and 1985, parts of North Third Street and *Green Bay* Avenue were renamed for the African American civil rights leader. Martin Luther King was born in Atlanta, Georgia in 1929. King, a Baptist minister,

won the Nobel Peace Prize for his nonviolent struggle for racial equality. He was murdered by James Earl Ray in Memphis, Tennessee in 1968. Opposition by downtown merchants prevented this name from extending south to Wisconsin Avenue (see *Old World Third*).

Martin Luther and Coretta King. (Milwaukee Public Library)

KINGSTON PLACE

700 North, between 4100 and 4200 West
Origin: *The Valley*

Kingston means a town named for a king. In 1930, Emery Place was given this more regal-sounding name.

KINNICKINNIC AVENUE

From 1700 South and 100 East/West to 3500 South and 2500 East
Origin: *Ordinance*

Looking south on Kinnickinnic Avenue at Potter Avenue. (Milwaukee County Historical Society)

This road was laid over an old Indian trail and named for the river to which it leads. After having been called, like almost all roads leading southward from the city, Chicago Road, the name was changed to Kinnickinnic by ordinance in 1865. The name, often shortened to "KK," comes from an Indian term meaning "it is mixed," referring to a smoking blend of tobacco, leaves, and bark.

142

KINNICKINNIC RIVER PARKWAY

3000 South, between 2000 and 7100 West
Origin: *Fairview*

This parkway along the Kinnickinnic River was named in the 1940s. Kinnickinnic is an Indian term meaning "it is mixed," and refers to a smoking blend of tobacco, leaves, and bark.

KINZIE STREET

5500 North, between 3000 and 3100 West
Origin: *Old North Milwaukee*

The Kinzies were active in Milwaukee and Wisconsin before the white settlement of the area. In 1804 John Kinzie Sr., who settled in Chicago, opened a trading post in Milwaukee. In 1821 the Superintendent of Indian Affairs forced Kinzie's son, James, to leave Milwaukee for having sold whisky to the local Indians. Another son, John Harris Kinzie, was appointed the Indian agent at Fort Winnebago (now Portage, Wisconsin), in 1829. In 1836 one of the city's early streets was named for Kinzie, though it was later changed to *Marshall* Street. This Kinzie Street, formerly called Smith Street, was renamed in 1929 because Smith was duplicated in Bay View.

KISSLICH PLACE

1400 North, between 3900 and 4000 West
Origin: *Washington Park*

Reinhold and Maria Kiesslich bought the land that now includes Kisslich Place in the late 1880s, when Reinhold was a shipping clerk at the Pabst Brewing Company. In 1905, after Reinhold had died, Maria subdivided their land as the Kisslich Subdivision. In 1927, the street renaming commission named this alley, using the subdivision spelling rather than the family spelling.

KLEIN AVENUE

5700 South, between 1300 and 2200 West
Origin: *Mitchell Field*

Jacob and Mathilda Klein platted Klein Avenue as part of Klein's Subdivision in 1937. Jacob Klein, who died in 1958 at the age of 83, was a cattle buyer and tavern operator.

KLONDIKE PLACE

2700 South, between 400 and 500 West
Origin: *Lincoln Village*

A gold strike in the Klondike Region sparked the Alaska-Yukon gold rush of 1898. Caught in the fever, *Clifford Chase* named this short South Side street that same year. Chase wasn't alone in his enthusiasm; two Wisconsin villages and a lake memorialized the Klondike Region, which derived its name from the salmon fishing technique used by the local residents.

KNAPP STREET

1300 North, between 100 East/West and 1200 East
Origin: *Yankee Hill*

Gilbert Knapp, the first settler and founder of Racine, was born in Massachusetts in 1798. After serving as a boy in the War of 1812, Knapp settled in Racine in 1834. He was elected to the Wisconsin legislature and is credited with choosing the name for his city. Racine, from the French word for "root," is located on the Root River. This street was named for Knapp, who also owned land in Milwaukee County, in 1837. Knapp died in 1887.

KNEELAND STREET

1400 North, between 600 and 2000 West
Origin: *Park View*

When the city changed the name of Union Street to Kneeland Street

144

in 1880, it was honoring either or both of the Kneeland brothers, James and Moses.

James Kneeland, born in New York State in 1816, arrived in Milwaukee in 1841. He came from Illinois where he had been a canal contractor. During his first ten years in the city, he was a general merchant who tried to fill the needs of his customers, even going so far as finding a wife for one of them. Kneeland's interests included politics, real estate, banking, canals, and railroads.

An athletic man, Kneeland bragged that in his youth he had been unafraid to walk through *Tory Hill* among the tough Irish gangs. However, he was also described as a lover of nature, but it was a cultivated nature. Out-of-doors for Kneeland was his grounds, which were probably the best manicured and most parklike of any in the city. James Kneeland died in 1899.

Moses Kneeland followed his younger half-brother, James, to Milwaukee in 1842. He was a businessman and railroad promoter who served as village trustee, alderman, and county board member. Moses Kneeland died in 1864.

James Kneeland. (Conard's History of Milwaukee County)

145

LAFAYETTE PLACE

2100 North, between 1600 and 2200 East
Origin: *Northpoint*

It would be almost un-American not to have a street named for the Frenchman, Marquis de LaFayette. After the Revolutionary War, where LaFayette gained his fame, American cities began a new practice in street naming. Instead of just calling their thoroughfares for trees or destinations or functions, developers and city leaders started the now popular tradition of naming streets for people, particularly those whom they admired. LaFayette was much admired, as demonstrated by the nearly one thousand streets named for him around the country.

Milwaukee got its LaFayette when Second Street was changed to LaFayette Place in 1875.

LAFAYETTE HILL ROAD

2100 East and 1800 North
Origin: *Northpoint*

Until 1989 the road leading down the hill from LaFayette Place to Lincoln Memorial Drive was unnamed. Then it was decided that it should have a name to refer to in emergency situations and the name Lafayette Hill Road was selected.

146

LAGOON DRIVE

1800 East, between 1200 and 1700 North
Origin: *Lake Park*

The road through Veterans' Park, along the lagoon, was named in 1989 by the Park Commission to provide an address in emergencies.

The lagoon at
Veterans Park.

LAKE DRIVE

From 2000 East and 1800 North to 3000 East and 3500 North
Origin: *Northpoint*

Lake Drive, which runs along Lake Michigan for most of its length, was formerly known as Fourth Avenue until an ordinance renamed it in 1875.

LAKEFIELD DRIVE

From 2800 West and 3500 South to 7200 West and 3100 South
Origin: *Jackson Park*

Lakefield Drive was named as part of the Concord Hill Subdivision. The other streets in the development have names with literary allusions. This street though, may have been named for a feature. In 1929, when the street was named, there was a field to the east that was crisscrossed with streams (see *Paine*).

147

LAKE PARK DRIVE

7700 North, between 11000 and 12000 West
Origin: *Park Place*

Lake Park Drive is not, as might be expected, in Lake Park. It is in the western part of the city, far from Lake Michigan. The road passes two ponds, which apparently serve as lakes, as it winds its way through Park Place. Trammel Crow, the developers of Park Place, requested that part of Fountain Avenue be renamed Lake Park Drive in 1985. In a major departure from a longstanding policy of not duplicating street names (*Lake* Drive in this case), the city agreed.

LAKE PARK ROAD

3200 East, between 2700 and 3100 North
Origin: *Lake Park*

The road through Lake Park was nearly a century old when it was named in 1989. The Park Commission chose the name to provide a specific destination for emergency response.

LANCASTER AVENUE

5100 North, between 2200 and 10700 West
Origin: *Village of Whitefish Bay*

Elizabeth Street was changed to Lancaster Avenue by Whitefish Bay ordinance in 1926, probably for its regal connotation. The Lancasters, from Lancaster, England, were the English royal family during the 13th and 14th centuries.

LAND PLACE

1800 North, between 900 and 1100 East
Origin: *Lower East Side*

This street, on a bluff over the Milwaukee River, had the appropriate name of Highland until 1926 when it was shortened to Land (see *Highland, Hillcrest*).

LANDERS STREET

7200 West, between 6400 and 6700 North
Origin: *Menomonee River Hills East*

This street may have been named for Lander, Wyoming. Finley Fisler, of the City Engineer's Office, named many streets at this time for western cities. Fisler was a frequent traveler through the western United States and a Civil War buff. Frederick Lander was a general during the War between the States and Lander Peak, Lander Mountain, and the city of Lander, all in Wyoming, are his namesakes. Other streets in this subdivision are named for western cities, such as *Yuba* and *Cody*.

LANGLADE STREET

6100 North, between 9500 and 12200 West
Origin: *Parkway Hills*

Charles Michel de Langlade has been called the "Father of Wisconsin." He was a fur trader (his father was a Frenchman) and an Indian military leader (his mother was an Ottawa Indian). During the French and Indian War he, along with Indians from Milwaukee, ambushed and defeated the English near Pittsburgh. After the English won the war Langlade moved to Green Bay and, except for his military campaigns supporting the English against the rebels in the Revolutionary War, remained there until his death in 1800.

The county and town of Langlade were named for him in the 1800s, and Langlade Street was named for him by the City Engineer's Department in 1958.

LAPHAM STREET, BOULEVARD

1600 South, between 100 East/West and 3800 West
Origin: *Clock Tower Acres*

Increase Allen Lapham, born in New York State in 1811, came to Milwaukee in 1836 to assist Byron *Kilbourn* in surveying and promoting the city. During the next 39 years, Lapham produced maps of Milwaukee and Wisconsin, published books on botany, zoology, geography, geology,

149

archeology, and history, and was responsible for the establishment of the United States Weather Bureau. He was an alderman, a school commissioner, and a founder of *Downer* College. Lapham died of a heart attack while boating in 1875.

Besides this street named for him in 1856, "Laphamia," a genus of plant, carries his name, as does a peak in southern Wisconsin.

Increase Lapham.
(Buck's Pioneer History of
Milwaukee)

LARAMIE ROAD

9400 North and 9400 West
Origin: *Village of Bayside*

Jacques Laramie was a French Canadian trapper who was killed by Indians in 1818 in Wyoming, where there is a river, a city, a county, a fort, and a mountain range named for him. This road was named by the old Town of Milwaukee in 1940, although it may have been in existence before that date.

LAWN AVENUE

5300 North, between 1300 and 10700 West
Origin: *Milwaukee River Parkway*

John Stewart owned the land where Lawn Avenue was laid out in the 1920s. This appears to be a promotional name, as there was no one named Lawn associated with it.

LAWRENCE AVENUE

4500 North, between 8500 and 9100 West
Origin: *Lindsay Park*

Lawrence Avenue was developed in 1955. The significance of the name is not recorded.

150

LAYTON AVENUE

4700 South, between 1200 East and 2700 West
Origin: *City of Cudahy*

Frederick Layton has two Milwaukee streets named for him. This one
was named in 1892 by Patrick *Cudahy* when he founded his town and named
most of the streets after men associated with the meat industry. Layton's
wealth was amassed through his meatpacking business. He was born in
England in 1827 and, in 1843, with his father John, came to Milwaukee
where they established a meat trade.

Cudahy, who could trace the lineage of his own meatpacking
company back to Layton's pre-Civil War business, was fond of Layton and
said, "He was always cheerful, and appreciated men who endeavored to do
what was right." Layton, who died in 1919, returned the compliment when
he said Cudahy was wonderful and "the strongest man I ever knew."

Layton Avenue in Cudahy,
where it began.
(Cudahy Public Library)

LAYTON BOULEVARD

2700 West, between 500 and 2300 South
Origin: *Ordinance*

When Frederick Layton died in 1919, the "Milwaukee Sentinel"
proclaimed, "Milwaukee has lost its best loved, most honored citizen." In
1888 Layton had given the city its first art museum, and he continued to

furnish it with European works of art the rest of his life. Layton was a philanthropist to such an extent that by the time he died at the age of 93 he had given away most of his wealth.

When this boulevard was named by ordinance in 1909, it was the only street in the city to bear Layton's name. A second was added later as Milwaukee expanded southward and *Layton* Avenue became part of the city.

LEEDS PLACE

2700 South and 3400 West
Origin: *Layton Park*

This short street along railroad tracks was named by ordinance in 1926. The name comes from Leeds, England, a city known, coincidentally, for its locomotive manufacturing.

LEFEBER AVENUE

7200 West, between 2700 and 2900 North
Origin: *City of Wauwatosa*

Abraham Lefeber, Jr., born in Holland in 1844, settled on his Wauwatosa farm in 1868. Three years after his death in 1922, his heirs sold the farm for a subdivision and Lefeber Avenue was created. Milwaukee changed the name of part of 73rd Street to Lefeber Avenue in 1938 to conform to the Wauwatosa name.

LEGION STREET

1900 South, between 2400 and 2700 West
Origin: *Muskego Way*

The American Legion was founded in Paris in 1919 to further the political and social interests of veterans of World War I. In 1926, members of the Legion were unsuccessful in having their mates who fell in battle memorialized with the street name *Argonne* (*Capitol* Drive was selected instead). They were more successful in 1932 when Pratt Street was renamed Legion Street. Today, the American Legion includes veterans of both World Wars as well as those of Korea and Vietnam.

LENOX STREET, PLACE

900 East, between 2000 and 4700 South
Origin: *Bay View*

With the construction of the Milwaukee Iron Company's rolling mill in Bay View, nearby farmer Joseph *Williams* subdivided his farm in 1870. Besides giving one of the streets his name, he named another Lenox Street. Lenox, a name that can be traced to Scotland, has been used as a surname and a placename. Why Williams chose it is not known.

LEON TERRACE

From 3800 North and 4400 West to 6900 North and 10600 West
Origin: *Ordinance*

This intermittent street runs parallel to Fond du Lac Avenue. It was known as Oak Terrace until 1928, when it was changed so as not to conflict with other streets with Oak in their names. It is not known why Leon, a first name that means "lion," was selected.

LEROY AVENUE

4200 South, between 1400 and 5700 West
Origin: *City of St. Francis*

In 1930, the old Town of Lake changed the name of Villa Avenue to Leroy Avenue, presumably because it was too similar to the North Side's Villard Avenue. Leroy is a French name for "the king."

LIMA STREET

6700 North, between 6800 and 7300 West
Origin: *Menomonee River Hills East*

When this street was named in 1958, the City Engineer's Office was naming streets for Wisconsin cities. There are several towns and villages of this name in the state. Ultimately, they derive their names from Lima, Peru, which was named for an Indian god.

LINCOLN AVENUE

2300 South, between 1400 East and 4400 West
Origin: *Lincoln Village*

Abraham Lincoln, born in Kentucky in 1809, led the country during the most severe crisis in its history. Lincoln, the first Republican elected president, helped end slavery and preserve the *Union*. Many consider him the most important person in United States' history. His life was ended by an assassin's bullet in 1865. In 1871, six years after his death, Lincoln was honored by developers *Burnham*, *Rogers*, and *Becher* with this street named in his memory (see *Grant*).

Statue of Abraham Lincoln at the head of Lincoln Memorial Drive.

LINCOLN CREEK DRIVE, PARKWAY

From 6300 West and 4800 North to 2200 West and 5200 North
Origin: *Lincoln Creek*

Lincoln Creek, earlier known as Mud Creek, runs into the Milwaukee River at Lincoln Park, which was named for Abraham Lincoln. The road along the creek was named by the old Town of Wauwatosa in 1933.

LINCOLN MEMORIAL DRIVE

From 2400 South and 1600 East to 3100 North and 3000 East
Origin: *Lake Park*

The result of over twenty years of landfill work, Lincoln Memorial Drive, formerly part of Lake Michigan, was opened in 1929. The drive, and the beaches and parks subsequently created along it, allow access to lake activities from downtown north to Lake Park. The road was named for Abraham Lincoln, whose statue overlooks the drive from the Lincoln Memorial Bridge.

The northern part of Milwaukee Bay before a landfill created Lincoln Memorial Drive. The flushing station at center right still stands at the intersection of LaFayette Hill Road and Lincoln Memorial Drive.
(Milwaukee's Great Industries, 1892)

LINDEN PLACE

1000 North, between 3500 and 4000 West
Origin: *Miller Valley*

Linden Place was named by ordinance in 1928. The linden tree, the European version of the American Basswood, was brought to this country by immigrants from the Linden area of Germany, the source of this name.

LINDSAY STREET

1000 West, between 2100 and 2300 North
Origin: *Triangle North*

Bernice Copeland Lindsay, born in Indiana in 1899, came to Milwaukee in 1928, where she was the director of the Northside Y.W.C.A. for 22 years. She also worked as a case worker for the County Department of Public Welfare. During that time she helped the first African American teachers to be hired by the public school system and founded a center to help people learn new skills. Lindsay served on human rights and interracial relations commissions and was involved in other projects of community benefit. Lindsay Street was named in 1967.

Bernice Copeland Lindsay.
(Milwaukee Sentinel Photo)

155

LINEBARGER TERRACE

1700 East, between 2700 and 2900 South
Origin: *Bay View*

When he named Linebarger Terrace in 1911, Paul Linebarger fulfilled one of his mother's last wishes. *Ellen Estes* Linebarger, the daughter of Elijah Estes and Zebiah *Wentworth*, had hoped that the last street platted on her parents farm, settled in 1835, would be named for her husband's family.

Paul Linebarger was born in Warren, Illinois in 1871, and lived much of his youth in Bay View. He spent the early days of his career as an attorney in Milwaukee and later served in the Philippines as a federal judge. He died in Washington, D.C. in 1939.

LINK PLACE

5200 West, between 7800 and 8000 North
Origin: *Bradley Estates*

Link Place, whose name was inspired by the Brynwood and Tripoli golf courses nearby, was named in 1955 (see *Fairway*).

LINNWOOD AVENUE

3000 North, between 1500 and 3100 East
Origin: *Cambridge Heights*

Linnwood, usually spelled Linwood, refers to the *linden* or basswood tree. This street was platted as part of the Evergreen Park Subdivision in 1891.

LINUS STREET

2400 South, between 500 and 1000 East
Origin: *Bay View*

Aside from the "Peanuts" character with the security blanket, a few popes, and a minor Greek god, the first name Linus is not common. Linus Street was named by Joseph *Williams* in 1870 when he subdivided his farm. Why he named it Linus remains a mystery.

156

LINWAL LANE

4900 North, between 2300 and 2700 West
Origin: *Lincoln Park*

Linwal is a combination of LINdsey and WALter. Lindsey Hoben was an editor for the "Milwaukee Journal" and Walter P. Blount was a physician. Both were officers of the real estate company that platted Linwal Lane in 1940.

LISBON AVENUE

From 1000 North and 2000 West to 4000 North and 10100 West

The Lisbon Plank Road was built in the 1840s and led to the town of Lisbon in Waukesha County. The town, established in 1838, was the namesake of Lisbon, the capital of Portugal.

LLOYD STREET

2100 North, between 600 East and 6000 West
Origin: *Brewers Hill*

In 1837 a group of Chicago speculators platted Sherman's Addition and named the streets for themselves. Streets named for Francis Sherman, Cyrenius Beers, Isaac Harmon, and Mark Beaubian have since been renamed, but Lloyd Street remains. The Lloyd in question was likely Alexander Lloyd, (1805-1871), a lumberman and builder, who was the Chicago mayor from 1840 to 1841.

LOCUST STREET

2900 North, between 3100 East and 9200 West
Origin: *North Division*

Haertel's Addition, platted in 1858, included Maple, Willow, Elm and Locust Streets. Locust trees are not native to Milwaukee but line some of its streets as ornamental trees.

LOGAN AVENUE, COURT

1000 East, between 2300 and 4700 South
Origin: *Bay View*

John Logan. (The Life of
Logan: The Warrior Statesman)

John Alexander Logan was a U.S. Congress-man, a Civil War general, and a U.S. Senator. As commander-in-chief of the Grand Army of the Republic, he issued an order to honor the Civil War dead that led to the first Memorial Day observance on May 30, 1868.

Logan, of Scots-Irish parentage, was born in 1826 in Illinois, a state he represented as U.S. Congressman at the beginning of the Civil War. As a civilian he raised his own regiment and led it in battle. He gained distinction on the battlefield, where he was wounded twice and had his horse shot from under him. By the end of the war he was a major-general.

After the war Logan's life was devoted to politics. He was the Republican vice-presidential candidate on the losing ticket in 1884, and was being considered as a presidential nominee for the 1888 election when he died late in 1886. Logan was very popular in Milwaukee and the next spring an opportunity to name a street after him arose.

In March of 1887 Bay View was annexed by Milwaukee, giving the city one too many *Mitchell* Streets. In May, that duplication was resolved when this Bay View avenue was named for John Alexander Logan.

LOLITA AVENUE

7800 North, between 7600 and 9700 West
Origin: *Village of Brown Deer*

The old Town of Granville approved the naming of Lolita Avenue in the Fountain Acres Subdivision in 1932. The reason this name was selected is not known.

LONG ISLAND DRIVE

2100 West, between 5300 and 5600 North
Origin: *Lincoln Park*

158

Long Island, an island that includes part of New York City, has a larger population than 41 of the fifty states. This street was platted as part of the Long Island Subdivision in 1953.

LOOMIS ROAD

From 2700 West and 3600 South to 3300 West and 3800 South

In the 1840s, when this road was built to connect Milwaukee with Wind Lake and other southwesterly points, the Loomis family owned vast tracts of land in the town of Franklin, which the road passed through.

In the early 1840s, the J.C. Loomis residence was the site of the first meetings of the town's officers, with the Loomis clan well represented. Isaac C. Loomis was elected road viewer and Justice of the Peace. J.N. Loomis and Jonathan J. Loomis were both given posts, the latter that of assessor. Other Loomises whose land the road passed through were T.N. and J.I. Loomis.

By 1850, there was no trace left of the family, who probably moved with the westward flow. Now we have just a street name as a reminder of their presence for a few years, a century and a half ago.

LORENE AVENUE

3500 West, between 5500 and 5700 South
Origin: *Gra-Ram*

Lorene Avenue was named in a subdivision of women's first names in 1957. The reason the name was chosen is not recorded.

LORRAINE PLACE

2800 North, between 7600 and 9700 West
Origin: *Cooper Park*

This street was called Hadley Place until 1927, when it was changed so it would not cause confusion with nearby *Hadley* Street. Lorraine is a province in eastern France that spawned the feminine first name that became popular in the 1800s and 1900s. The person for whom this street was named, if there was one, is not known.

LOUISE PLACE

3200 North, between 5400 and 5500 West
Origin: *Sunset Heights*

Clyde Fuller and Charles Wild platted this short street in 1923. None of their mothers, wives, or children were named Louise, leaving the reason for the name of this street a mystery.

LOUISIANA AVENUE

2200 West, between 4300 and 4500 South
Origin: *Wilson Park*

Louisiana Avenue was named in 1955 in the Villa Mann Subdivision with two other state names, *Kentucky* and *Tennessee*. The state of Louisiana was named for the French king, Louis XIV (see *Alabama*).

LOVERS LANE ROAD

From 4800 North and 11300 West to 6000 North and 11500 West

In 1925, Lovers Lane Road extended from Hales Corners to Capitol Drive over what is now called *Mayfair* Road and 108th Street. Today, the name still exists in fragments from Franklin to Appleton Avenue. The emerging popularity of the automobile after World War I undoubtedly led to lovers seeking seclusion in places along this road.

Traffic was light on
Lovers Lane Road.
(Milwaukee County Historical
Society)

160

LUEBBE LANE

7900 North, between 5100 and 5800 West
Origin: *Village of Fox Point*

In the late 1800s, Carl Luebbe had a farm in the old town of Milwaukee. By the 1940s it was subdivided, with Luebbe Lane the only reminder of the farm.

LUSCHER AVENUE

4900 North, between 4200 and 8400 West
Origin: *Old North Milwaukee*

George D. Luscher, president of the Franklin State Bank, platted this street in 1923 as part of the Oakdale Subdivision.

LUZERNE COURT

5100 South, between 1800 and 1900 West
Origin: *City of Cudahy*

In order to not duplicate Milwaukee's *Pulaski* Street, the old Town of Lake changed the name of Pulaski Avenue to Luzerne Avenue in 1930. Anne Cesar Luzerne, (1741-1791), was the French minister to the United States during the Revolutionary War. Luzerne, Pennsylvania is named for him.

LYDELL AVENUE

200 West and 4800 North
Origin: *Village of Whitefish Bay*

Formerly called Second Street, this avenue had its name upgraded to Lydell by the Village of Whitefish Bay in 1929. Lydell was apparently chosen for its marketing value.

LYNMAR COURT, TERRACE

4200 North, between 7800 and 8300 West
Origin: *Arlington Gardens*

Val Zimmermann, a real estate dealer and home builder, named this street for his daughters, LYNne and MARy, in 1954.

LYNNDALE AVENUE

3700 South, between 4800 and 5000 West
Origin: *Southpoint*

Win *Morgan* developed the Lynndale Subdivision in 1895, naming it for his four year old son, Lynn. Lynndale Avenue was named in 1926 for the subdivision. Lynn Morgan, later a captain in the infantry during the First World War, died in 1942.

LYNX AVENUE, COURT

6200 North, between 8400 and 12300 West
Origin: *Little Menomonee Parkway*

Until the 1930s, the Lynx golf course was located between Appleton and Silver Spring Avenues. Lynx Avenue, named by 1949, is the last reminder of the former course.

LYON STREET

1500 North, between 300 and 1100 East
Origin: *Lower East Side*

Lucius Lyon was a U. S. Senator from Michigan when this street was named for him in 1837. Lyon, along with William *Ogden* and others, founded the Wisconsin Land Company, which owned land throughout the state, including Milwaukee. Lyon, born in Vermont in 1800, died in Detroit in 1851.

Lucius Lyon. (Milwaukee Public Library)

162

MABBETT AVENUE

1900 East, between 2800 and 3200 South
Origin: *Bay View*

Hiram J. Mabbett, a Milwaukee lumberman, platted Mabbett Avenue as part of H. J. Mabbett's Addition in 1887. Mabbett Avenue runs both north/south and east/west and intersects itself, creating the corner of Mabbett and Mabbett.

MADELINE AVENUE

3600 West, between 5600 and 5900 South
Origin: *Gra-Ram*

Madeline Avenue was named in 1958. It may not have been named for a particular Madeline, as there are other streets in this neighborhood named for women.

MADISON STREET

1300 South, between 200 East and 3300 West
Origin: *Walker's Point*

James Madison, (1751-1836), was the fourth President of the United States, from 1809 to 1817. Madison fought against British colonial policy and was a strong supporter of the Revolutionary War. The principal event of his presidency was another war with England, the War of 1812. Madison Street was named by developers in 1838.

MAGNOLIA STREET

7500 North, between 8600 and 10000 West
Origin: *Melody View*

Magnolia trees are native to the southern part of the United States. This street was named in 1965 as part of the Melody View Subdivision (see *Tupelo*).

MAIN STREET

600 South, between 5700 and 9500 West
Origin: *Johnson's Woods*

This may have been the main street in the Euclid Park Subdivision, platted in 1888. The developer, F.T. *Adler*, would have had to have been quite optimistic to hope that it would grow to be a traditional Main Street. Milwaukee's original Main Street was changed to *Broadway* in 1870.

MALLORY AVENUE

5400 South, between 600 and 2400 West
Origin: *City of Cudahy*

Mallory Avenue was platted in 1892 and, like other *Cudahy* streets, was named for people in the meat industry. Herbert and Henry Mallory worked in Michigan before starting their livestock commission business in Chicago in 1863. The Mallorys claimed that they handled more hogs than any other firm in Chicago.

MALVERN PLACE

3400 South, between 2300 and 2400 East
Origin: *Fernwood*

164

Malvern, England, is the source of this name. Malvern Place was platted in 1923 by George *Meredith*, whose English-born parents were from a place near Malvern (see *Falling Heath*).

MANCHESTER AVENUE

5100 South, between 2300 and 2600 West
Origin: *Clayton Crest*

Manchester was chosen as the name for this street in 1978 because it "rolled well off the tongue" and was popular at the time. Manchester, England, is an industrial city known for its textile industry.

MANGOLD AVENUE

6200 South, between 100 and 2700 West
Origin: *Goldman Park*

Leopold and Leo Goldmann of Goldman Realty reversed the syllables of their name to come up with Mangold Avenue in 1931. They started Goldmann's Department Store with their father in 1898. Leo Goldmann died in 1963, a few years after Leopold had passed away (see *Goldcrest*).

MANITOBA STREET

3000 South, between 1600 East and 6500 West
Origin: *Bay View*

This street was named for the Canadian province by the *Herman Mann* family in 1882. The name is an Indian word referring to the narrow part of Lake Manitoba and is thought to mean "the straits of the Great Spirit" (see *Montana*).

MANOR COURT

9100 North and 9400 West
Origin: *Village of Bayside*

The Suburban Investment Company platted Manor Court in 1927 and gave it this promotional name.

MAPLE STREET

1800 South, between 100 East and 3800 West
Origin: *Clock Tower Acres*

Maple trees line the streets of Milwaukee and, earlier, they filled the forests the city replaced. Maple Streets have been common too, but this is the only survivor. It's also the oldest, platted in 1857 by Judge A.D. Smith.

MAPLEWOOD COURT

5400 South, between 600 and 1500 West
Origin: *Greendale*

Maplewood Court was platted in 1955 by the Milwaukee Community Development Corporation.

MARCELLE AVENUE

6900 North, between 9500 and 9800 West
Origin: *Golden Gate*

Marcelle Avenue was named for developer Francis Schroedel's grandson, Marc, in 1962.

MARCIA ROAD

8300 North, between 7000 and 7300 West
Origin: *Land Bank*

This street was named for Marcia Endrizzi, the wife of alderman Thomas Nardelli, in 1990. She was born in Superior, Wisconsin in 1944.

MARCY STREET

6600 West, between 3700 and 3900 South
Origin: *Root Creek*

Marcy Street was platted in 1959. For whom the street was named, if anyone, is not known.

166

MARGARET PLACE

1300 South, between 3700 and 3800 West

Origin: *Silver City*

John Johnston named this street in 1893. There were two Margarets in his life, his mother and his first wife.

His mother was Margaret Mitchell Johnston, sister of Alexander *Mitchell*. John was three years old when his uncle Alexander left Scotland for Milwaukee, and his fortune, in 1839. After Johnston earned his master's degree in Scotland in 1856, he came to Milwaukee where he worked in his uncle's bank. Margaret died a few years after Johnston left.

John Johnston named Margaret Place. (Illustrated News Annual)

Shortly before his mother's death, another Margaret came into his life. He married fellow Scot, Margaret Hunter, in 1861. They had three children, two of whom died before Margaret's death in 1880 (see *Dorothy*).

MARIETTA AVENUE

3000 East, between 2800 and 3300 North

Origin: *Downer Woods*

Marietta Avenue was named by Clarence *Shepard* in 1891. The reason he chose the name, which means "little Maria," is not known.

MARILYN STREET

3100 West, between 5500 and 5900 South

Origin: *Gra-Ram*

Harold and B.J. Sampson platted Marilyn Street in 1957. The City Engineer's Department named this street, but no one there now remembers why they chose this name.

MARINA DRIVE

500 East and 1900 South
Origin: *Bay View*

Public boat storage and launching facilities on the Kinnickinnic River at Mound Street prompted the change of name from *Mound* to Marina Drive in 1986. Fred Vogel III, of P&V Atlas, recommended the change.

MARINE DRIVE, COURT

9000 North, between 6800 and 7500 West
Origin: *Northridge Lakes*

The artificial lake in the Northridge Lakes Subdivision was the inspiration for the naming of Marine Drive by the Kohl family in 1972.

MARION STREET

4300 North, between 3500 and 10000 West
Origin: *Village of Shorewood*

Anthony Dallman and Zachara Merrill platted Marion Street in 1887. The reason for the name is not known.

MARKET STREET

200 East, between 800 and 1300 North
Origin: *Juneautown*

Market Street was platted by Solomon *Juneau* and Morgan L. *Martin* by 1840. In its early days, it truly was a market street, with Market Square near where the city hall now stands.

Market Hall stood at the intersection of Market and Water Streets where City Hall now stands. (Milwaukee, ca1890)

168

MARSHALL STREET

900 East, between 500 South and 1800 North

Origin: *Juneautown*

John Marshall, (1755-1835), was the fourth chief justice of the U.S. Supreme Court. His decisions established the Supreme Court as an important part of the federal government and increased the national government's influence over the states. A few weeks after Marshall died in 1835 Solomon *Juneau* and Morgan L. *Martin* named this street in their village of Milwaukee.

MARTIN DRIVE

1100 North, between 4100 and 5700 West

Origin: *Martin Drive*

Morgan L. Martin, a Green Bay lawyer and speculator, bought half of Solomon *Juneau's* Juneautown property for $500 in 1833. In 1835 they co-founded their new village, with Martin responsible for the legal and promotional aspects while Juneau took care of local issues. Martin, born in Martinsburg, New York in 1805 (his father founded the town), was a Wisconsin congressman, assemblyman, and state senator, as well as Oneida Indian Agent in Green Bay. He died in 1887.

A street in the village was named for Martin, but during the 1920s renaming program it was changed to *State* Street. To appease those who complained that Martin deserved a place on the city's map, this street, one block south of Juneau Avenue, was renamed Martin Drive in 1926.

Morgan L. Martin. (Buck's Pioneer History of Milwaukee)

MARTIN LANE

4400 South, between 100 East/West and 500 West
Origin: *Town of Lake*

Since the mid-1920s, the city street naming policy has been that no two streets should have the same name, or even names that sound alike, and that a street should have only one name for its entire length.

But every system must have its exceptions, and this street, Martin Lane, breaks both the duplication rule and the continuous name dictum. The lane, which runs west from Howell Avenue, was part of the land owned by A.E. and Lafayette Martin. They donated it as a thoroughfare in 1940, when the area was part of the old town of Lake.

In 1955, after the Town of Lake had ceased to exist and Milwaukee had taken over this part of it, Martin Lane became a duplicate of *Martin Drive* near the Miller Brewery. Martin Lane was changed to *Whitaker Avenue*, so that the street would have one name throughout its length. But the residents of the street were unhappy with the change and they petitioned the city to have their street name back, and in 1956 Martin Lane was returned to the city's map.

MARYLAND AVENUE

2200 East, between 2300 and 3500 North
Origin: *Murray Hill*

Charles I of England gave the land rights to the area that became Maryland to George Calvert in 1632. The colony was named for Charles' wife, Henrietta Maria, although the Catholic founders preferred to consider it "the land of the Virgin Mary." James *Murray* platted this street in 1856.

MASON STREET

800 North, between 100 and 1000 East
Origin: *Juneautown*

The year 1835 was a big one for 23 year old Tom Mason, as Stevens Thomson Mason was familiarly known. That year he had a street named for him, founded a major Wisconsin city, started a war that defined Wisconsin's northern border, and was elected Michigan's first governor.

At the age of 19, Mason had become acting governor of the Michigan Territory, an area that included Wisconsin. As Michigan's statehood approached, the issue of its border with Ohio heated up. The Northwest Ordinance of 1787 had set the border between the two states as a line due east from the southern tip of Lake Michigan. Ohio was admitted as a state in 1803 with a border slightly north of where it should have been, a border that included the harbor of Toledo as part of the state.

Tom Mason. (The Life and Times of Stevens Thomson Mason)

Tom Mason, deciding to take back that which was rightfully Michigan's, sent territorial troops to take control of Toledo, beginning the "Toledo War." The Ohioans fled as the Michigan troops moved in; the Michiganders won the battle but not the war.

The United States Congress, in a move to settle the dispute, offered Michigan the northern portion of what would have been Wisconsin in exchange for the Toledo Strip. Michigan thought it was a poor swap, that the Upper Peninsula was too wild for settlement. But they had to take it or leave it, because Congress wouldn't allow Ohio to lose Toledo. Michigan accepted and became a state, and Mason, the Toledo War hero, became its first governor.

That same year, Mason and James D. *Doty* bought land in Wisconsin that would become the city of Madison two years later. Meanwhile, Solomon *Juneau* and Morgan *Martin* were laying out their village of Milwaukee and naming some of their streets, including Mason Street, for Democratic politicians and statesmen.

Mason City and Mason County, Michigan, also memorialize Mason's name, as do street names in other communities throughout the Midwest.

MASSACHUSETTS AVENUE

7500 West, between 3500 and 3900 South
Origin: *Wedgewood*

A more recent addition to the South Side's state name streets, Massachusetts Avenue was platted in 1955. The Indian word means "blue hill" and referred to the hills at Massachusetts Bay. The selection of the

171

name Massachusetts for this street seems peculiar; the city named it at a time when it rejected Connecticut as too difficult to spell.

MAXWELL PLACE

4100 North and 5400 West
Origin: *Lincoln Creek*

The old Town of Wauwatosa named Maxwell Place in 1933 during the county-wide street renaming program. The reason for the name is unknown.

MAYFAIR ROAD

10800 West, between 100 North/South and 400 North
Origin: *Zoo*

Mayfair Road, formerly known as *Lovers Lane* Road, was renamed in 1964 when the Mayfair Shopping Center requested the change from the Wauwatosa Common Council. Milwaukee followed suit in 1988.

The original May Fair took place in London during the first two weeks of May in 1688. Cattle and other goods were traded but over the years the fair became an excuse for lewdness and uninhibited pleasure. The bawdy festivities continued annually for twenty years, but due to public outrage it was banned in 1708. Mayfair is now a respectable London area known for its elegance.

MAYFLOWER COURT

700 West and 1600 North
Origin: *Hillside*

The Mayflower carried 120 pilgrims from Southhampton, England to Plymouth, Massachusetts in 1620. In 1963, Mayflower Court was named in the Plymouth Hill Subdivision.

The Mayflower. (Milwaukee Public Library)

McAULEY PLACE

500 North, between 800 and 900 West
Origin: *Kilbourntown*

Raymond R. McAuley was the executive vice-president of Marquette University until he left in 1970. When a new street was created by freeway construction that year, it was named for McAuley by alderman William R. Drew. Drew had become close friends with the priest when he had worked at Marquette some years earlier.

McKINLEY AVENUE, BOULEVARD, CT

1300 North, between 300 and 5800 West
Origin: *Ordinance*

William McKinley, (1843-1901), was the 25th U.S. President and the third to be assassinated while in office. McKinley, a Republican, was serving his second term when he was killed. He was succeeded by Theodore *Roosevelt*. Although the recommendation to rename Cold Spring Avenue for McKinley was made in 1913, it wasn't until 1926 that the change finally occurred.

MEDFORD AVENUE

From 2400 West and 2400 North to 10900 West and 6900 North
Origin: *Ordinance*

Medford Avenue was chosen as the new name for Kilbourn Avenue (not to be confused with the downtown *Kilbourn* Avenue) in 1929 during the renaming program. It was probably named for Medford, Wisconsin, which was named for Medford, Massachusetts.

MEINECKE AVENUE

2400 North, between 1300 East and 6000 West
Origin: *North Division*

Adolph Meinecke named this avenue Meinecke in 1887 and he wanted it to remain Meinecke Avenue. When he donated land to the city for a firehouse, he stipulated that if the name of the street was changed, the land would revert to his family. Forty years later, in 1927, when the city was trying to make sense out of its street naming chaos, the name of this street came under scrutiny.

It was known as Lee Street for part of its length and Meinecke for the rest. The choice was obvious. Lee was easy to pronounce and simple to spell, so Meinecke became Lee. But Meinecke's grandson, Ferdinand, pointed out the provision in his grandfather's donation. The land, with the firehouse, was now worth over $100,000. The street was quickly renamed.

Adolph Meinecke was born in Germany in 1831 and came to Milwaukee in 1855. He founded the Milwaukee Willow Works, a business that produced wicker baskets, furniture, and toys. In its early days, the wicker material was supplied from Meinecke's 37-acre willow fields at 15th and North Avenue.

Meinecke's Willow Works.
(Milwaukee's Great Industries)

MELINDA STREET

3400 West, between 5600 and 5900 South
Origin: *Gra-Ram*

Melinda Street was platted in 1957. It is in a neighborhood of feminine street names.

MELVINA STREET, PLACE

3900 North, between 900 East and 9800 West
Origin: *Williamsburg*

Jonas Cohen named this street in 1888. Perhaps, like Chicago's Melvina Avenue, this street was the namesake of Melvina, Wisconsin in Monroe County.

MENOMONEE STREET

100 North/South, between 200 and 600 East
Origin: *Juneautown*

The Menominee Indians, part of the Algonquin language family, once lived throughout most of Wisconsin and Upper Michigan. The tribe is now centered in Menominee County and is the only Wisconsin tribe not scattered or removed from the state. The street was platted in 1837 by Solomon *Juneau* and Morgan *Martin*.

Another unique street sign in the Third Ward.

MENOMONEE PARK COURT

5900 North, between 9800 and 9900 West
Origin: *Parkway Hills*

This street, off the Little Menomonee Parkway, had its name changed in 1968. The word "menomonee" is from the Algonquin-speaking tribes and means "good grain." The grain in this case was the wild rice growing along the river, a diet staple of local Indians (see *Menomonee River Parkway, Menomonee Street*).

MENOMONEE RIVER PARKWAY

9800 West, between 2700 and 3200 North
Origin: *City of Wauwatosa*

There are many places named Menominee, Menomonie, or Menomonee in Wisconsin. All were named either for wild rice or for the Indian tribe that gathered the plant. The Menomonee River may have been named for either since it was the source of wild rice and its banks were occupied by Menominee Indians. The parkway was named in the 1920s.

MEREDITH STREET

3000 South, between 2200 and 2500 East
Origin: *Bay View*

John T. Meredith built furnaces for the iron and steel industry in England, where he was born in 1840. He left his native land in 1867 for similar work in the United States. With his sons, he started a business in Bay View that built steel plants and furnaces throughout the Midwest.

Meredith served as president of the Village of Bay View before it became part of the City of Milwaukee. His son, George, was an alderman representing Bay View in 1900 when Union Street was changed to Meredith Street. John Meredith died in 1911 (see *Malvern, Falling Heath*, and *Swain*).

MERRILL STREET

2000 South, between 2300 and 2400 West
Origin: *Muskego Way*

A diamond was picked off the top of a dirt pile near Eagle, in Waukesha County, during the winter of 1884. William P. Merrill quickly bought up the four acres of land surrounding the mound of earth that had come from the bottom of a newly dug well. Merrill sold stock in his Eagle Diamond Fields and began to drill. But all he and his supporters got for their time and money were more wells, not more diamonds.

William Merrill. (Buck's Pioneer History of Milwaukee)

176

William Merrill, a native of Maine and one of the city's early white settlers, moved to Milwaukee in 1836 when he was a 19 year old. He helped install a state of the art water system in early Milwaukee; hollowed out tamarack logs laid underground to carry water from a Wisconsin Avenue spring to a nearby hotel.

Merrill, who served the city as alderman, was a farmer and real estate dealer, although he dabbled in other ventures, such as his ill-fated diamond mine. Merrill Street is located on what was Merrill's farm, which was subdivided in 1885.

MESSMER STREET

4100 North, between 700 and 1000 West
Origin: *Grover Heights*

Messmer Street was known as Maurice Street until 1929, when Messmer High School was on built it. The school was named for Sebastian Gebhard Messmer, who was born in Switzerland in 1847. When he was 24 years old, Messmer arrived in America and taught Catholic theology for twenty years on the East Coast, until he was appointed bishop of Green Bay. He became archbishop of Milwaukee in 1903. Messmer died during a visit to his homeland in 1930.

Messmer High School. (Capitol, 1962)

METCALF PLACE

From 3500 North and 8900 West to 3900 North and 10000 West
Origin: *Golden Valley/Kops Park*

William H. Metcalf, a partner with Charles T. Bradley in one of the country's largest boot and shoe manufacturing businesses, was born in New York City in 1821. He and Bradley, who were clerks in the same New York shoe store, came to Milwaukee, traveling mostly by sleigh, in the winter of 1843. They opened a small boot store that was the foundation of their enterprise, which eventually employed hundreds.

Metcalf, who died in 1892, spent part of his wealth on art. He made several art hunting expeditions to Europe and Japan, using the trophies to furnish his home, which became the city's unofficial art museum. Before Frederick *Layton* donated an art museum to the city, on Sunday afternoons Metcalf would open the doors of his collection to the public.

In 1887, Bradley and Metcalf donated the statue of Solomon *Juneau* that stands on the bluff in Juneau Park. Metcalf Place was named in 1927 by city ordinance.

MICHELE STREET

9500 West and 8900 North
Origin: *North Meadows*

Clarence Miller, alderman on the city's Northwest Side from 1964 to 1978, named this street for his granddaughter. Michele Miller was one year old when this street became her namesake in 1969 (see photo on back cover).

MICHIGAN STREET

600 North, between 1100 East and 9300 West
Origin: *Historic Third Ward*

Lake Michigan was the source for this street name. Michigan means ''great or big lake'' in Algonquin Indian languages. The street was platted by Solomon *Juneau* and Morgan *Martin* in 1837.

MIDDLEMASS STREET

2100 South, between 2100 and 2300 West
Origin: *Layton Park*

Archibald Middlemass was born in Edinburgh, Scotland in 1846. He came to Milwaukee when he was twenty years old to garden on the estate of a wealthy Scotsman. Within a few years he started a well-known floral business that lasted until his death in 1900.

Not unexpectedly, Middlemass' interests were in things Scottish. He won awards in curling, a game popular with Scots in Milwaukee, and at Scottish get-togethers he led in the singing of ballads from the homeland. He was also a member of the St. Andrew's Society and a Presbyterian. Middlemass' partner, John Dunlop, also a Scotsman, named this street in 1881.

MIDLAND DRIVE

From 3200 South and 4400 West to 3600 South and 5500 West
Origin: *City of Greenfield*

Midland Drive was named as part of William Mitchell's Mitchell Highlands Subdivision in 1920. Perhaps it was named Midland because it was the middle street in the development.

MILL ROAD, COURT, PLACE

6400 North, between 2800 and 12400 West
Origin: *Mill Valley/City of Glendale*

It was inevitable that this road would be called Mill Road. On its western end, where it crosses the Menomonee River, there was a mill, called Ver Bryck's Mill, by 1842. On the eastern portion, where it crosses the Milwaukee River, there was Bender's Mill by 1852. The mills used waterpower to grind grain and saw wood. The street was known as Mill Road well before the old Town of Milwaukee formalized the street name in 1917.

MILLER LANE

900 North and 3700 West
Origin: *Miller Valley*

Frederick Miller, a German immigrant who died in 1888, bought Charles Best's brewery near here in 1855. The land this lane is on was the site of his home. In 1900, Ernest G. and Fred A. Miller, his sons, platted Miller Lane, a north-south street. In 1926, it was replatted as the east-west street that it is today. The Miller brewery is now Milwaukee's largest.

The Miller Brewery a century ago. (Stadt Milwaukee)

MILWAUKEE STREET

400 East, between 100 South and 1500 North
Origin: *Juneautown*

It is a common belief that the name Milwaukee comes from a Potawatomi phrase meaning ''Gathering place or council ground by the river.'' With a rendering of something like ''Mahnah-wauk-seepe,'' it has been assumed that the current spelling of Milwaukee comes from this phrase. The evidence does not support this theory, however.

There seems little reason to doubt that Milwaukee means ''good, fine, rich or beautiful land.'' Frederic *Baraga*, the man who wrote the dictionary and grammar for Ojibwa, the universal language of the Wisconsin Indians, said that it means ''good land.'' Louis Moran, an Ojibwa interpreter, described it as meaning ''rich, or beautiful land.'' French traders translated Milwaukee as ''la Belle Terre.'' The Potawatomi and Menominee languages, like the Ojibwa, are part of the Algonquin group of languages, and scholars of both give it this meaning. And finally, place-name experts, comparing it to the meaning of similar names in North America, have arrived at the same conclusion.

Milwaukee Street is one of the original village streets platted by Solomon *Juneau* and Morgan L. *Martin* in 1835. During the first decade or so of the city's founding, there was a lack of consensus as to whether the name should end in ''ie'' or ''ee.'' In 1844, in the midst of the debate, James Clyman, who had lived here since 1835, was taken with wanderlust and moved to the West Coast where he founded Milwaukie, Oregon, spelling it ''ie.'' But by the time that homesteaders from this city had settled Milwaukee Lake, South Dakota later in the century, the ''ee'' had long become standard.

MILWAUKEE RIVER PARKWAY

1200 West, between 5100 and 5600 North
Origin: *Milwaukee River Parkway*

The old Town of Milwaukee named this parkway along the Milwaukee River in 1940. Whether the name Milwaukee was first used for the river, or for the place it led to, is not known. Evidence that it may have

180

been used for the city can be found in the meaning of the word, "fine or good land." But the term "land" here could be more general and mean the good land of the river.

MINER STREET

3100 West, between 3800 and 3900 South
Origin: *Southpoint*

Miner Street was named in 1959. The reason for the name is not known.

MINERAL STREET

1000 South, between 200 East and 2700 West
Origin: *Walker's Point*

Mineral Street was platted in 1836 by George *Walker*. The mineral referred to was the product of the Lead Region in southwestern Wisconsin, near Mineral Point. Lead mining was flourishing at the time, with most of the non-Indian population of Wisconsin in that region. Street name lore says Mineral Street was named because it led to the so-called Mineral Road, a route that supposedly led to the Lead Region. There were reports of ox-drawn lead wagons coming to the city before 1836, but the route into town is not documented (see *Galena*).

MITCHELL STREET

1700 South, between 100 East and 3800 West
Origin: *Historic Mitchell Street*

Lemuel Weeks named this street in 1857 for his business partner, Alexander Mitchell. Mitchell immigrated to Milwaukee from Scotland in 1839 to run the banking business of a fellow Scotsman. He was a mature 21 years old at the time.

Before he died in 1887, Mitchell was one of the wealthiest and most influential men in the state. Banker, railroad executive, and congressman were among his titles. As president of the Chicago, Milwaukee and St. Paul Railroad, he had two cities in South Dakota named for him, Alexandria and

Mitchell. Mitchell Park is named for his son, John, and Mitchell International Airport is the namesake of his grandson, Billy.

One of Mitchell's most interesting, and least pleasant, experiences occurred during the Bank Riot in the summer of 1861. Banks in the state had just made a decision that many people felt would lead to the loss of their deposits. Five hundred irate citizens marched on Mitchell's bank near Michigan and Water Streets. Mitchell's attempt to soothe the group outside his bank was quickly ended with a thrown paving stone. He sought refuge inside his business but was followed by the mob, who took everything that wasn't nailed down, and some things that were.

The Bank Riot of 1861. (Wisconsin: A History, blank left corner on original)

The crowd built a bonfire with the bank's furnishings. Other financial institutions were looted as well, their possessions feeding the fire. The assembly was eventually dispersed, but the riot was effective. The banks soon reversed their decision, and a week later a crowd marched again on Water Street, this time in celebration of the success of the Bank Riot.

MOHAWK AVENUE

200 West and 4800 North
Origin: *Village of Fox Point*

The Mohawks, "cannibals" in Algonquin, gained their name by eating their captured enemies. This street was platted by Bay Shore Realty in 1927 (see *Navajo*).

MOLTKE AVENUE

3100 North, between 6400 and 7200 West
Origin: *Enderis Park*

Helmuth Von Moltke was a favorite with Milwaukee's German population. Von Moltke, (1800-1891), was given control of the Prussian Army in 1858. When Prussia defeated France in 1870, the city's Teutons celebrated by marching with bands leading them through downtown, as they partied and drank from the parade's beer wagons. During the next few decades, a park and two streets were named for Von Moltke and a statue was erected in his honor.

This street was named in 1916 by Paul Hartung in what may have been a pro-German statement prior to U.S. involvement in World War I (many local Germans supported Germany before the United States entered the war). After the war, German names fell into disfavor. During the 1920s renaming program, the city's older and more German sounding Von Moltke Place was renamed Laurel Street.

MONARCH PLACE

800 North, between 4200 and 4500 West
Origin: *Miller Valley*

In 1891 Henry Niedecken, president of the Monarch Stone Quarry Company, developed Monarch Park, which included Monarch Place.

MONROE STREET

From 1800 West and 2200 North to 2600 West and 2700 North
Origin: *Triangle North*

James Monroe, born in Virginia in 1758, was the country's fifth President, serving two terms between 1817 and 1825. While a teenager, Monroe was wounded at the Battle of *Trenton* during the Revolutionary

War. His administration is best remembered for the "Monroe Doctrine," which prohibited European colonization in the Americas. Monroe died in 1831. This street was changed from Bismarck to Monroe in 1908.

MONROVIA AVENUE

6100 North, between 8600 and 9000 West
Origin: *Village of Whitefish Bay*

Monrovia is the capital city of the west African country, Liberia. The city was named for American President James *Monroe*. The country was established for the resettlement of African American slaves. Monrovia, an unusual name for a street, had been Pinewood until it was renamed in 1926.

MONTANA STREET

2800 South, between 1300 East and 7200 West
Origin: *Bay View*

This street was named for the Montana Territory in 1882 by the *Herman* Mann family. Montana means "mountainous region" in Latin. It became a state in 1889 (see *Nevada*).

MONTREAL STREET

3600 West, between 4000 and 4200 North
Origin: *Lincoln Creek*

Fearing that East Edgebrook Drive and West Edgebrook Drive, short streets near one another, could cause confusion, particularly in emergency situations, the city changed their names in 1926. Additionally, Edgebrook was similar to *Edgewood*, and the city was stamping out sound-alike names at the time. One of the Edgebrooks became Montreal Street, the other *Toronto*. Montreal is a version of the French "Mount Royal."

MONTROSE AVENUE

2400 South, between 4600 and 4900 West
Origin: *Jackson Park*

Montrose, Scotland may have been the inspiration for this street, named by Frank and Elisabeth Kirkpatrick in 1948.

MORGAN AVENUE, PLACE

3500 South, between 2800 East and 10000 West
Origin: *Morgandale*

Win Morgan. (Illustrated News Annual)

Win Morgan was born in Milwaukee in 1862; his father was an Irish immigrant, his mother a New Yorker. Win (his name was really Winfield but he always went by Win) began his business career when he was nine years old, as a paperboy. At 16, he started a grocery store with his brother, but sold his interests before he was twenty, when he went into sales. While still in his twenties, he set up a real estate office and soon handled more land sales and development than anyone in the city. He named this street for himself in 1892. Morgan died in 1912.

MOUND STREET

500 East, between 2100 and 2300 South
Origin: *Bay View*

Mound Street was platted in 1867 by future mayor Ammi R.R. Butler, and industrialist Edward P. *Allis*. There were Indian mounds in the neighborhood (near Sixth Street and Lincoln Avenue), but the small hill this street runs over is not one of them, as street lore has claimed.

MOUNT COURT

2600 North and 5500 West
Origin: *Uptown*

This short street, which runs uphill, was platted as part of the Mount Heights Subdivision in 1920 by R.S. Witte.

MT VERNON AVENUE

300 North, between 1200 and 9500 West
Origin: *Merrill Park*

Mount Vernon, the Virginia plantation, was George *Washington's* home for most of his life. This street was platted in 1857 by James *Greves* and Edwin Palmer.

MURIEL COURT, PLACE

From 8100 West and 5400 North to 11200 West and 7000 North
Origin: *Valhalla*

Harold and B.J. Sampson platted Muriel Place in 1954. According to Harold Sampson, the City Engineer's Department named it, but there is no record of the reason for the choice.

MURRAY AVENUE

2000 East, between 2300 and 3500 North
Origin: *Ordinance*

James Murray owned the land north of North Avenue that Murray Avenue runs through. Murray, whose charity provided nearby land for orphans and the aged, was a Scotsman who

James Murray. (Buck's Pioneer History of Milwaukee)

immigrated to Milwaukee in 1835. He initially worked as a painter and glazier but later went into land development and farming.

Like many 19th century Scots in Milwaukee, Murray was a member of the St. Andrew's Society and a curler. He died in 1863, 19 years before a city ordinance named this street for him.

MUSKEGO AVENUE

From 1500 West and 400 South to 2500 West and 2300 South

This road dates from the 1840s and was named because it led to the Muskego area. Muskego, Wisconsin, like Muskegon, Michigan, is named from the Algonquin language for "swamp or swampy."

186

NASH STREET

3700 North, between 1100 East and 10000 West
Origin: *Arlington Heights*

Charles Dennis Nash learned the banking business from his father in Vermont, where he was born in 1819. After settling in Milwaukee in 1853, Nash founded the Bank of Milwaukee. In 1859 he was one of the men who brought the Northwestern Mutual Life Insurance Company to Milwaukee. When the company was confronted with its first death claim and didn't have the resources to pay, Charles Nash came to the rescue, lending the money for the claim.

Both of Nash's sons worked for the insurance carrier, from which he retired in 1892. His son George, the company's loan officer, named this street in 1889. Nash died in 1897.

NATIONAL AVENUE

From 800 South and 200 East to 1300 South and 3900 West
Origin: *Ordinance*

In 1877, the "Milwaukee Sentinel" reported that Elizabeth Street had been renamed National Home Avenue. The paper was wrong, the word "Home" wasn't in the new name, but the mistake was understandable. The

National Home, also known as the National Soldiers' Home, or just the Soldiers' Home, was a facility built to care for men disabled during the Civil War. Its parklike grounds at 45th and National drew picnickers from the city, and the area became an attraction. And in 1877, the way to get to the National Home for much of the city's population was via National Avenue.

Picnics and concerts drew people to the grounds at the National Home. (Milwaukee Illustrated)

NAVAJO AVENUE

100 West and 4800 North
Origin: *Village of Fox Point*

The Navajo Indians, the largest tribe in the United States, live in Arizona, New Mexico, and Utah. In 1927 the Bay View Realty Company named four streets in their Bay Shore Manor Subdivision for Native American tribes.

NEBRASKA AVENUE

From 5200 West and 3300 South to 6300 West and 3800 South
Origin: *Lyons Park*

An Indian term applied to the Nebraska River, it means "flat or spreading water." The street was named in 1954, adding still another state-named street to the South Side, as part of the King's Addition by Thomas and Grace King (see *Alabama*).

NEIL PLACE

5400 North, between 2200 and 2400 West
Origin: *Lincoln Park*

Neil Place was named as part of the Long Island Subdivision in 1953. The reason for the designation is unknown.

NEVADA STREET

1400 East, between 2900 and 4100 South
Origin: *Bay View*

This is one of the western state streets named by the *Herman* Mann family in 1879. The state took its name from the Sierra Nevada mountain range which is on its border with California. Nevada means ''snow-covered'' in Spanish (see *Oklahoma*).

NEWBERRY BOULEVARD

2800 North, between 1800 and 3100 East
Origin: *Riverside Park*

Wealthy Chicagoan Walter Loomis Newberry was buried in a barrel. On a trip to Europe in 1868, Newberry died aboard ship and his body was sent back to Chicago in a rum barrel that served as his coffin.

Newberry was born in 1804 in Connecticut, and moved to Chicago in 1833. He was one of the largest land owners in Wisconsin and Upper Michigan. Newberry had owned the land that this street was platted on in 1887. Besides real estate, he made his fortune in banking and railroads. In Chicago his name has been memorialized with a street and a library named for him. The Newberry Library was established with an endowment left for it in Newberry's will.

NEWHALL STREET, LANE

1600 East, between 2300 and 3500 North
Origin: *Riverside Park*

When Newhall Street was platted in 1857, the up and down career of Daniel Newhall was at its peak. The former grocer, born in Massachusetts, was the foremost wheat dealer in the world. Newhall, also a real estate developer, was building the Newhall House, the leading hotel in the Midwest. At the time he was 36 years old. Over the next 17 years, Newhall made and lost fortunes. At the age of 53 he retired to his Waukesha County farm. He died in 1895.

In 1883, well after Newhall had sold his hotel, the Newhall House burned down, claiming more lives than any other city disaster except the sinking of the "Lady Elgin." Seventy-one bodies were found, but due to the intensity of the fire, there may have been others consumed by the flames (see *Elgin*).

The Newhall House, where the city's second largest loss of life disaster occurred.
(Buck's Pioneer History of Milwaukee)

NEW JERSEY AVENUE

3700 South, between 6700 and 8300 West
Origin: *Root Creek*

The state of New Jersey was named for the Island of Jersey in the English Channel. New Jersey Avenue was named for the state in 1956 as part of the Wedgewood Subdivision (see *Alabama*).

190

NEWPORT AVENUE, COURT

3400 North, between 1500 and 3100 East
Origin: *Cambridge Heights*

Newport Avenue is another of John *Stowell*'s 1887 East Coast city
street names. Newport, Rhode Island was a new port when it was founded;
it may have been named for Newport, England (see *Providence*).

NEWTON PLACE

5700 North, between 4200 and 4300 West
Origin: *Thurston Woods*

Stedman S. Newton was a speculator in the booming of North
Milwaukee. When Newton Place was named in 1893, Newton lived in
Columbus, Wisconsin, selling pianos and organs. Shortly thereafter he
moved to Milwaukee and began his own real estate firm, a business he was
active in until 1926.

NEW YORK AVENUE

2500 East, between 3000 and 3500 South
Origin: *Fernwood*

This is another of the eastern state streets in Bay View named by
Thomas Lathrop Kennan in 1888. Kennan, of Scottish ancestry, was born in
Morristown, New York in 1827. The state name memorializes James, Duke
of York, who later became James II, King of England from 1685 to 1688
(see *Ohio*).

NICHOLAS STREET

400 South and 500 West
Origin: *Walker's Point*

Robert Sulkowski, an alderman in 1967, was teased about naming
two streets on the South Side for his six month old grandson, *Alexander*
Nicholas Sulkowski. The alderman responded that when the names were
suggested by fellow alderman Eugene L. Woeher, "I didn't object." Neither

did anyone else. There was no one living on either of these short streets to complain. The two streets carry traffic between 5th and 6th Streets at the south end of the 6th Street Viaduct.

NOCK STREET

2800 South, between 1800 and 2300 East
Origin: *Bay View*

Henry Nock, merchant and Bay View village treasurer during the first half of the 1880s, moved to Denver, Colorado in 1886. The next year, when Bay View became part of Milwaukee, its Division Street became redundant and was renamed for the departed Henry Nock.

NORTH AVENUE

2300 North, between 2500 East and 6000 West
Origin: *Ordinance*

When this street was named by ordinance in 1856, it defined the northern limits of the city. The name did not reflect reality for long. Within a year the city limits had been pushed a mile north to Burleigh Street.

NORTHRIDGE COURT

9200 North, between 8300 and 8400 West
Origin: *Northridge*

Herbert Kohl, later owner of the Milwaukee Bucks and U.S. Senator, and his family platted this street in 1972. The name was chosen as the northern counterpart to Southridge Mall in Greendale.

NORTHRIDGE LAKES BOULEVARD

9100 North and 7500 West
Origin: *Northridge Lakes*

Herbert Kohl and family platted this street in 1972 as part of the Northridge Subdivision that includes an artificial lake.

Northridge Lakes.

NORWICH STREET, COURT

4000 South, between 1900 East and 8100 West
Origin: *Tippecanoe*

New street names in the Howell Avenue Park Subdivision, platted in 1892, included names of Wisconsin cities. Besides *Waterford* and *Plainfield* there is Norwich, the former name of the city of Plainfield. The Norwich name spread from England to Connecticut, to New York, and then to Wisconsin. The Wisconsin community was named Norwich by its first settler, a New Yorker.

NORWOOD PLACE

5500 West, between 3200 and 3300 North
Origin: *Grasslyn Manor/Sunset Heights*

Norwood Place was named as part of the Norwood Subdivision developed by the Atlas Land Company in 1923. Perhaps, like Chicago's Norwood Street, it was named for Henry Ward Beecher's novel, "Norwood: or Village Life in New England." Or it may be a shortened version of "North Woods." Or possibly, like the Norwood in Massachusetts, the name was chosen because it "had a pleasing sound, was easy to write, and had no 'i' to dot or 't' to cross."

NOTRE DAME COURT

1100 North, between 5400 and 5700 West
Origin: *Wick Field*

The School Sisters of Notre Dame, who began their organization in Milwaukee in 1850, platted this street in 1927. The sisters opened missions and schools throughout the United States and Canada (see *Tower View*).

194

OAK STREET

2400 North and 2400 West
Origin: *Park West*

In 1889 a group of short streets in this neighborhood was named for trees native to Milwaukee. They included *Ash, Hickory, Tamarack,* and an old favorite, Oak Street.

OAKLAND AVENUE

1800 East, between 1800 and 3500 North
Origin: *Ordinance*

The naming of this street has been attributed to six year old Willie Selby. In 1877, when High Street was being extended northward between the Selby and Mariner farms, a new name was to be selected. Listening to a family discussion that centered on Oakland, California, Willie suggested Oakland as the street name. His father, Dr. Selby, passed the idea on and that summer High Street was changed to Oakland Avenue.

OAK PARK COURT

5700 West and 600 South
Origin: *Johnson's Woods*

This quiet street forms a rectangle. It was named in 1925 by the Distinctive Homes Realty Company.

O'CONNOR STREET

200 South, between 5900 and 8400 West
Origin: *Ordinance*

In 1963 this street, created by the new freeway, was named for Charles W. (Chick) O'Connor. O'Connor, who was born in Milwaukee in 1886, was an alderman for 24 years. He died in 1961.

ODELL STREET

1600 South, between 1500 and 1600 West
Origin: *Historic Mitchell Street*

Odell Street was platted in 1871 on land owned by farmer Galutia Odell. Odell, whose farm and home were in what was then known as Odell's Grove, died in 1876.

OGDEN AVENUE

1400 North, between 100 East/West and 1100 East
Origin: *Yankee Hill*

William Butler Ogden, (1805-1877), moved to Chicago from New York State in 1835 to handle his family's Chicago real estate holdings. Not limiting his speculation to Chicago, he purchased land with Lucius *Lyon* in the fledgling village of Milwaukee. In 1837 he became Chicago's first mayor and had Milwaukee's Ogden Avenue named for him. Ogden died in 1877.

OHIO AVENUE, COURT

3300 South, between 2800 East and 9900 West
Origin: *Fernwood*

Ohio means "beautiful" in the Iroquois language. This street, platted in 1888, is one of seven Bay View streets named for states by Thomas Kennan. Kennan and his wife were married in Ohio, where he received his law education before coming to Wisconsin in 1855 (see *Pennsylvania*).

OKLAHOMA AVENUE, PLACE

3100 South, between 3000 East and 10000 West
Origin: *Bay View*

When this street was named in 1882 by the *Herman* Mann family, Oklahoma was an Indian Territory; it wasn't admitted as a state until 1907. The word, from the language of the Choctaw Indians, means "red people" (see *California*).

OLD WORLD THIRD STREET

300 West, between 700 and 1700 North
Origin: *Kilbourntown*

"Old World" was added to this section of Third Street in 1984 to promote the old German businesses, like Mader's Restaurant and Usinger's Sausage, which had long been on it. The name change came as a reaction to efforts to rename Third Street for Martin Luther *King*, Jr. A compromise changed this portion to "Old World," while Third Street north of downtown was named for King.

Old World Third Street, 1994.

OLIVE STREET

4200 North, between 1100 and 8900 West
Origin: *Village of Shorewood*

Zachara Merrill platted this street in 1887 and may have named it for his cousin, Olive E. Merrill. Of the first names coined from plants during the 19th century, Olive was one of the more popular.

ONTARIO STREET

2500 South, between 1700 and 1800 East
Origin: *Bay View*

When Bay View was platted in 1866, a street was named for each of the Great Lakes. The force behind the community was Eber *Ward*, who had a shipping business on the lakes, carrying the products of his iron and steel business. In 1887, when Bay View was annexed by Milwaukee, which already had some of its own streets named for the Great Lakes, the village lost the names Michigan, Erie, and Huron. Milwaukee's Huron Street was later changed to *Clybourn*, leaving the city with only four of the lake names. Ontario is an Iroquois term that has been variously interpreted as a lake that is either fine, beautiful, handsome, or great.

ORCHARD STREET

1500 South, between 200 East and 4300 West
Origin: *Historic Mitchell Street/Clock Tower Acres*

James Sanderson, an early settler and a Great Lakes captain, had an orchard south of Greenfield Avenue. In 1853 he ran into business difficulties, sold his land, and moved to California. Orchard Street was platted two years later by Charles Bradley and William *Metcalf*.

OREGON STREET

300 South, between 200 East and 800 West
Origin: *Walker's Point*

Oregon wasn't a state in 1842 when George *Walker* named this street. Patriotic fervor and strong anti-English sentiment were the reasons for the street name; many places in the United States, including a village and a town in Wisconsin, were named Oregon during this time.

The Oregon Country covered present day Oregon, Idaho, parts of Montana and British Columbia, and, the source of conflict, the state of Washington. The English wanted the western half of Washington. The United States, in no mood for a compromise, said if England didn't agree to give up its claim to Washington, the U.S. would take it and part of British Columbia as well. The argument was convincing, and England decided it was content with British Columbia, so in 1846 the current border between the United States and Canada was agreed on.

ORINDA COURT

7100 North, between 9400 and 9500 West
Origin: *Golden Gate*

When it was platted in 1962, this street was called Euclid Court. When the subdivision was annexed by the City of Milwaukee a short time later, Euclid became a duplicate and needed to be changed. The street's lone resident, a former resident of Orinda, California, suggested the name that became official later that year. The name "Orinda" was the pseudonym for poet Katharine Fowler Philips.

ORIOLE DRIVE

5800 North, between 2700 and 3500 West
Origin: *Thurston Woods*

This colorful orange and black bird summers in Milwaukee's shade trees. Erwin and Irma Wallschlaeger applied the name in 1925 (see *Bobolink*).

OTJEN STREET

2600 South, between 500 and 1100 East

Origin: *Bay View*

The Otjen brothers were born on a farm north of Detroit, Michigan; Christian in 1846 and Theobald in 1851. The young boys, sons of German immigrants, lived with the Eber *Ward* family near Detroit after their mother died. Ward was the founder of the rolling mills in Bay View.

Christian was made a foreman at the mills at age 22 and assistant superintendent at 24. Theobald became a foreman at 19, but left to pursue a career in law. Both men later served as officers of the Village of Bay View; Christian as treasurer, Theobald as attorney. After the village was annexed by Milwaukee, Theobald represented Bay View as alderman for seven years and then as U.S. Representative for 12 years.

The brothers added a real estate business to their interests in 1883, the year this street was named for them (see *Rhode Island*).

Christian Otjen. (Conard's History of Milwaukee County)

Theobald Otjen. (Conard's History of Milwaukee County)

PABST AVENUE

2600 South, between 3100 and 3500 West
Origin: *Layton Park*

He gave up the sea for her love, and ultimately, for her father's brewery.

Frederick Pabst, born in Germany in 1836, began his Great Lakes career as a cabin boy at 15, and by 21 he captained a steamer. At 26 he married Jacob Best's daughter, Marie, and went to work at Best's brewery. Largely through his efforts the brewery became one of the world's largest. When Pabst was 54, the brewery's name was changed to the Pabst Brewing Company. He was 67 when he died in 1904.

This short South Side street was named in 1889 and, like Pabst

The Pabst Brewing Company, looking at the intersection of Ninth Street and Juneau Avenue from the southeast. (Milwaukee, Picturesque and Descriptive)

201

Avenue in Cudahy, led to railroad tracks and trains carrying the brewery's product. The marquee beer at taverns on each of these streets is, of course, Pabst Blue Ribbon.

PAINE STREET

3200 South, between 3100 and 3300 West
Origin: *Jackson Park*

Thomas Paine's writings had strong influence on the leaders of the Revolutionary War, and he was a significant figure in the French Revolution. Paine, (1737-1809), is best known for writing "The Rights of Man" and "The Age of Reason." This street was platted in 1929 (see *Poe).*

PALMER STREET

200 East, between 1700 and 4000 North
Origin: *Ordinance*

Henry L. Palmer, president of Northwestern Mutual Life Insurance from 1874 to 1908, was born in Pennsylvania in 1819. He moved to Milwaukee in 1849 hoping to relieve his asthmatic condition. It worked; he had a long and varied career. Palmer practiced law and served as state legislator and state senator. He ran unsuccessfully for governor in 1865 and was school board president from 1865 to 1868. The City of Milwaukee memorialized his name when this street's name was changed from Island to Palmer in 1929.

PALMETTO AVENUE, COURT

From 9200 West and 4500 North to 7700 West and 5000 North
Origin: *Long View*

All the trees referred to in Milwaukee street names were native to the area until 1926, when Palmetto Street was christened. Exotic Palmetto trees occur from Florida to Texas along the Gulf of Mexico, and could only survive as a name on Milwaukee's frigid winter streets. Real estate dealer Fred Hartung named this street as part of the Marion Ridge Subdivision.

PARK PLACE

2700 North, between 1400 and 3000 East
Origin: *Murray Hill*

The city's first Park Place was named in 1882 by Frederick Johnson and Moses Brand. It may have been named in anticipation of the nearby Riverside Park, which was developed a few years later.

PARK PLACE

From 10700 West and 7200 North to 12400 West and 7900 North
Origin: *Park Place*

In 1983, Park Place was named by ordinance at the request of the Trammel Crow Company, which built the business park known as Park Place. There are only two sets of duplicate street names in the city, *Pierce* Street and this one, Park Place. There are others with the same name, including *Layton*, *Washington*, *Grant*, and *Wilson*, but they each have different suffixes (boulevard, drive, avenue, street, etc.). While the naming of this street would probably cause those who labored to rid the city of duplicate names during the 1920s renaming program to roll over in their graves, the fact that the two Park Places are so far apart (the other is on the East Side) probably accounts for the city's approval of the name.

(Daniel J. Baehr)

203

PARK HILL AVENUE

200 North, between 3100 and 9500 West
Origin: *Merrill Park*

Park Hill Avenue, overlooking the Menomonee Valley, was platted by Edward R. Paine in 1883. Paine, a physician, was born in Pennsylvania. After moving to Milwaukee in 1866 he changed his profession, switching from medicine to selling coal and wood.

PARKLAND AVENUE, COURT

7800 North, between 5100 and 5200 West
Origin: *Bradley Estates*

Parkland Avenue was laid out in 1955 and runs near Algonquin Park.

PARK MANOR DRIVE

9400 West, between 6800 and 7200 North
Origin: *Golden Gate*

Park Manor Drive was platted in 1962. The "park" in the name comes from the Menomonee River Parkway that parallels the street. The "manor" portion was added for its promotional value rather than as a local feature. There are no estate houses on this street.

PARKWAY AVENUE

1600 West, between 4600 and 4750 North
Origin: *Lincoln Park*

This avenue was platted as part of the Lincoln Park Gateway Subdivision in 1924 by the Concordia Land Company.

PARKWAY DRIVE

From 4700 West and 4400 North to 6000 West and 4700 North
Origin: *Lincoln Creek*

This drive along Lincoln Creek was platted by Nicholas Ewins and John Wiersum in 1926.

PARNELL AVENUE

5700 South, between 1400 and 3800 West
Origin: *Village of Hales Corners*

Parnell Avenue first shows up on a 1937 town of Greenfield atlas, as a short road east of 108th Street. There were no Parnells in the area and there had been no prominent Parnells in the city's background. The city's 1913 Street Renaming Commission had recommended changing the name of *Park Hill* Avenue in the Merrill Park area to Parnell Street. If acted on, that would have given the Irish neighborhood a street named for Charles Stewart Parnell, champion of Irish Home Rule. Someone may have had a similar idea when naming Parnell Avenue; the old town of Greenfield was heavily settled by Irish.

PEARL STREET

From 1600 West and 1500 South to 2100 West and 1900 South
Origin: *Muskego Way*

By the end of the 19th century there were over 400 Pearl Streets in the principal cities of the United States. That was twice as many as streets named for Elizabeth, four times more than for Mary or Ann, and twenty times more than for Ruby or Emerald. Pearl as a feminine first name was never so popular that the number of streets named Pearl would be so disproportionately high. What would account for so many Pearl Streets? Pearl Street in New York City may be the answer.

During the 1800s, New York's Pearl Street was a commercial center second only to Wall Street. And, like Wall Street, it was imitated by developers and town fathers in cities around the country, who hoped that some of New York's success would rub off on their communities. The New York street wasn't named for a woman, but for the oyster shells that littered the shore of the East River, where Pearl Street began. The Milwaukee street was named by developers in 1855.

PEARSON STREET

1700 North, between 700 and 1100 East
Origin: *Lower East Side*

In 1836 Hiram Pearson, along with other Chicago speculators, platted *Hubbard* and Pearson's Addition, naming the streets after themselves. While some, like Hunter and Kinzie Streets, have since been changed, *Hamilton* and Pearson remain. Hiram Pearson was a Chicago alderman and treasurer in the late 1830s.

PECK PLACE, COURT

4600 North, between 4200 and 8600 West
Origin: *Old North Milwaukee*

George W. Peck, born in New York State in 1840, was a humorist, writer, mayor, and governor. Peck wrote the classic ''Peck's Bad Boy'' and published ''Peck's Sun,'' a popular Milwaukee paper. He was elected mayor in 1890 but only served a short time before being elected governor. He died in 1916. This street was named during the 1920s renaming program.

Peck's Bad Boy made
George Peck famous.

PEMBERTON AVENUE

2600 North and 3000 West
Origin: *Metcalfe Park*

In 1888, Robert Pierce named this street for a fellow member of Veteran Post #8, R. Eves Pemberton.

PENNSYLVANIA AVENUE

2400 East, between 3000 and 3500 South
Origin: *Fernwood*

Pennsylvania Avenue was named for the state, which honored William Penn's father, William Penn Sr. It is taken to mean "Penn's woods." Thomas Kennan named seven streets in Bay View for states, this one in 1888 (see *Texas*).

PERKINS PLACE

4000 North, between 7400 and 7600 West
Origin: *Capitol Heights*

Forest Street, because it was a "near" duplicate of Forest Home Avenue, was renamed Perkins Place by the old Town of Wauwatosa in 1933. The reason for the selection of the name Perkins is not known.

PETERSIK STREET

6900 North, between 8600 and 8800 West
Origin: *Menomonee River Hills*

Edward Petersik probably knew more about Milwaukee street names than anyone. He began working for the City Engineer's Office around 1910. He served on the first Street Renaming Commission in 1913 and on the second commission in 1923. When the City Engineer's Office was given the responsibilty for renaming streets in 1926, Petersik played a major role. And he was involved in the naming of new streets for the next thirty years. A 1941 newspaper article said that Petersik was planning a book on the origins of Milwaukee street names, although none was ever published. Unfortunately, Petersik, who died at the age of 99 in 1985, took the reasons for many street names with him to his grave. This street was named for him in 1957, one year after his retirement.

PETTIBONE PLACE

600 North, between 2300 and 2500 West
Origin: *Avenues West*

Sylvester Pettibone, born in Connecticut in 1793, arrived in Milwaukee in February of 1836. That summer Pettibone graded the first street in Milwaukee when he cut through *Water* Street behind eight oxen and a plow. Pettibone, who died in 1876, owned a farm of 250 acres along Wisconsin Avenue that included the land where this street (it's really an alley) was named. Pettibone Place was named by developer Ephraim Mariner in 1902.

PHILIP PLACE

3400 North, between 5500 and 6000 West
Origin: *Grasslyn Manor*

Charles Wild and Clyde Fuller, officers of the Atlas Land Company, named Philip Place in 1923. Neither of them had a father or son called Philip, leaving one to wonder for whom this street was named.

PIER STREET

500 South and 900 East
Origin: *Historic Third Ward*

Pier Street, at 25 feet long, is the shortest street in town. It is a fraction of the length of the piers for which it was named. They extended a third of a mile into the lake. Piers were necessary in the city's early days when lake vessels could not navigate the river into downtown. The city named this street in 1856, the year before the harbor entrance was cut at its present site, allowing access to the inner harbor and making the piers obsolete (see *Abert*).

The pier with the tower extended from the foot of Pier Street. (Milwaukee of Today, 1892)

PIERCE STREET

700 South, between 100 East/West and 3900 West
Origin: *Walker's Point*

In 1852, Franklin Pierce was a good-looking 48 year old and the youngest president to be elected up to that time. Pierce, a Democrat, was popular for favoring the Compromise of 1850, which was billed as the answer to the slavery issue. Milwaukee aldermen came up with a compromise of their own on May 5, 1853, two months after Pierce was inaugurated, when they named a Walker's Point street for Pierce, and another for his Whig opponent, Winfield *Scott*. Franklin Pierce, the country's 14th President and a Northerner, died in obscurity in 1869 after arguing against the Civil War.

Many consider Franklin Pierce to have been America's most handsome President. (Milwaukee Public Library)

209

PIERCE STREET

600 East, between 2400 and 3500 North
Origin: *Riverwest*

Jonathan Peirce spelled his name with the "e" before the "i," but almost no one paid any attention to it. People who took censuses didn't, nor did directory publishers. They spelled it with the "i" first. So did biographies and histories. County records show his 1856 subdivision as "Pierce's Addition." So it's really not surprising the way the street was spelled on the 1857 plat map registered by developer George Julius Franke. And it's just as well; everyone would probably spell it with the "i" first anyway.

Jonathan L. Peirce, born in New Hampshire in 1799, came to Milwaukee in 1849 and opened a dry goods store before branching out into land speculation. He is responsible for naming at least four Milwaukee streets, all of them with their letters in the proper sequence. There was one place his name was spelled the way he wanted it to be, though probably not when he wanted; that was in his 1875 death notice. His death was caused by exposure while surveying in the subdivision whose street bears his name.

PINE AVENUE

800 East, between 2600 and 4700 South
Origin: *Bay View*

Pine is one of the most common trees in Wisconsin, whether Red, White, or Jack, and one of its most prevalent street names. Milwaukee has had its share of streets named Pine, but during the 1920s the city eliminated duplicate street names, leaving only this one, which was named by Henry Mann in 1887.

PINECREST STREET

4800 West, between 200 and 500 South
Origin: *Story Hill*

Hiram *Story* and his family liked the name "Pinecrest." In 1922, they gave the name to four streets in their subdivision. The crest in the name

210

is appropriate; the streets were on high land over the Menomonee Valley. When the city sought to eliminate duplicate street names in 1926, Pinecrest Avenue, Pinecrest Avenue West, and Pinecrest Court were all changed, and Pinecrest Avenue East was renamed Pinecrest Street.

PINGREE AVENUE

10200 West, between 8000 and 8200 North
Origin: *Pheasant Run*

Finley G. Fisler, of the City Engineer's Department, named this street for a friend in 1963.

PITTSBURGH AVENUE

200 South, between 300 East and 300 West
Origin: *Walker's Point*

Lake Street was renamed Pittsburgh Avenue in 1926. It was named not for the city, but for the Pittsburgh Plate Glass Company, which was located on Lake Street. The company dealt in paints, varnishes, and stains.

PLAINFIELD AVENUE

4200 South, between 600 East and 6000 West
Origin: *Tippecanoe*

Plainfield, Wisconsin was probably the source for this street name. The town of Plainfield was named for Plainfield, Vermont, the home of Plainfield's first postmaster (see *Norwich*, *Waterford*).

PLANKINTON AVENUE

100 West, between 200 and 900 North
Origin: *Kilbourntown*

Two weeks after arriving in Milwaukee in 1843 at age 22, John Plankinton started a butchering business. Over the years, he became wealthy in successive partnerships with meatpackers Frederick *Layton,* Philip *Armour,* and Patrick *Cudahy.* Plankinton, born in Delaware, later branched

This statue of John Plankinton stands in the Grand Avenue Mall.

out into banking and railroads. He built Milwaukee's finest hotel of the time and was instrumental in the building of the city's public library. He died in 1891 at age 71.

Plankinton, South Dakota was named for him as the director of a railroad. Plankinton Avenue in Cudahy was named for him as a meatpacker by Patrick Cudahy. The Plankinton Canal in the Menomonee River Valley carries his name as a packing plant owner. And, to honor the city's "foremost citizen" of his era, downtown's West Water Street became Plankinton Avenue in 1929.

PLEASANT STREET

From 1600 North and 1100 East to 1700 North and 300 West
Origin: *Lower East Side*

Hilly, forested land provided the inspiration for the name Pleasant Street. Planned before the financial depression of 1837, this street became a reality in the 1840s.

POE STREET

3300 South, between 3300 and 3500 West
Origin: *Jackson Park*

Poe Street was named for Edgar Allan Poe, (1809-1849), an American poet and short story writer. Among Poe's more famous works are "The Raven," "The Fall of the House of Usher," and "The Masque of the Red Death." Poe Street was named in the literary Concord Hill Subdivision in 1929 (see *Ruskin*).

POINT TERRACE

3000 West, between 3500 and 3700 South
Origin: *Southpoint*

Point Terrace was the name suggested in 1963 by the operators of the Point Loomis Shopping Center that the street borders.

POLCYN STREET

400 West and 1300 South
Origin: *Walker's Point*

John W. Polcyn was Milwaukee police chief from 1945 to 1957. Born in LaMont, Illinois, he worked as a streetcar conductor before joining the police force in 1916. During his tenure as police chief he streamlined functions, reduced the work week from 48 to 40 hours, and instituted rewards for service above and beyond the call of duty. Polcyn died in 1959, and when this short street was created by the new freeway system in 1968, it was named in his honor.

John W. Polcyn. (Milwaukee County Historical Society)

POLK STREET

300 South, between 500 and 900 East
Origin: *Historic Third Ward*

James Knox Polk, (1795-1849), was the nation's 11th President. Polk's claim to fame, one that hasn't been duplicated since, is that he achieved each goal he promised before his election. Polk's term of office was from 1845 to 1849, and he expired a few months after his term did. Polk Street was named by ordinance in 1856.

PORT AVENUE

7800 North, between 5600 and 8800 West
Origin: *Bradley Estates*

Port Avenue was named by developer Francis Schroedel in 1955 for one of the many corporations in which he was involved.

PORTAGE AVENUE, STREET

7500 North, between 3800 and 9100 West
Origin: *Village of Fox Point*

Portage Avenue was named in 1930 by the Village of Fox Point. It may be named for the Wisconsin city of Portage, which was the site of a canoe portage between the Wisconsin and Fox Rivers, used by Indians and French traders.

PORT SUNLIGHT WAY

440 North, between 2500 and 2700 West
Origin: *Garden Homes*

Five English "Garden Cities" were memorialized in the names of the Garden Homes Subdivision streets in 1921. Garden Cities were planned communities that included parks and open spaces for their residents. Garden Homes, financed by the City of Milwaukee, included a small park in the center of the subdivision. The houses were designed to be bright and pleasant, with enough space around them to admit light to all sides of the structure.

This street was named for Port Sunlight, a model industrial village near Liverpool, England, which was developed by Lever Brothers, of soap fame, in 1888. The community was designed around the soap manufacturing facility, but with the employees' comfort in mind. Besides living in homes in garden surroundings, the workers shared in the profits and had many benefits not available elsewhere. The other streets in the Garden Homes Subdivision were originally named Ealing, Bourneville, Letchworth, and Hampstead for the other English planned towns of the late 1800s. These street names were changed during the renaming program of the late 1920s.

214

The plat map of the Garden Home Subdivision included five streets named for English Garden Communities.

(Milwaukee County Register of Deeds)

PORT WASHINGTON AVENUE, ROAD

600 West, between 3400 and 4800 North

Like the city it led to, this pre-Civil War road was known as Washington Road. When the lakeshore community added a pier to encourage lake commerce, it also upgraded its name by adding the "Port." The road also became known as Port Washington. George *Washington* was the honoree in both cases.

POTOMAC AVENUE

From 3700 North and 7200 West to 5500 North and 9900 West
Origin: *Vogel Park*

The Potomac River's Indian trade gave it the name Potomac, or "where the goods are brought in." The Glenwood Land Company gave this street its name in 1927.

POTTER AVENUE

From 500 East and 2700 South to 1400 East and 2500 South
Origin: *Bay View*

Orrin Woodard Potter, born in Rochester, New York in 1836, was president of the North Chicago Rolling Mills for 25 years. Potter started working for Eber *Ward's* Michigan rolling mills in 1857. The next year he

215

married Ward's niece, and became the superintendent of the Bay View Rolling Mills when they were established after the Civil War. When farmer Joseph *Williams* subdivided his farm near the mills in 1870, he named a street for Potter. A short time later, Potter took over the presidency of the company from Stephen *Clement* and moved to Chicago, where he died in 1907.

PRENTISS STREET

7300 West, between 5400 and 5600 North
Origin: *Silver Spring*

Massachusetts-born William Prentiss was a mature old-timer compared to many settlers of 1836 Milwaukee. He was 37; most of the others were under 30, with many in their late teens or early twenties. His experience in the Vermont legislature was useful to him in representing Milwaukee in the Wisconsin territorial, and then state, legislatures.

He was an official of Juneautown before it was united with Kilbourntown, and then represented the area east of the river as part of a united Milwaukee during its village days. After Milwaukee became a city, Prentiss was elected to four terms as alderman and one as mayor. Prentiss also served three years as county board chairman and 11 years as justice of the peace.

In 1872 Prentiss retired, after helping, probably more than anyone else, to guide the city through its formative years. In 1954, based on the recommendation of the City Engineer's Office, an ordinance named this street for Prentiss, 62 years after his death.

PRICE AVENUE, COURT

4600 South, between 600 and 1000 East
Origin: *Town of Lake*

David Price was shot in the head twice. The first one, received in battle during the Civil War, he survived. The second one was self-inflicted and fatal.

Price, born in Minersville, Pennsylvania in 1838, returned there after the war. A few years later he and his family moved to Bay View. During the

216

1870s Price was appointed village postmaster, started a successful grocery business, became involved in village politics, and prospered. In 1880 he was elected to represent Bay View in the state legislature.

It was political life that led to Price's downfall. While he was in Madison, his business failed. A second business, a saloon, didn't last long. Lawsuits resulted and he started drinking heavily. In March of 1882 he was arrested for disorderly conduct. A few weeks later, after failing in an attempt to kill his wife, he shot himself. He left four children, the youngest five years old.

The old Town of Lake changed Plankinton Avenue to Price Avenue in 1930.

PRINCETON AVENUE

3600 West, between 3300 and 3500 South
Origin: *Harder's Oaks*

This street was named in 1926, shortly after the city took over the responsibility for street nomenclature. It was probably named for Princeton University, located in Princeton, New Jersey. The name Princeton became popular in colonial America, where towns were named for the prince of the reigning royal family of England (see *Purdue*).

PROSPECT AVENUE

From 800 North and 900 East to 3100 North and 2400 East
Origin: *Yankee Hill*

James H. Rogers named this street in 1847. The street, on the bluffs, offered a pleasing view, or prospect, of Lake Michigan. Rogers, born in New York in 1794, put a $1,200 value on his land along Prospect Avenue from Juneau Avenue to Brady Street, and west to Humboldt Avenue. He died in 1863.

Prospect Avenue around the turn of the century.
(Milwaukee Illustrated)

217

PROVIDENCE AVENUE

3400 North, between 1500 and 1800 East
Origin: *Cambridge Heights*

This street was named for Providence, Rhode Island by John M. *Stowell* in 1887. The city was named by Roger Williams ''for God's merciful providence to me in my distress'' (see *Hartford)*.

PRYOR AVENUE

2700 South, between 1100 and 1900 East
Origin: *Bay View*

William J. and Elizabeth Pryor, who were Bay View residents at the time, platted this street in 1872. When William died in 1876 at the age of 52, the Pryor family moved back to Waupun, Wisconsin.

Pryor Avenue is the site of Milwaukee's only public well. The well, opened a few years after Pryor's death, has been a public source of water ever since. Over the years, legends and theories about the water's origins and properties have abounded. But the fact is that the water flows from Waukesha County and contains no special ingredients; just iron, calcium and fluorine.

The Pryor Avenue Well.

PULASKI STREET

1300 East, between 1700 and 1900 North
Origin: *Lower East Side*

Casimir Pulaski, a Polish nobleman who volunteered his services to the Continental Army during the American Revolution, died leading the Pulaski Legion in an attack on Savannah in 1779. This street, in a Polish neighborhood, was named by ordinance in 1875. It ran through a gully that was called the filthiest spot in the city in 1885 and was deemed a health hazard which the city health department ordered be cleaned up (see *Bremen*).

PURDUE STREET
4700 North, between 1900 and 2400 West
Origin: *Lincoln Park*

Purdue University, in West LaFayette, Indiana, was named for John Purdue, a benefactor of the school. Northway Street was changed to Purdue Street in 1929 (see *Cornell*).

QUINCY AVENUE, COURT

600 East, between 2700 and 4700 South
Origin: *Bay View*

This street was named in 1909 and is assumed to be named after President John Quincy Adams since the other streets in the Humboldt Park Subdivision (*Adams* and *Taylor)* carry presidential names.

John Quincy Adams, (1767-1848), was the sixth President of the United States and the son of the second President, John Adams. Quincy Adams' presidency (1825-1829) was unremarkable. He was better known as James Monroe's secretary of state before he became president and as an anti-slavery congressman afterwards.

RAE AVENUE

5400 North, between 10300 and 10600 West

Origin: *Timmerman West*

Rae Avenue was named in 1954. It may have been named for the wife of Melvin Raskin, a developer active at the time.

RAMSEY AVENUE

5900 South, between 1300 and 3900 West

Origin: *City of Cudahy*

In 1930 the old Town of Lake renamed Garden Terrace as part of the county-wide program to rid the area of duplicate street names. Many of the new street names introduced during this period were for Milwaukeeans with significant public contributions. Ramsey Avenue was probably named for Thomas Ramsey, a real estate man who was a Milwaukee alderman and museum trustee during the 1890s.

RANDOLPH STREET, COURT

3400 North, between 1400 East and 500 West
Origin: *Harambee*

Because Morton Place sounded too similar to *Morgan* Avenue and *Martin* Drive, it was changed to Randolph Place in 1926. Why the name Randolph was selected is not known.

RAVINE ROAD

2800 North, between 3200 and 3400 East
Origin: *Lake Park*

This 1920s road, which runs down a ravine between Newberry Boulevard and Lincoln Memorial Drive, finally got a name in 1989. The County Board named it to provide a location for emergency response.

A biker descends Ravine Road. (George Olson)

REICHERT PLACE

5700 North, between 2700 and 9800 West
Origin: *Thurston Woods*

Conrad K. and Joseph B. Reichert platted Reichert Place as part of the Reichert Brothers Subdivision in 1893. Conrad Reichert ran a tobacco business and Joseph managed a wine company.

222

RENEE STREET

1600 West, between 900 and 1000 North
Origin: *Avenues West*

In 1970 a new street was created, connecting 16th and 17th Streets between Kilbourn Avenue and State Street. It was named for alderman Robert Ertl's daughter, Renee.

RESERVOIR AVENUE

1900 North, between 500 East and 1400 West
Origin: *Ordinance*

The first city-wide water service began when the reservoir in Kilbourn Park was filled in 1873. In 1875 the bluff road (then called Beers Street) leading to the park (then called Reservoir Park) was renamed Reservoir Avenue.

REYNOLDS PLACE

600 South, between 1700 and 1900 West
Origin: *Mitchell Park*

Thomas Reynolds was a South Side saloonkeeper and socialist alderman. He served on the Common Council from 1916 until his death in 1924 at age 57. Reynolds Place was named by ordinance in 1940.

RHODE ISLAND AVENUE

3200 South, between 2800 and 3000 East
Origin: *Fernwood*

After the *Herman* Mann family named seven Bay View streets for states and territories around 1880, and Thomas Kennan named seven more by 1890, Theobald *Otjen* added two more in 1891. There are two theories about how the state of Rhode Island got its name. The first is that it was named for the island of Rhodes near Greece; the second is that it was named "Roodt Eylandt," or "red island," by a Dutch explorer (see *Vermont).*

223

RICHARDS STREET

300 East, between 2300 and 4400 North
Origin: *Harambee*

Daniel Hamilton Richards is best known for publishing Milwaukee's first newspaper, the "Milwaukee Advertiser," which made its debut in July 1836. Richards, who had come to Milwaukee the previous winter, had learned the printer's trade as a 16 year old in Canada. He was born in New York in 1808.

Richards was also involved in farming and real estate, and served several terms as state assemblyman from Milwaukee. He died in 1877. This street was named for him in 1857 by Otis Hopkins.

RICHARDSON PLACE

900 North, between 2700 and 2900 West
Origin: *Concordia*

Ray Richardson, who was born in Tulsa, Oklahoma about 1923, began working at the Neighborhood House in 1950 and became executive director of the social service agency in 1960. The Neighborhood House, which assisted people through programs and classes designed to help them recognize their skills, was located on Dunbar Place. In 1975 Dunbar Place was renamed for Richardson, who died in 1987 while still director of the agency.

Ray Richardson holds his namesake street sign.
(Milwaukee Sentinel Photo)

224

RICHMOND AVENUE

2800 North, between 6100 and 6400 West
Origin: *Enderis Park*

Paul *Hartung* named Richmond Avenue when he subdivided the family farm in 1916. His subdivision, Lenox Heights, and this street may have been named for the Duke of Richmond, Charles Lenox.

RIDGE COURT

From 4800 West and 3700 North to 4300 West and 3900 North
Origin: *Grasslyn Manor/Roosevelt Grove*

Ridge Court was named as part of the Rainbow Ridge Subdivision. It was platted by the Finance and Investment Company in 1922.

RING STREET

3300 North, between 300 East and 1700 West
Origin: *Harambee*

Jonathan Peirce named this street for a relative, Hannah Ring, in 1856 (see *North Pierce*).

RIO STREET

6100 North, between 9500 and 12200 West
Origin: *Parkway Hills*

Rio Street was named in 1958, during an era when streets were being named for Wisconsin towns. Ohio was to be the name of this Columbia County community, but apparently the word ''Ohio'' was misread on the Post Office application as ''Rio'', leading to the misnaming of the community.

RIPON PLACE

8200 West, between 3400 and 3500 North
Origin: *Nash Park*

The Wisconsin city, known as the birthplace of the Republican Party, was named for Ripon, Yorkshire, England. The street was changed from 82nd Street to Ripon Place in 1930.

RIVER BEND DRIVE

3300 South, between 7200 and 7500 West
Origin: *River Bend*

River Bend Drive was platted as part of the River Bend Subdivision in 1955. The subdivision was laid out at a bend in the Honey Creek.

RIVERBOAT ROAD

1100 East, between 2100 and 2200 North
Origin: *Riverside Park*

In 1972 this street, then known as *Commerce* Street, was renamed for the Riverboat Cocktail Lounge and Restaurant that was located on it. Tom Terris, the proprietor, was credited with ''the most outstanding job of riverside beautification of any business entity along either bank of the Milwaukee River.''

RIVERSIDE PLACE

2700 North, between 1700 and 1800 East
Origin: *Riverside Park*

Riverside Park, along the Milwaukee River, was the inspiration for the naming of this street. Riverside Place, next to the park, was changed from South Park Front in 1908.

226

RIVER TRAIL DRIVE

12300 West, between 6000 and 6300 North
Origin: *Park Knoll*

This drive was aptly named in 1963. It follows the Menomonee River.

ROADSMEET STREET

2900 North, between 1200 and 1300 East
Origin: *Riverwest*

When short Roadsmeet Street was named by Charles *Whitnall* in 1926, the roads that it met were Dousman and Bolton Streets.

ROBERTS STREET

1800 North, between 3700 and 4000 West
Origin: *Walnut Hill*

Roberts Street was named in 1902 for Robert Christian Reinertsen, who claimed to have surveyed and platted more land in Milwaukee than anyone else. His career began in the City Engineer's Office forty years before and included a ten-year stint as county surveyor. Later Reinertsen went into business for himself, providing civil engineering and real estate services.

He was born in Farsund, Norway in 1846, where his family had been involved in ship design and navigation. They came to Milwaukee when he was ten months old, prompting Reinertsen to claim that he "was a full-blooded Norwegian, fully Americanized."

ROBINSON AVENUE

200 East, between 2100 and 2300 South
Origin: *Bay View*

Chauncey Clark Robinson had better business instincts than most physicians. The New Yorker's career as a physician began in Milwaukee shortly before a cholera epidemic in 1849. His vigor in fighting the disease,

227

and use of the newest diagnostic methods, quickly built up his practice.

Within a few years, Robinson was buying real estate and erecting buildings and docks along the Kinnickinnic River. In 1872 he named a street in this subdivision for himself and another for his wife, Mary Alexander, although Alexander was later changed to *Austin* Street.

ROCHELLE AVENUE

7100 North, between 3700 and 9800 West
Origin: *City of Glendale*

Horace Graham and Herman Lange platted Rochelle Avenue in 1926. The name Rochelle ultimately comes from La Rochelle, a French seaport on the Atlantic, although why it was selected in this case is not known.

RODER COURT

1100 North, between 5600 and 5700 West
Origin: *Wick Field*

Roder Court was named as part of the Highland Park Subdivision, platted by the School Sisters of Notre Dame in 1927. The reason that Roder was selected as the name is a mystery (see *Notre Dame*).

ROGERS STREET

2000 South, between 500 and 3700 West
Origin: *Historic Mitchell Street*

Daniel G. Rogers, a lawyer from West Point, New York, joined George *Burnham* and John *Becher* in naming streets for themselves in the subdivision they platted in 1871. That year Rogers was elected as alderman for the first of several terms. Rogers, who also invested in gold and silver mines, was born in 1824. He came to Milwaukee when he was 32 and died at the age of 79.

ROHR AVENUE

5300 North, between 2200 and 12400 West
Origin: *Old North Milwaukee*

John H. Rohr, physician and North Milwaukee village president, was born in 1869 in Racine County. Rohr, of Swiss and German parents, served as county physician for more than twenty years. A man of many talents, he was town assessor, treasurer, and postmaster. This street was named in the 1920s.

ROOSEVELT DRIVE

From 6000 West and 3100 North to 2000 West and 4400 North
Origin: *Roosevelt Grove*

An insane man, John Schrank, attempted to assassinate Teddy Roosevelt in Milwaukee in 1912. Schrank shot Roosevelt near 3rd Street and Kilbourn Avenue. A fifty-page speech in Roosevelt's breast pocket absorbed much of the impact of the bullet, enabling the former president to deliver his speech, although in a blood soaked shirt. In 1922, the Finance and Investment Company named this street for the one-time Rough Rider who died in 1919.

Teddy Roosevelt.
(Milwaukee Public Library)

ROSEDALE AVENUE

2700 South, between 400 East and 500 West
Origin: *Bay View*

The western portion of *Pryor* Avenue was changed to Rosedale Avenue in 1926 during the renaming program. Street names formed by combining words such as ''rose'' and ''dale'' proliferated at this time, regardless of whether those features were nearby or not.

ROYALL PLACE

1800 North, between 1500 and 1700 East
Origin: *Lower East Side*

Royall Houghton, land developer, banker, dry goods merchant, and lumberman, was born in Vermont in 1831. The Houghton family, which moved to Milwaukee when Royall was 13, were owners of large parcels of land that eventually became part of the city. This street was officially given the name Royall Place by ordinance in 1875, although it had been informally in use earlier. Houghton died in 1892.

RUBY AVENUE

4500 North, between 2200 and 8800 West
Origin: *Village of Shorewood*

Charles F. Seefeld named this street for his daughter, Ruby, in 1888. Ruby was one of the 19th century names that was coined from precious stones.

RUSK AVENUE

2900 South, between 1600 and 2400 East
Origin: *Bay View*

In 1886, after Jeremiah Rusk gave the order to shoot, four men and a boy lay dead in Bay View. Nine years later, a Bay View street was named for the man responsible for the "Bay View Massacre."

The shootings occurred during a city-wide strike for an eight-hour workday. Strikers marched from Milwaukee to the steel mill in Bay View, hoping to garner the support of workers there. Governor Rusk's militia was there when the strikers got out of hand and their gunfire quickly ended the demonstration.

"Uncle Jerry" Rusk, already popular in the state, became even more popular. Newspapers throughout the country praised him and people talked of making him president. Rusk's evaluation of his actions, well known to millions at the time and enough to make English teachers everywhere cringe, was "I seen my duty and I done it."

Jeremiah Rusk. (Political History of Wisconsin)

Rusk, of Scots-Irish ancestry, was born in Ohio in 1830. Before moving to Wisconsin in 1853, he farmed, drove a stage coach, and worked on a railroad. After his arrival he ran a tavern, became a banker, and then

230

bought a stage coach line. He entered politics as assemblyman, was later governor, and became the country's first secretary of agriculture. Rusk died in 1893.

RUSKIN STREET, COURT

3400 South, between 3000 and 3800 West
Origin: *Jackson Park*

John Ruskin, (1819-1900), was an English critic who wrote about art, architecture, literature, and social and economic issues. Ruskin was included in the literary Concord Hill Subdivision in 1929 (see *Drury Lane).*

RUSSELL AVENUE

2700 South, between 400 and 1700 East
Origin: *Bay View*

Thomas Russell was born in Ireland in 1843, the year before his family immigrated to New York. He came to Bay View in 1871 from Michigan, where he worked in the iron industry. Russell, employed at the rolling mills as a rail straightener, was elected as village trustee in 1880, the same year the village changed the name of the street he lived on to Russell Avenue.

ST CLAIR STREET

1400 East, between 2400 and 2700 South
Origin: *Bay View*

When the Village of the Milwaukee Iron Company was platted in 1866 in what was later called Bay View, its streets were named for the five Great Lakes and for three other bodies of water along the route to the Atlantic Ocean. Some have since been changed. St. Lawrence Street, named for the river leading from the Great Lakes, is now *Russell* Avenue. Niagara Street, for the river between Lakes *Ontario* and *Erie*, we know as *Potter* Avenue.

St Clair Street was named for the lake that joins Lakes Erie and Huron. The lake was originally named for St. Clare by the French explorer, LaSalle. It was later renamed, and respelled, for Arthur St. Clair, the first governor of the Northwest Territory. St. Clair, an American general in the Revolutionary War, was born in 1736 and died in 1818.

ST PAUL AVENUE

400 North, between 700 East and 9500 West
Origin: *Ordinance*

232

St Paul Avenue is the namesake of the Chicago, Milwaukee, and St. Paul Railroad, which was often called the St. Paul Road (now known as the Milwaukee Road). Fowler and Hill Streets, which ran parallel to the railroad's tracks, were renamed St Paul Avenue in 1889.

The Chicago, Milwaukee & St. Paul Railway passenger station, on a spur north of St. Paul Avenue. (Milwaukee's Great Industries, 1892)

SALEM STREET

6400 South, between 1700 and 2000 West
Origin: *College Heights*

Salem, in Kenosha County, was the likely source for this street name. Salem is the Americanized version of the Hebrew "shalom," for "peace." It is also the shortened version of "Jeru*salem*," the "City of Peace." This street was platted in 1958, when many of the city's new streets were given names of Wisconsin communities.

SANTA MONICA BOULEVARD

300 East and 4800 North
Origin: *Village of Whitefish Bay*

Whitefish Bay's desire to rename some of its streets for glamorous California cities created a bitter religious controversy that lasted for six years and led to the resignation of two members of its village board. Renaming a street Hollywood Avenue in 1925 was no problem, but calling *Richards* Street Santa Monica Boulevard in 1926 caused a fuss.

By coincidence, although some felt there was a connection, St. Monica Catholic Church was on Richards Street. About one-fifth of the Richards Street property owners objected, saying they didn't want their street named after the parish. In spite of the argument that the street name had nothing to do with the church name, the name reverted to Richards

233

Street. But after six years of petitions, letters, debate, and the resignation of the two board members, Richards Street was changed permanently to Santa Monica Boulevard in 1932.

SARASOTA PLACE

4000 North, between 9400 and 10000 West
Origin: *Grantosa*

Sarasota, Florida was named for a Seminole village whose name means "point of rocks." Originally, this development of 1926 also had a street named for Tampa. The developers were Gilbert J. Davelaar and William O. Meilahn.

SARNOW STREET

From 1700 North and 3500 West to 1900 North and 4000 West
Origin: *Washington Park*

German-born Christian Sarnow came to Milwaukee in 1854, when he was 17 years old. After serving in the Civil War, first as a rifleman, then as an officer, Sarnow worked as a carpenter, as a U.S. revenue officer, and finally as a real estate developer. His political career included two terms in the state assembly and two years as an alderman. This street was named for him by ordinance in 1901.

SAVELAND AVENUE

3700 South, between 1800 East and 500 West
Origin: *Tippecanoe*

Tennis Saveland, a Norwegian sea captain, came to Milwaukee in 1844, where he adapted to captaining on the Great Lakes. His six sons followed him in his profession, each at one time or another commanding vessels on the lakes.

His son John had interests on shore as well. In 1868 he established a business in Walker's Point, supplying lake-going vessels with food and equipment, but also retailing fish, lumber, coffee and spices. He developed a recreation center on six acres of land near Saveland Park in the old town of

Lake. It included an artificial lake and a pavilion. Lake Tippecanoe, as it was called, dried up when wells were drilled in the area.

John Saveland, who served as a county board supervisor for two years, died in 1907. This street was named by ordinance in 1929.

SCHILLER STREET

2800 South, between 300 and 400 East
Origin: *Bay View*

Johann Von Schiller was a German playwright whose drama, "The Robbers," attacked political tyranny and inspired German revolutionaries in 1848. In the years that followed their unsuccessful rebellion, many of the intellectual revolutionaries who immigrated to America came to Milwaukee. They brought culture with their liberal ideas, including Schiller's "Robbers," which was performed in Milwaukee for the first time in 1853.

There was also a North Side Schiller Street but it was renamed as a duplicate in 1926. This short Schiller Street was platted by Anna Koenen in 1886 (see *Fratney*).

SCHLINGER AVENUE

700 South, between 8400 and 9000 West
Origin: *Fair Park*

George Schlinger and his brother Michael settled at what is now 92nd Street and Schlinger Avenue before 1876. The brothers, who also spelled their name Schlenger, were wolf hunters. In the 1870s they found their prey in Elm Grove, Brookfield, and other parts of Waukesha County. By the 1880s the declining wolf population forced the brothers to wander

The Schlinger Farm. (Illustrated Atlas of Milwaukee County, 1876)

as far as Iowa to conduct their business. The "Milwaukee Sentinel" reported in March of 1887 that the Schlingers killed seven grey timber wolves in that state. What had been Pierce and Spring Meadow Streets became Schlinger Avenue in 1926 by ordinance of the old Town of Wauwatosa.

SCOTT STREET

1200 South, between 200 East and 3800 West
Origin: *Walker's Point*

According to Milwaukee historian John Gregory, Scott Street was named in the late 1840s for Wisconsinite Martin Scott. Martin, a major, died bravely in 1847 during the Mexican War. Aside from his death being noted in the newspaper, there seems to have been no particular significance attached to Scott.

And Gregory was wrong about when this street was named. It was May 5, 1853. Two Milwaukee streets were renamed that day. Division Street became *Pierce* Street and Beaubian Street was changed to Scott Street. A few months earlier, Franklin Pierce and Winfield Scott had been presidential opponents.

Winfield Scott. (Winfield
Scott: The Soldier and the Man)

Winfield Scott was the best known American general since George *Washington*. Scott became a national hero during the War of 1812, wrote the first United States manual on military tactics in 1825, and became general-in-chief of the army in 1841. After he successfully concluded the Mexican War of 1847, his popularity was at its peak.

When Scott ran for president as a Whig in 1852, he had the support of many Milwaukeeans who organized Scott Clubs around the city. Scott lost the election to Franklin Pierce, but shortly after Pierce's inauguration, during an era of great compromise, these two Walker's Point streets were renamed. During the Civil War, the soldiers' camp that was set up on Wisconsin Avenue between 12th and 14th Streets was named Camp Scott for Winfield Scott. He died at age 80 in 1866.

SCRANTON COURT, PLACE

From 4600 West and 3600 North to 11300 West and 7000 North
Origin: *Grasslyn Manor*

Several city streets were given the names of cities during the renaming program of the 1920s. Scranton, Pennsylvania was named for the Scranton brothers, who founded the iron business that made that city known. This street, formerly Avondale, was renamed in 1928.

SEEBOTH STREET

200 South, between 300 East and 300 West
Origin: *Walker's Point*

The Seeboth brothers, Michael, Albert, and Adam, started their scrap iron business in 1878. The Seeboths, who were German immigrants, had their business at what is known today as 2nd and Seeboth Streets. A portion of South Water Street was changed to Seeboth in 1929.

SEELEY STREET

2700 South, between 1200 and 1500 East
Origin: *Bay View*

Francis and Edward Seeley (sometimes spelled Seely) were steel workers from Norfolk, England where they were born in the 1840s. Both moved to Bay View during the 1870s and were employed at the steel rolling mill. Frank was elected to the village board in 1886 and Edward was the steel workers' union representative. The street was named by steel mill foreman, village treasurer, and real estate developer, Christian *Otjen* in 1880.

SENATOR AVENUE

3100 North, between 3200 and 3300 West
Origin: *Roosevelt Grove*

Senator Christian August Koenitzer, who developed this short street in 1892, represented Milwaukee in the state senate from 1891 to 1895. Koenitzer, born in Wauwatosa in 1852, was a livestock dealer.

SERCOMBE ROAD

3800 West and 4200 North
Origin: *Lincoln Creek*

The Sercombe family, from Cornwall, England, arrived in Milwaukee in the mid-1830s and settled on a farm that was then four miles out of the city. The first mention of the road occurs in the 1844 old Town of Wauwatosa highway record that describes the "so called Sercomb Road" that "runs to a post in the clearing of Samuel Sercomb's, then over Mud Creek." Mud Creek is now Lincoln Creek.

SERVITE DRIVE

From 7600 West and 8400 North to 8100 West and 8800 North
Origin: *Servite Woods*

What sounds like a contemporary corporate name was the name of a Catholic religious group who settled in this part of the old town of Granville in the 1890s. The Servite Fathers of Chicago built a school for boys and a five-story limestone monastery, named Mount St. Philip, in this area. Servite Drive is part of the Servite Woods Subdivision developed in 1976.

SHARON LANE

4300 North, between 10000 and 10300 West
Origin: *Grantosa*

Sharon Lane was named in 1971 as part of the Madison Park Heights Subdivision. The reason for the designation is unknown.

SHEA AVENUE

3200 West, between 700 and 800 South
Origin: *Silver City*

Thomas Shea.
(Illustrated News Annual)

Thomas Shea platted this street in 1880. Shea was a transportation executive who served as alderman and police commissioner. His Walker's Point residence was described as "unquestionably the most sumptuous on the

238

South Side." Shea, who immigrated to Milwaukee from Ireland in 1850, was a survivor of the sinking of the "Lady Elgin" in 1860 (see *Elgin*).

SHELBY STREET

6600 North, between 6600 and 6800 West
Origin: *Menomonee River Hills East*

Shelby Street was named in 1958 during an era when many Milwaukee avenues were named for Wisconsin communities. Shelby, in LaCrosse County, was named for a hero of the American Revolution, Isaac Shelby.

SHEPARD AVENUE

2900 East, between 2700 and 3500 North
Origin: *Downer Woods*

Clarence Shepard named this street in 1891, the year before he died. Shepard, born in New York State in 1810, settled in Milwaukee in 1843, where he began a hardware business. He owned 72 acres of land east of what is now the University of Wisconsin - Milwaukee, but lived downtown. Shepard and his wife actively supported the Milwaukee Orphan Asylum.

SHERIDAN AVENUE, COURT

5500 North, between 1300 and 10700 West
Origin: *Old North Milwaukee*

After Ulysses S. *Grant* and William Tecumseh *Sherman*, Philip Sheridan, (1831-1888), was the most popular Union general to come out of the Civil War. As an Irishman, Sheridan was particularly popular with Milwaukee's Irish, who renamed their military company the Sheridan Guards. How did Sheridan feel about Milwaukeeans? "I have a warm feeling for the people of the Cream City," he was quoted as saying in 1880. Sheridan and *Custer* Avenues were named by Henry Clay Payne in 1892.

SHERMAN BOULEVARD

4300 West, between 2100 and 6400 North
Origin: *Sherman Park*

William Sherman.
(Milwaukee Public Library)

William Tecumseh Sherman, (1820-1891), was a general in the Union Army during the Civil War. He is best remembered for his "march to the sea" from Atlanta, Georgia, when his troops devastated the countryside, hoping to end Southern resistance by destroying their resources. After the war Sherman served as commanding general of the U.S. Army until 1883. This street was named in 1909 by the Boulevard Park Land Company (see *Grant Boulevard*).

SHOLES AVENUE

6600 West, between 2700 and 2900 North
Origin: *Enderis Park*

Sholes Avenue was known as Stratford Avenue until 1926. Christopher Latham Sholes, born in Pennsylvania in 1819, was a Milwaukee newspaper editor credited with the invention of the typewriter. Sholes died in 1890.

SHORE DRIVE

From 2400 South and 1700 East to 2900 South and 2900 East
Origin: *Bay View*

In 1929, the renaming commission decided that Shore Drive was a better name for the road along the lake than was Beulah Street. Beulah Brinton was a cousin of the industrialist founder of Bay View, Eber *Ward*. Beulah Street was one of four streets in Bay View with the names of Ward's family and associates (see *Clement*, *Otjen*, *Potter*).

SIEBEN PLACE

3200 North, between 4200 and 4300 West
Origin: *Sherman Park*

240

In the early 1900s, John Sieben, the president of a wine and liquor business, owned the land where this street was developed. The Bonny Park Subdivision, including Sieben Place, was platted in 1913.

SIEGFRIED PLACE

500 South, between 5800 and 6000 West
Origin: *Johnson's Woods*

August M. Siegfried, the son of a German immigrant, operated his saloon near Siegfried Place and Hawley Road when this street was named in 1901 as part of the Hawley Avenue Subdivision. With his wife, Emma, he later ran a grocery store from the same site. Siegfried died about 1929.

SILVER SPRING DRIVE, ROAD

5600 North, between 900 and 12400 West
Origin: *Town of Milwaukee*

Edward J. Cuyler, an official with the Chicago and Northwestern Railroad, named the company's station near Green Bay Road and what became known as Silver Spring Road. He chose the name Silver Spring Station because a nearby manufacturer advertised using "silver springs" in his factory. The business may have been Herman's Silver Springs Mills near Green Tree Road, which produced starch and cereals. The springs referred to supplied settlers in the area with water before well drilling dried them up. In 1917, the old Town of Milwaukee made official the name that had been in use for many years.

SINGER CIRCLE

3700 North, between 1100 and 1300 East
Origin: *Riverwest*

Anthony Singer was president of Singer Brothers, a landscape gardening business at this location. The brothers subdivided their land in 1927, creating Singer Circle.

241

SLESKE COURT

7700 West, between 8100 and 8300 North
Origin: *Land Bank*

Sleske Court was known as Fountain Court until 1984. It was changed then to honor Donald Sleske, one of the original members of the city's Division of Economic Development, which developed the land bank program. Sleske had recently passed away at the time of the naming.

SMITH STREET

2400 South, between 200 and 600 East
Origin: *Bay View*

Milwaukee Smith.
(Bruce's History of Milwaukee)

Uriel B. Smith and his family were among the county's first Yankee-Yorker settlers when they came to Milwaukee in 1835. That same year, Mrs. Smith gave birth to a girl, Milwaukee's first white child. She was named Milwaukee Smith. (The area's first Native American birth probably occurred about 10,000 years earlier).

Milwaukee Smith's brother, Tully H. Smith, who platted this Bay View subdivision in 1871, was named for his father's birthplace, Tully, New York.

SOMERS STREET

1500 North, between 700 and 1000 West
Origin: *Hillside*

Peter J. Somers, born of Irish immigrant parents in 1850 in Waukesha County, advocated an Irish revolution in 1884. He proposed that 40,000 Irishmen take over every English-held fort and barrack in Ireland. His views assured his popularity with Milwaukee's Irish citizens. His good looks and unfashionably long hair made him popular with enough of the rest of the

242

population for him to be elected as city attorney that year, in spite of an opponent's claim that he was "long on hair and short on law."

Somers was later elected mayor and then U.S. representative. He died in 1924. Central Street, because it was too much like *Center* Street, was renamed Somers Street in 1926. Somers Avenue in Cudahy was named for his brother, John, who had been superintendent of schools in Milwaukee.

Peter Somers, long on hair, short on law?
(Men of Progress, 1897)

SPAULDING PLACE

2100 North, between 4200 and 4300 West
Origin: *Washington Park*

Eiring Place was renamed Spaulding Place in 1926 because it was too similar to *Irving* Place on the East Side. Why Spaulding was selected is not known.

SPENCER PLACE

From 3800 North and 4400 West to 7000 North and 10500 West
Origin: *Lincoln Creek*

Spencer Place was named in 1928 as part of the Franklin Gardens Subdivision. It may be named for Robert C. Spencer, born in Ohio in 1829, and founder of Spencerian Business College in Milwaukee. He served on the school board and had a special interest in the education of the hearing impaired. Spencer died in 1916.

SPOKANE STREET

6900 North, between 6000 and 11500 West
Origin: *Menomonee River Hills*

In 1957 Spokane, Washington was represented in this subdivision of western street names. The city was named for the Spokane Indians.

SPRING LANE

7700 North, between 5300 and 5600 West
Origin: *Village of Fox Point*

The village of Fox Point named Spring Lane in 1930. Although later renamed Beach Drive in Fox Point, the name remained in Brown Deer and Milwaukee.

SPRINGFIELD AVENUE

2100 East, between 3200 and 3400 South
Origin: *Fernwood*

In 1927, Walter *Bennett* subdivided part of the farm that had been in his family for nearly a century. The Bennett Hill Subdivision included Springfield and *Dayfield* Avenues.

STACK DRIVE, COURT

3000 South, between 5200 and 6500 West
Origin: *White Manor*

Brothers Stephen Sylvester Stack, a physician, and Earl L. Stack, a gas station operator, named Stack Drive as part of their White Manor Subdivision in 1939.

STANLEY PLACE

1200 East, between 2350 and 2400 North
Origin: *Riverwest*

Stanley as a first name was in vogue when Stanley Place was named in 1898. The name had gained popularity thanks to Henry Stanley and his African explorations with David Livingstone two decades earlier. The street was platted by Ephraim Mariner. No Stanley appears in Mariner's family, so perhaps he named it for the man whose remark, "Doctor Livingstone, I presume?" became legendary (see *Congo*).

STARK STREET

4900 North, between 1700 and 11000 West
Origin: *Old North Milwaukee*

Stark Street was named in 1892 as part of the village of North Milwaukee. It was probably named for a farmer named Stark who owned the land this street is located on.

STATE STREET

1000 North, between 1100 East and 6000 West
Origin: *Kilbourntown*

New York City's State Street was well known during the 19th century as one of the most fashionable and elegant residential addresses in the world. Chicago's State Street was the retail center of that city. In 1866, Milwaukee got a State Street of its own when it renamed *Tamarack* Street. It was a logical street to name State Street; it ran to Watertown Plank Road, also known as the Madison Road, then on to the state's capital. The "Milwaukee Sentinel" wasn't impressed with the new name. It sarcastically reported that, "as a consequence the value of the property on the upper portion of that drive has increased $10 per foot."

STEVEN ROAD

7300 West, between 8300 and 8400 North
Origin: *Land Bank*

Steven Nardelli was born in Milwaukee in 1974, the son of alderman Thomas Nardelli. The street was named in 1990 (see *Marcia*).

STEVENSON STREET

200 North, between 6000 and 9500 West
Origin: *Merrill Park*

Clifton Avenue, because it was too similar to the now renamed Clinton Street, was renamed Stevenson Street in 1926. Because it is in line with *Hawthorne* Avenue, it has been suggested that the two streets are

245

named for literary figures, one for Nathaniel Hawthorne, the other for Robert Louis Stevenson.

STEWART STREET

2000 South, between 300 and 500 East
Origin: *Bay View*

Alexander Stewart, born in Scotland in 1799, and his wife Elizabeth settled on their 160-acre farm where Kinnickinnic Avenue meets the Kinnickinnic River. Besides farming, Stewart supplied fuel wood to the lake steamers of the era, a business taken over by his son Robert when Alexander died in 1873.

After the Civil War the Stewarts began to subdivide their farm, and in 1879 a city ordinance named this street for them. Over the years the landscape changed from farmland to railroad tracks and factories, and in 1889, tired of the noise and grime, Robert and his family left for the relative calm of Wauwatosa.

STORY PARKWAY

4800 West, between 100 and 600 North
Origin: *Story Hill*

Hiram Story, born in Vermont in 1818, settled in the Story Hill area in 1845. After farming for a decade, he realized he was on a stone mine when a tree overturned, exposing the stone beneath the soil. Story's stone quarry became one of the most valuable in the state and provided building stone for Milwaukee for decades. The quarry later became the site of County Stadium. Hiram Story died in 1887, and Story Parkway was named by his son, Albert, in 1922.

(Department of City Development)

246

STOWELL AVENUE

2500 East, between 2500 and 3100 North
Origin: *Murray Hill*

John Maxwell Stowell was the city's mayor when developer Edmund Burke named this street for him in 1883. Stowell, born in New York State in 1824, worked as a publisher, grocer, and saw mill operator in St. Louis before arriving here in 1856. Stowell's saw mill experience led to the founding of the Filer and Stowell Company in Bay View, a manufacturer of milling machinery. He was also a real estate developer and served as state assemblyman and city alderman before being elected Democratic mayor in 1882. Stowell died in 1907.

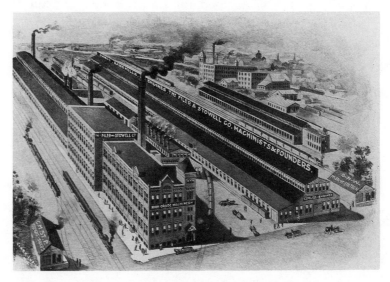

The Filer and Stowell Company, Bay View. (Milwaukee, Picturesque and Descriptive)

STRATHMORE AVENUE

6900 West, between 5400 and 5600 North
Origin: *Silver Spring*

This aristocratic sounding name can be traced to Kensington, London, England where the Earl of Strathmore developed the Strathmore Gardens. The street was named in 1953.

SUMAC PLACE

2500 South, between 4400 and 4800 West
Origin: *Jackson Park*

In 1948 Frank and Elisabeth Kirkpatrick named Sumac Place, after the bush common to the Milwaukee area.

SUMMIT AVENUE

From 1800 East and 1800 North to 2800 East and 2700 North
Origin: *Northpoint*

Third Avenue was renamed Summit Avenue by the Common Council in 1875. It undoubtedly was named for its place on the bluff above Lake Michigan.

SUNBURY COURT

3400 South, between 2200 and 8300 West
Origin: *Harder's Oaks*

The origin of this name is Sunbury, England. Sunbury Court was platted in 1926 by Frank Harder.

SUNNYSIDE DRIVE

300 North, between 4800 and 5000 West
Origin: *Story Hill*

Sunnyside Drive was named by Albert and Alice *Story* in 1922 as part of the Story Hill Subdivision.

SUNSET DRIVE

7100 West, between 3500 and 3800 South
Origin: *Wedgewood*

Sunset Drive was named as part of the Wedgewood Subdivision in 1954.

248

SUPERIOR STREET

From 2400 South and 1300 East to 3200 South and 3000 East
Origin: *Bay View*

Superior Street is one of the eight streets named for bodies of water during the founding of Bay View in 1866 by Captain Eber *Ward* of Detroit. Ward's steel business used ports on Lake Superior, the largest of the Great Lakes (see *St Clair*).

SUSSEX STREET

3900 West, between 6900 and 7400 North
Origin: *Town & Country Manor*

Platted in 1959, Sussex Street was named for the Waukesha County community. Sussex was settled by immigrants from Sussex, England in 1834.

St. Alban's Episcopal Church in Sussex, Wisconsin is similar to the one left behind by settlers from Sussex, England.

SWAIN COURT

2300 East, between 3200 and 3300 South
Origin: *Fernwood*

George S. *Meredith* and his half-brother, Horatio Samuel Meredith, named this short street for their mothers in 1923. George's mother, Sarah Ann Swain, the wife of John T. Meredith, died in Bay View in 1872 when George was two years old. His father then married her sister, Eliza, and their son Horatio was born in 1874.

John Meredith, both his wives, and their father, Samuel Swain, a mining engineer, were from Wolverhampton, England. They all died in Bay View.

SWAN ROAD, CIRCLE

9200 West, between 4800 and 5700 North
Origin: *Kops Park*

In 1837 Emery Swan farmed in the old town of Wauwatosa, where there were no roads and no other settlers around. He had to mark the trail between his place and the Menomonee River, his water route to Milwaukee. When he got lost in the forest around his farm, he would fire his gun, hoping he was close enough to draw a responding shot and a way home. Swan was born of English ancestry in Vienna, New York in 1801 and died in 1887. The first plat map that shows this road with the name Swan is dated 1925.

SYLVIA STREET

8400 North, between 10300 and 10500 West
Origin: *Pheasant Run*

German-born Ludwig Haas was the engineer in charge of the northwest district for the City Engineer's Office during the 1960s. In 1967 this street was named for his wife, the former Sylvia Meyers, who was born in Milwaukee in 1928.

250

TACOMA STREET

9000 West, between 6800 and 7100 North
Origin: *Menomonee River Hills*

Tacoma Street, like other streets in this 1957 subdivision, was named for a western city. Tacoma, Washington gets its name from an Indian language, and one theory says it means "near to heaven."

TALLMADGE PLACE, COURT

5300 North, between 6900 and 7200 West
Origin: *Silver Spring*

John J. Tallmadge was the agent of a Buffalo steamship line when he came to Milwaukee in 1855. He was born in Calverick, New York in 1818 and lived in Buffalo before steaming into Milwaukee Bay. Ten years later he was elected to the first of two terms as mayor of the city. Tallmadge's vigor in promoting the city had given him the presidency of the Chamber of Commerce, where his administrative abilities led to his selection as Democratic Party mayoral candidate in 1865. He won, but his inauguration, the day after President *Lincoln*'s assassination, was a somber affair.

Tallmadge ran for governor of Wisconsin after his success as mayor, but lost. He died in 1873. On recommendation of the City Engineer this street was named for him in 1954.

251

TAMARACK STREET

2600 North and 2500 West
Origin: *Park West*

When the first Yankee settlers arrived in Milwaukee, the downtown area was covered with tamarack trees. The Grand Avenue Mall rests over a tamarack swamp. Tamaracks were cut for poles for bridges and dwellings from the swamp now covered by the Auditorium. Hollowed out tamarack logs were used as water mains in the city's early days.

One of the first streets in the new community was named Tamarack Street by Byron *Kilbourn* in 1835, the same year he contracted to have tamaracks and other downtown trees cut down. That Tamarack Street was renamed *State* Street in 1866. This newer Tamarack Street was named in 1889, along with a group of other short, tree-named streets (*Oak, Ash, and Hickory*) along Fond du Lac Avenue near 27th Street and North Avenue.

A grove of tamaracks like these covered much of Kilbourntown.

TAYLOR AVENUE, COURT

700 East, between 2700 and 4600 South
Origin: *Bay View*

This street was named in 1909 and is assumed to have been named after President Zachary Taylor, since the other streets in the Humboldt Park Subdivision (*Quincy* and *Adams*) carry presidential names.

Zachary Taylor, (1785-1850), a military hero, was the 12th President of the United States. Taylor fought Chief Black Hawk and his followers in Wisconsin and Seminole Indians in Florida, but gained most of his fame during the Mexican War, the year before he was elected president in 1848. He died of cholera after one year and four months in office.

252

TENNESSEE AVENUE

2200 West, between 4300 and 4500 South
Origin: *Wilson Park*

Tennessee, *Kentucky*, and *Louisiana* Avenues were named in 1955 in the Villa Mann Subdivision. The state got its name from a Cherokee village called Tennessee.

TERESA LANE

6900 North, between 9700 and 9800 West
Origin: *Golden Gate*

Teresa Lane was named by developer Francis Schroedel in 1962. The name was selected with no one particular in mind.

TERRA AVENUE

8100 North, between 9300 and 10500 West
Origin: *Village of Brown Deer*

Terra, or earth, was the name given to this street by Francis Schroedel in 1956.

TERRACE AVENUE

From 2000 East and 1800 North to 3000 East and 2700 North
Origin: *Northpoint*

One of the World Book Dictionary definitions of terrace is "a street along the top of a slope." What could better describe Terrace Avenue, a street on the bluff overlooking Lake Michigan? The former Fifth Avenue was renamed Terrace Avenue in 1875.

TESCH AVENUE

4100 South, between 4800 and 8100 West
Origin: *City of St. Francis*

German-born Charles Tesch owned a farm near the St. Francis

Seminary until his death in 1881. Charles' son, August, was the victim of an early Milwaukee murder. In 1867, 19 year old August was walking to his parents' St. Francis home from downtown Milwaukee. As he walked the Chicago and Northwestern Railroad tracks near Oklahoma Avenue, he was shot three times and robbed. The killers were found and sentenced to life imprisonment. Tesch Avenue was named by Julius Wechselberg in 1885.

TEUTONIA AVENUE

From 1200 West and 2200 North to 3800 West and 7600 North
Origin: *Ordinance*

Teutonia refers to the Teutons, the Latin word for the German people. The term was used in 1852 by a German revolutionary group that named its new Milwaukee Turner Society "Teutonia." These "Teutonians" promoted concepts considered radical in Germany at the time; "Free speech, free press, and free assembly for discussion of all questions." A city ordinance renamed the Milwaukee and Fond du Lac Plank Road in 1857, calling it Teutonia Avenue.

TEXAS AVENUE

3000 South and 2700 East
Origin: *Bay View*

The Spanish word for allies is "tejas." The Indian interpretation is "texia." It came to mean the land north of the Rio Grande, now the state of Texas. This street, named in 1891, is one of seven named for states by Thomas Kennan (see *Delaware*).

THOMAS AVENUE

2400 North, between 1500 and 2100 East
Origin: *Murray Hill*

Thomas Avenue was named in 1856 by James *Murray*. It has been supposed that it was named for Thomas Roddis (and that nearby Edward Avenue, since renamed *North* Avenue, was named for Edward Roddis). The

Roddis brothers were meatpackers. Thomas Roddis, who died in 1864, was also involved in real estate, insurance, and grain.

THURSTON AVENUE, CIRCLE, COURT

5700 North, between 3100 and 9900 West
Origin: *Old North Milwaukee*

William J. Thurston was born in Ohio about 1836 and died in Los Angeles in 1902. Between Ohio and California, Thurston worked in Milwaukee as an oyster dealer who dabbled in real estate. He was active in local gun clubs and was an expert shooter. Thurston Avenue became part of the new industrial community of North Milwaukee in 1893.

TORONTO STREET

4100 North, between 3500 and 3800 West
Origin: *Lincoln Creek*

East Edgebrook Drive became Toronto Street in 1926 because Edgebrook was too much like *Edgewood* Avenue, the border between Shorewood and Milwaukee. The Canadian city name is an Indian word of uncertain meaning (see *Montreal*).

TORY HILL

400 North, between 1000 and 1300 West
Origin: *Marquette*

Tory Hill was named in 1965 as a reminder of one of the city's early neighborhoods. The area, which was settled by Irish who gave it a reputation as a tough neighborhood, has been largely paved over with freeway. Some claim that the name was given because of residents named Torrey, but it may have come from a 17th century English term for Irish outlaws who refused to accept British rule.

TOWER AVENUE

8200 North, between 7600 and 11000 West
Origin: *Village of Brown Deer*

Tower Avenue was named as part of the Kirkwood Subdivision, a former farm, in 1926. No one named Tower was associated with the farm or the subdivision. According to a man who farmed the land at the time, the closest thing to a tower nearby was the farm's silo.

TOWER VIEW BOULEVARD

2900 North, between 9700 and 9900 West
Origin: *Mount Mary*

The tower in view from Tower View Boulevard is part of Notre Dame Hall at Mount Mary College. The hall was built in 1929, and the street was platted in 1948, both by the School Sisters of Notre Dame.

TOWNSEND STREET

3400 North, between 1300 East and 9900 West
Origin: *Franklin Heights*

Contrary to city streetlore, this street was never the town's end. It was named for the Townsends, Edwin and Hamilton.

Edwin Townsend was born in 1803 in New York City, and in 1846 he brought his family, including son Hamilton, to Milwaukee. Townsend was a partner in a real estate business for many years, and in 1870 he and Hamilton decided to start their own realty company. Unfortunately, the family business was short lived; Edwin died a few weeks later.

Hamilton Townsend continued on his own and was involved in the city's dramatic growth through the 1890s. In 1897 he moved to New Orleans hoping to improve his health, but died there three months later. This street was named in 1887 by William H. Roddis.

TRENTON PLACE

1000 North, between 5600 and 5900 West
Origin: *Valley Forge*

This name commemorates the Battle of Trenton, where George *Washington*'s rebels defeated England's troops. The combat took place at Trenton, New Jersey in 1776. The street was named in 1928 (see *Valley Forge*).

TRIPOLI AVENUE

3800 South, between 1800 East and 9900 West
Origin: *City of St. Francis*

Tripoli is the name of cities in both Lebanon and Libya. Henry Niedecken and George Ziegler named the streets of their subdivision after exotic places like *Ahmedi* and Bombay in 1892.

TROWBRIDGE STREET

2900 South, between 1900 and 2200 East
Origin: *Bay View*

In 1835 William S. Trowbridge, of early English settler stock, came to Milwaukee. He was 22 years old and came from New York, where he had received an education in civil engineering. Before he died in 1886, Trowbridge was elected both city and county surveyor, and had surveyed much of Milwaukee.

Trowbridge surveyed the subdivision that includes this street in 1872. Besides having Trowbridge Street named for him, and the Trowbridge School

William Trowbridge.
(Conard's History of Milwaukee County)

257

located on it, he lived on Trowbridge Road (since renamed) in the West Milwaukee area.

TUCKER PLACE

8800 West, between 3600 and 3700 North
Origin: *St. Aemilian's*

In 1933 a portion of 88th Street was renamed Tucker Place. The name may have been chosen because it is easy to pronounce and spell.

TUPELO STREET, COURT

7300 North, between 3900 and 9800 West
Origin: *Melody View*

Tupelo joined a group of tree-named streets in 1959. The tupelo, which means "swamp tree," is not native to Milwaukee (see *Dogwood*).

UNCAS AVENUE

6100 South, between 100 East/West and 500 West
Origin: *City of Cudahy*

Many names were popularized by James Fenimore Cooper's "Leatherstocking Tales;" Iowa's Hawkeyes and Wisconsin's Horicon and Mingo Lake are among them. Frequently, as with Uncas of the "Last of the Mohicans," Cooper based his characters on real people. Uncas was a 17th century chief of the Mohegan Indians who helped the English settlers in fighting other tribes along the Connecticut River. In appreciation, the citizens of Norwich, Connecticut erected a monument to him. Bert J. Pander and Robert O. Betz platted this street near Lake Michigan in 1893.

UNION STREET

1700 West, between 1400 and 1600 South
Origin: *Muskego Way*

In the years leading to the Civil War, there were many threats by southern states to dissolve the union of the states. In 1855 five Milwaukeeans, Henry Brugman, Gustav Pfeil, Augustus Wilmann, Joseph Ody, and David Power, affirmed their belief in the Union by naming this street. This may be the only street in the city named for an ideal.

UPHAM AVENUE, COURT

5200 South, between 1400 and 1800 West
Origin: *Greenfield*

Don A. J. Upham, born in Vermont in 1809, was the city attorney in Wilmington, Delaware before coming to Milwaukee in 1837. He became the city's fourth mayor when he was elected in 1849. Upham, described as slow walking, slow talking, and fond of fun, presided over the banquet that celebrated the lighting of the city's streets. That occurred in 1852; the light source was gas. Upham also served as district attorney and in the territorial legislature, but lost his bid for governor in 1851. He died in 1877 and the street was named in 1934.

Don A. J. Upham.
(Conard's History of Milwaukee County)

UTAH AVENUE

5100 West and 3400 South
Origin: *Lyons Park*

The state of Utah was named for the Ute Indians. This street, one of many named for states on the South Side, was platted as part of the King's Addition in 1954 (see *Alabama*).

260

VALLEY FORGE DRIVE

900 North, between 5600 and 6000 West
Origin: *Valley Forge*

Valley Forge Drive, a short, hilly street, was known as Menomonee Drive until its renaming in 1928. Valley Forge, Pennsylvania is where George *Washington*'s revolutionaries suffered through the winters of 1777 and 1778. Valley Forge Drive memorializes their victory over bitter cold and lack of food and clothing, rather than a military encounter (see *Trenton*).

VAN BECK AVENUE, WAY

4000 South, between 1600 East and 8200 West
Origin: *Tippecanoe*

Gerhardt Van Beck, born in 1806, came to Milwaukee from Germany in 1854. After working as a laborer for several years he accumulated enough money to buy farm land in the old town of Lake, where the Van Beck name is still prominent in farm produce today. Gerhardt Van Beck died in 1884 and the street was named in 1926.

VAN BUREN STREET

700 East, between 300 and 1700 North
Origin: *Juneautown*

Martin Van Buren, (1782-1862), was Andrew *Jackson*'s vice-president when Solomon *Juneau* and Morgan L. *Martin* named this street in 1835. Van Buren, who had previously been governor of New York and Jackson's secretary of state, was elected the country's eighth president the following year.

Van Buren Street looking north from Mason Street in the days of the horse and buggy.
(Milwaukee Public Library)

VANCE PLACE

4300 North and 5600 West
Origin: *Lincoln Creek*

Vance Place was named as part of the Longview Subdivision in 1928. Named by the city, it may have been named for David Vance. The Irish-born Vance was president of the Chamber of Commerce and was active in the

Board of Trade during the late 1800s. He operated a vessel brokerage and marine insurance business.

VAN NORMAN AVENUE

4500 South, between 1000 East and 2300 West
Origin: *City of Cudahy*

George Bosworth Van Norman, a livestock commissioner, was the source for this street name in Patrick *Cudahy's* new community in 1892. Van Norman, born in New York State in 1842, moved with his family to western Wisconsin in 1855. After serving in the Civil War, he began purchasing cattle for shipment to Milwaukee meatpackers, a business which eventually brought him to live in this city. Van Norman was the president of the syndicate that organized the Town of South Milwaukee, and of the Eagle Horse Shoe Company, one of that community's first factories.

George Bosworth Van Norman. (Men of Progress, 1897)

VERA AVENUE

7000 North, between 3100 and 10500 West
Origin: *Town and Country Manor*

Vera Avenue was named by the old Town of Granville in 1942. Vera is Russian for "faith." The reason for its selection wasn't recorded.

VERMONT AVENUE

2900 East, between 3100 and 3300 South
Origin: *Bay View*

Vermont is French for "green mountain." Theobald *Otjen* named this street for the state in 1891, giving Bay View a total of 16 streets named for states or Canadian provinces (see *Delaware, Herman, Rhode Island).*

263

VERONA COURT

3500 South, between 2200 and 9100 West
Origin: *Harder's Oaks*

Verona Court was platted in 1926. It may be named for the Wisconsin city of Verona, a name that has its roots in Verona, Italy.

VIEAU PLACE

1100 South, between 2300 and 2400 West
Origin: *Clarke Square*

Vieau is one of the oldest names associated with Milwaukee. Jacques Vieau, a French Canadian born in Montreal in 1757, was a farmer and a fur trader. He spent his summers farming in Green Bay and then went south for the winter, to Milwaukee, for the trading season. Vieau's trading post, a few blocks north of this short street, was in operation during the fall and winter each year starting about 1795.

Vieau, who married a French and Menominee Indian woman, brought Solomon *Juneau* to Milwaukee as his clerk about 1818. A short time later Juneau married Vieau's teenage daughter, Josette, and took over the Milwaukee fur trade. Vieau returned to Green Bay where he died in 1853. Vieau Place, formerly Washington Street, was named in 1905.

Vieau's trading post in 1795.
(Buck's Pioneer History of Milwaukee)

VIENNA AVENUE, COURT

3800 North, between 1300 East and 10000 West
Origin: *Williamsburg*

Vienna, the capital of Austria, was a center of science, music, and literature when this street was named in 1891 by the Vienna Park Land Company.

VILLA AVENUE

8300 North, between 10300 and 10500 West
Origin: *Village of Brown Deer*

A villa can be a large, luxurious residence, although another definition - any house in the suburbs - more closely fits the homes on Villa Avenue. It was named in 1957 by Francis Schroedel.

VILLARD AVENUE

5200 North, between 1800 and 12400 West
Origin: *Old North Milwaukee*

In 1856, Bavarian-born Henry Villard came to Milwaukee as a 21 year old from Chicago, trying to sell books of American literature. After three weeks he left town with his expenses exceeding his sales and the realization that the city's German citizens weren't interested in American literature.

In 1892, when Henry Clay Payne named this street, Villard, then living in New York, was president of the Milwaukee Street Railway Company. After his Milwaukee book selling days, Villard gained fame as a Civil War correspondent for Eastern newspapers, then later as a financier who owned railroads and street railways. He was also the founder of the General Electric Company. Villard, who was born Henry Hilgard, died in 1900.

Henry Villard. (Illustrated News Annual)

VILTER LANE

2100 South, between 2000 and 2200 West
Origin: *Muskego Way*

Ernst Vilter and his wife Elise emigrated from Germany to Milwaukee after the Civil War. Elise had been a widow with young children when Ernst married her. Her sons, Theodore and William, took their stepfather's name and followed him in the family machine business. After Ernst died, the brothers, joined by their half-brother Emil, expanded the business from several employees to over seven hundred workers, making it a major Milwaukee employer. The company changed its product line from the manufacture of brewers' machinery to ice-making and refrigeration equipment. The Vilters, Theodore in particular, were active in city affairs, contributing to the welfare of the community in many ways.

In 1926, during the city's street renaming program, Inland Street was changed to Vilter to avoid confusion with Island, although Island was later changed to *Palmer* Street.

VINE STREET

1800 North, between 300 East and 6000 West
Origin: *Midtown*

Patrick Mallon, a Cincinnati attorney, and his wife Sophia platted Vine Street in 1869.

VIRGINIA STREET

500 South, between 100 and 900 West
Origin: *Walker's Point*

George *Walker*, the founder of Walker's Point, named this street in 1842 for his home state. Walker was born in Lynchburg, Virginia in 1811. The state of Virginia was named for Elizabeth I of England, "the Virgin Queen."

266

VLIET STREET

1400 North, between 300 and 6000 West
Origin: *Kilbourntown*

Garrett Vliet was a surveyor and a friend of Byron *Kilbourn*. He surveyed Kilbourn's future townsite west of the river where this street was named for him in 1835. Vliet, of Dutch ancestry, was born in New Brunswick, New Jersey in 1790 but grew up in a frontier community in Pennsylvania. After stints as a hunter and then a soldier in the War of 1812, Vliet turned to surveying, a career that led him west.

Vliet surveyed portions of Wisconsin and laid out the city of Mineral Point and towns along the Mississippi River, including Dubuque, Iowa. He died in Milwaukee in 1877.

VOGEL AVENUE, COURT

5000 South, between 200 and 2600 West
Origin: *City of Cudahy*

Pfister and Vogel Leather Store. (Milwaukee, 1883)

Frederick Vogel and his cousin Guido Pfister began the Pfister & Vogel Leather Company in the late 1840s, soon after arriving in Milwaukee. Both were born in Germany and lived in Buffalo, New York before coming here. Besides helping to build a successful tanning business with offices throughout Europe, Vogel served as a Milwaukee alderman and in the state legislature.

He died on October 24, 1892, during the height of a real estate boom. A week later, this street was named for him in the new meatpacking community of *Cudahy*. Pfister Avenue was platted nearby, and had things developed as planned, there would have been an intersection of Pfister and Vogel on land now occupied by Mitchell International Airport.

VOLLMER AVENUE

3400 South, between 2100 and 2300 East
Origin: *City of St. Francis*

Before settling down in St. Francis when he was 39, German-born Francis Vollmer moved around. His family immigrated to Baltimore in 1838 when he was seven years old. At twenty he came to Milwaukee, and when he was 33 he left for Prairie du Chien. At 39 he settled near the St. Francis Seminary, where he farmed and ran a boarding house. He died in 1884. The street was platted by John M. *Stowell*, a former Milwaukee mayor, in 1892.

Francis Vollmer Residence. (1876 Illustrated Atlas of Milwaukee County)

268

WABASH AVENUE, COURT

8600 North, between 7200 and 10700 West
Origin: *Town of Milwaukee*

In 1940, Washington Court was changed to Wabash, possibly to avoid confusion with nearby Port Washington Road. Wabash, the name of the river between Illinois and Indiana, means "white water" in the Miami Indian language.

WAHL AVENUE

2600 East, between 2300 and 2700 North
Origin: *Northpoint*

Wahl Avenue, along Lake Park, was named to honor the first "Father of Milwaukee's Park System," Christian Wahl. Wahl, born in Germany in 1829, came to Milwaukee with his family when he was 17. He left the city five years later and, until he retired in 1886, lived primarily in Chicago where he founded a glue company. After selling his business to Philip *Armour*, Wahl came back to Milwaukee, where he devoted the last 15 years of his life to beautifying the city.

Wahl supported a plan of parks throughout the city, rather than one huge park, as in New York City with its Central Park. He was president of the Park Board when it made land purchases for the city's first five parks.

269

Before his death in 1901, Wahl spent much of his time overseeing the development of his favorite, Lake Park (see *Whitnall*).

WALKER STREET

900 South, between 200 East and 1600 West
Origin: *Walker's Point*

George Walker, the founder of the city's South Side, visited Milwaukee in 1833 when he was 22 years old. Walker, a Virginian who had become a fur trader at 18, built his trading post in the area now called Walker's Point the following year.

As the fur trade died out, Walker's interests turned to real estate promotion, politics, and railroads. The corpulent Walker served in the territorial legislature and as Milwaukee alderman and mayor. Unlike Byron *Kilbourn* and Solomon *Juneau*, he was the only one of Milwaukee's founders to remain in the city until his death in 1866. Walker named this street in 1836.

George Walker. (Bruce's History of Milwaukee)

WALNUT STREET

1700 North, between 300 and 4000 West
Origin: *Kilbourntown*

In 1993, "Mad" magazine's Alfred E. Neuman observed that "they cut down all the trees and then name the streets after them." In 1835, Byron *Kilbourn* and his group did just the opposite. They named the streets first, then cut the trees down. The streets were named *Tamarack*, Cedar, Poplar, Sycamore, Chestnut, *Cherry* and Walnut. The next year, 1836, Kilbourn contracted to have the trees in the downtown area felled. The walnut tree common to the Milwaukee area is the Black Walnut.

WALTON PLACE

8000 West and 3300 North
Origin: *Nash Park*

This short street which connects 80th and 81st Streets was known as 80th Street until it was renamed Walton Place in 1930. The name may have been selected simply because it is easy to pronounce and to spell.

WALWORTH STREET

2300 North, between 1100 and 1200 East
Origin: *Riverwest*

It was illegal for Clinton Walworth, a lawyer and future judge, to do what he and other settlers did in 1839. But it was understandable, considering what the land sharks were going to do.

After the Federal government had acquired Milwaukee lands through treaties with Indians, the settlers came. They cleared the land and built homes on it, without having title to it. When the government was ready to auction the land, the sharks, whose methods were well known, came to town. They would approach a squatter and offer not to bid on his land if the settler would pay them off. Or they would bid on a homesteader's land and then offer to sell it back to him for a profit. The settler would lose either his money, if he had any, or his land and home.

Walworth and the others came up with a plan to outfox the con men. The auction was held in the open air of downtown Milwaukee. When a parcel of land was auctioned, a designated settler would bid the minimum price. A settlers' committee of brawny men stood by to take any bidding shark on a trip to the river. The plan worked, and no one lost his land or his money.

Walworth, who was about 24 years old at the time, was born in Burlington, New York around 1814. By the time he died in 1862, Walworth had been an editor of the "Milwaukee Sentinel," a probate judge, and a police judge. His family subdivided their land and named this short street in 1887.

WANDA AVENUE

5600 South, between 1400 and 4000 West
Origin: *City of Cudahy*

This street was named by the Reliance Land Company as part of

271

Cudahy in 1893. The name Wanda had become popular with the publication of the novel, "Wanda," by Marie Louise de la Ramee in 1883. Previously, the name had not been used in the English-speaking world.

WARD STREET

2200 South, between 200 and 400 East
Origin: *Bay View*

Eber Brock Ward, (1811-1875), was the founder of Bay View. Ward, of Detroit, turned his career as a seaman into the ownership of a Great Lakes steamship line. When he branched into ironworks, he formed companies on the shores of the lakes. In 1866 Ward platted the Village of the Milwaukee Iron Company, now known as Bay View. In 1872 C.C. *Robinson* developed a part of north Bay View and named this street for Ward. Bay View streets named for people with connections to Ward include *Clement* (business partner), *Otjen* (foster sons), and *Potter* (son-in-law). Beulah Street, now South *Shore* Drive, had been named for Beulah Brinton, said to be his cousin.

WARNIMONT AVENUE, COURT

3600 South, between 1600 East and 9100 West
Origin: *Tippecanoe*

Eugene Warnimont served as a supervisor on the county board for 35 years. Warnimont was born in the old town of Lake in 1886, the son of immigrants from Luxembourg. Warnimont Avenue, near the family farm, was named by ordinance in 1929. Warnimont Park was also named for Eugene Warnimont, who died in 1950.

WARREN AVENUE

1200 East, between 1500 and 2000 North
Origin: *Lower East Side*

In 1884 the city passed an ordinance that changed Doty Street to

Warren Avenue. One theory says the street was named for a Nathaniel Warren who owned a marble yard nearby. Another is that it honors a Revolutionary War patriot, Joseph Warren. Judging by the city's naming habits, the Revolutionary Warren is more likely. The city tended to rename streets for the prominent, either local or national. No Nathaniel Warren, with or without a marble yard, shows up in directories of the time. Nor were there other Warrens of note in the area. Joseph Warren, the patriot, died at the Battle of Bunker Hill.

WASHINGTON BOULEVARD

1700 North, between 4700 and 6000 West
Origin: *Washington Heights*

George Washington, "Father of our Country," was born in Virginia in 1732. Before his death in 1799, he led the country to independence, served as president of the Constitutional Convention, and was the first President of the United States. This boulevard, west of Washington Park, was named in 1912.

WASHINGTON STREET

George Washington.
(Milwaukee Public Library)

1100 South, between 300 East and 2000 West
Origin: *Walker's Point*

Prior to the Revolutionary War, American streets were primarily named for features or for kings or saints. After the war, Americans began naming their streets for people, particularly patriots. George Washington, as commander of the army and then president, was the most frequently honored. This street was named by James *Doty* and others of his group in 1838, as part of their subdivision called Milwaukee Proper.

WATER STREET

From 300 East and 1100 South to 900 East and 1900 North

Origin: *Juneautown*

Before 1836, Water Street was a trail along the Milwaukee River. In June of 1836 it became the first street in the city. Sylvester *Pettibone*, behind a plow pulled by eight oxen, graded the new street to the cheers of early Milwaukeeans. The group then began a Milwaukee tradition of celebrating significant (and sometimes not so significant) events with food or drink. They consumed 30 baskets of champagne to mark the event. The street was platted by Solomon *Juneau* and Morgan L. *Martin* in 1835.

Sylvester Pettibone grades Water Street between Michigan and Clybourn Streets. (Buck's Pioneer History of Milwaukee)

WATERFORD AVENUE

4100 South, between 1200 East and 8200 West

Origin: *Tippecanoe*

Waterford, Wisconsin was likely the inspiration for this name. The Racine county community was apparently named because the Fox River

274

could be forded there. J.V. Quarles and George A. West, both from Racine, named this street in 1892 (see *Plainfield*).

WATER TOWER ROAD

2200 North and 2500 East
Origin: *Northpoint*

This street, which winds down the bluff at the foot of North Avenue, was named in 1994. The road needed a designation for emergency response purposes, and the name was taken from the Northpoint water tower at the top of the bluff.

WAUSAUKEE ROAD

Washington-Ozaukee County border

This name is apparently a misspelling of a contraction of WAShington and OzAUKEE, the two counties it separates. It is spelled Wasaukee in Mequon and Germantown, while Ozaukee County and Milwaukee spell it this way. The city acquired the triangle of land, which is not in Milwaukee County, when a restaurant owner there wanted police and fire protection. Milwaukee, in an expansion mode and willing to provide the protection, annexed its only land in Washington County.

Washington County was named for the country's first President. Ozaukee County was named for the Sauk Indians. Ozaukee is an older spelling of Sauk and means "yellow earth people."

WAVERLY PLACE

1100 East, between 1000 and 1200 North
Origin: *Yankee Hill*

In 1833, a year after Walter Scott's death, the citizens of Greenwich Village in New York City petitioned to name one of their streets Waverly Place. The name was chosen to honor Scott for his "Waverley" novels, a series of romantic stories of England's past. Over the next few decades other cities, including San Francisco, Milwaukee, and St. Paul, followed suit.

Milwaukee's Waverly Place was named by Charles Parker Cole in

1850. It was probably the inspiration for the naming of Northpoint's *Ivanhoe*, *Kenilworth* and *Woodstock* Places, titles of novels in Scott's "Waverley" series, 25 years later.

Waverly Place. (Stadt Milwaukee)

WEBSTER PLACE

2600 North, between 1600 and 2600 East
Origin: *Murray Hill*

Webster Place was known as Summit Place until 1903 when it was changed because it was a duplicate of nearby Summit Avenue. There had been an earlier Webster Place, between Ogden Avenue and Lyon Street, but that was changed in 1896, leaving the city without a Webster.

Since the street was named by ordinance, it's likely that it was named for a prominent Webster. That leaves two candidates; one local, the other national.

Nelson Webster was born in Massachusetts in 1818 and arrived in Milwaukee in 1850. Besides running a wine and liquor business with his brothers, Webster was elected alderman and sheriff before his death in 1866. However, his one term as alderman, two years as sheriff, and relatively short residency in Milwaukee may not have made him prominent enough to have a street named for him.

The more likely candidate is Daniel Webster, (1782-1852), a statesman, lawyer, and orator, who gained fame as a strong supporter of national government. His energetic advocacy of the *Union* made him popular throughout the North, where streets named for Webster are common.

WEDGEWOOD DRIVE, COURT

3600 South, between 6800 and 7600 West
Origin: *Wedgewood*

Wedgewood Drive was named in 1953 as part of Wedgewood Park. This promotional name likely came from Wedgwood, the pottery, spelled without the second ''e'' and made famous by Josiah Wedgwood.

WEIL STREET

1000 East, between 2200 and 3900 North
Origin: *Riverside Park*

Baruch Schleisinger Weil was the biggest Weil around when this street was named for him in 1857. He was a state senator and had the village of Schleisingerville named for him (it was shortened to Slinger during the anti-German sentiment of the World War I era).

Baruch Schleisinger, a Jew, was born in the Alsace region of France in 1802. He took his wife's name and became Baruch Schleisinger Weil before coming to Wisconsin in 1845, where he eventually owned thousands of acres in the Slinger area. His political career, spanning 30 years, was interrupted by scandals involving residency requirements and railroad payoffs with Byron *Kilbourn*. He died in 1893.

Benjamin Weil, a real estate developer active in the late 1800s, has been credited with being the source of this street name. But he was a seven year old living in Baltimore in 1857 when Julius Franke platted the street.

WELLINGTON PLACE

5000 North and 7100 West
Origin: *Long View*

In 1925 the Wellington Park Land Company subdivided Wellington Park and named Wellington Place. Arthur Wellesley, the 1st Duke of Wellington, has had towns, cities, and streets named for him throughout the English-speaking world. Wellington gained fame for defeating Napoleon at Waterloo in 1815. He later served as prime minister of England.

WELLS STREET

800 North, between 1200 East and 5700 West
Origin: *Kilbourntown*

Wells Building. (Bruce's History of Milwaukee)

During Daniel Wells' 67 years in Milwaukee he seemed to be involved in everything. He dealt in lumber, wool, grain, railroads, real estate, banking, insurance, hotels, and roads. Besides these businesses, at one time or another he was a surveyor, farmer, justice of the peace, probate judge, undersheriff, representative to the Territorial Council, and U.S. congressman.

Wells, whose ancestors were New England settlers, was born in Maine in 1808. When he came to Milwaukee in 1835 he was well-to-do, and when he died he was thought to be the richest man in the state. His death in March of 1902, at the age of 93, prevented him from seeing the completion of his Wells Building on Wisconsin Avenue. Wells Street was named in 1835 by Byron *Kilbourn*.

WENTWORTH AVENUE

From 2400 South and 1300 East to 3100 South and 2700 East
Origin: *Bay View*

278

Zebiah Wentworth, who was born in Maine in 1810, settled in the Bay View area with her husband, Elijah *Estes*, in 1835. In 1871 she platted both Estes Street and Wentworth Avenue. She has been credited with naming Bay View. Zebiah and her husband both died in 1887.

WHITAKER AVENUE, COURT

4300 South, between 1100 East and 2700 West
Origin: *City of Cudahy*

As with most of Patrick *Cudahy's* avenues named in 1892, this one was named for someone in the meat industry. Francis Whittaker, born in Ireland in 1810, was the founder of Whittaker and Sons Meatpacking of St. Louis. Whittaker, as both the man and the Cudahy street spell it, has two "t"'s, but Milwaukee incorrectly spells it with only one.

WHITE STREET

1600 South, between 1900 and 2000 West
Origin: *Muskego Way*

White Street was named by a group of investors in 1855. None were named White.

WHITNALL AVENUE

From 100 East and 3300 South to 1600 East and 4400 South
Origin: *Tippecanoe*

Charles (aka Charlie) B. Whitnall was a charter member of the Milwaukee County Park Commission and came to be known as the "Father of the Milwaukee County Parks." Whitnall, who served on the park commission from 1907 to 1947, also had Whitnall Park named for him. A florist, Whitnall originated the service of telegraphing flower orders for delivery in cities throughout the world.

It was probably his work as a socialist, though, that led to the renaming of Chicago Road for Whitnall in 1926. The change occurred in Bay View where socialism was strong. A few years earlier one of its streets had been renamed for social reformer Albert *Brisbane*, and it had a socialist alderman, Paul *Gauer*. Whitnall's tax payment reforms as the city's socialist treasurer and his establishment of a cooperative bank for the benefit of wage earners earned him support among Social-Democrats in Bay View. Whitnall was born in Milwaukee in 1859 and died in 1949.

WICK PLACE

2600 South, between 6700 and 6800 West
Origin: *Fairview*

Paul Wick, born about 1890, was a prominent real estate dealer in Milwaukee beginning in the 1920s. He was elected alderman from 1932 to 1936. Wick Place was named by ordinance in 1951. Paul Wick Playfield on Vliet Street was also named for him.

WILBUR AVENUE, COURT

3700 South, between 1800 East and 9700 West
Origin: *Saveland Park*

Wilbur Avenue was named as part of John *Saveland*'s Lincoln Park Subdivision in 1888. We don't know why he named this street Wilbur.

WILLIAMS STREET

800 East, between 2300 and 2600 South
Origin: *Bay View*

Joseph Williams, who settled in the Bay View area in 1836, was born in Amsterdam, New York in 1795. When the Milwaukee Iron Company moved into the area, Williams began subdividing his farm and platted this street in 1870. He died in 1877.

WILLIS PLACE

9500 West and 3800 North
Origin: *Golden Valley*

In 1930 a short portion of 93rd Street was changed to Willis Place. The reason for the name is unknown.

WILSON DRIVE

5400 North and 1300 West
Origin: *Village of Whitefish Bay*

Thomas Woodrow Wilson, the 28th President of the United States, was born in Virginia in 1856. Wilson, who was in office from 1913 to 1921, died early in 1924. The Village of Whitefish Bay passed an ordinance later that year to lay out this street and to name it Wilson Drive.

WILSON STREET

2400 South, between 300 and 500 East
Origin: *Bay View*

The intersection of Wilson and *Graham* Streets is one of two intersections in the city where the meeting streets are named for one person. As one of Milwaukee's first attorneys, Wilson Graham's name appears on many of the city's subdivision maps.

Graham served as lawyer for the survivors of Joseph *Williams*, an early settler in the area. Williams' son, Sanford, subdivided part of the family land and named Graham Street in 1879. Four years later Joseph's widow, Catherine, developed more of the farm and named Wilson Street (see *Alexander, Nicholas*).

WINCHESTER STREET

600 East, between 2100 and 2300 South
Origin: *Bay View*

In 1867, when Ammi R.R. Butler chose the name for this street, the name Winchester was well known. At Winchester, Virginia, in the fall of 1864, Civil War General Philip *Sheridan* rallied his fleeing Union troops and turned a defeat into a major moral victory. "Sheridan's Ride," a poem memorized and recited by America's schoolchildren for the next fifty years, popularized the names of Sheridan and Winchester. To mark the event, Sheridan had also changed the name of his horse to Winchester.

Ammi Butler, Milwaukee mayor from 1876 to 1878, attempted to memorialize heavy Union casualties at the Battle of Kennesaw Mountain by naming another street in this subdivision Kennesaw Street. However, it was later changed to *Woodward*.

The final charge at Winchester. (Library of Congress)

WINDERMERE COURT

2900 East and 3300 North
Origin: *Downer Woods*

The scenery around Windermere, the largest lake in England, inspired poets William Wordsworth and Samuel Coleridge. Windermere apparently also inspired Paula Uihlein, who named this court in 1928.

WINDLAKE AVENUE

From 1700 South and 700 West to 2700 South and 1900 West

This 1840s South Side road led to Wind Lake, Wisconsin. The lake, and the community near it, are supposed to have been named for the winds that swept across it.

WINDSOR PLACE

2100 North, between 1500 and 2000 East
Origin: *Northpoint*

Windsor, England, with its castle and royalty, has been the source of names throughout America since 1637, when a Connecticut town was named for it. Third Street was changed to Windsor Place in 1875.

WINFIELD AVENUE

6300 North, between 7700 and 9000 West
Origin: *Menomonee River Hills East*

The name Winfield was probably chosen for its promotional value. This street was named in 1954.

WINNEBAGO STREET

1200 North, between 700 and 1100 West
Origin: *Kilbourntown*

Their Algonquin-speaking neighbors gave the Winnebago their name. It means "dirty" or "foul-smelling," and does not refer to the people themselves, but to the smell of saltwater. The former home of the Winnebago was on the shores of Hudson Bay, a large body of saltwater. Winnebago Street first appears on Byron *Kilbourn*'s village map of 1835.

WINONA LANE

1700 West, between 1900 and 2000 South
Origin: *Muskego Way*

Winona was a Sioux Indian name usually given to the firstborn daughter. After the 1881 poem "Winona" by H.L. Gordon, the name came into general use as a woman's name. This short diagonal street, formerly called 13th Avenue, was renamed Winona Lane in 1926.

WISCONSIN AVENUE

700 North, between 1000 East and 9500 West
Origin: *Juneautown*

Wisconsin, the state, is named for the river flowing through it into the Mississippi. It's from an Indian language, although which one is not known, and its meaning, with many interpretations and spellings, is uncertain. The street name was chosen by Solomon *Juneau* and Morgan L. *Martin* in 1835 for one of the city's original streets.

Wisconsin Street ran through Juneautown between Lake Michigan and the Milwaukee River for nearly a century. On the other side of the river the street was named Spring Street when the neighboring Kilbourntown was laid out. Spring Street was named for springs in that area.

In 1876 Spring Street was changed to Grand Avenue, which it remained until the street renaming program of the 1920s, which recommended that the name be the same on both sides of the river. Grand Avenue merchants, like their Kilbourntown predecessors, wanted no part of Wisconsin Street, fearing that a less prestigious address would cost them business. Over their objections the street was renamed Wisconsin in 1926, although, perhaps to mollify them, the commonplace suffix ''Street'' was replaced by the more desirable ''Avenue.''

Facade of the Marc Plaza Hotel at 5th Street and Wisconsin Avenue.

WOOD AVENUE

6700 South, between 1700 and 2000 West
Origin: *College Heights*

284

Wood Avenue was named as part of the College Heights Subdivision platted in 1958. The pleasing name was selected by the city. Many city streets were given Wisconsin placenames during this era, so the name may have been inspired by Wood, Wisconsin.

WOODLAWN COURT

700 North, between 4700 and 5000 West
Origin: *Story Hill*

Woodlawn Court was named by the *Story* family in 1911.

WOODSTOCK PLACE

2300 North, between 2100 and 2300 East
Origin: *Northpoint*

"Woodstock," published in 1826, was one of Walter Scott's "Waverley" novels. In 1875, Fourth Street was renamed for the romantic story (see *Waverly*).

WOODWARD STREET

700 East, between 2100 and 2400 South
Origin: *Bay View*

Joseph *Williams* platted Woodward Street in 1870 when he laid out his farm for residential development. Why he chose the name Woodward is not known.

WOOLWORTH AVENUE

6300 North, between 4300 and 5700 West
Origin: *Graceland*

The offices of the F.W. Woolworth variety stores, then known as five-and-ten cent stores, were at the corner of Hopkins and Industrial Streets. In 1956 Industrial Street was renamed Woolworth Avenue.

WREN AVENUE, COURT

5900 North, between 3300 and 12300 West
Origin: *Thurston Woods*

Wrens can be found in parks and yards throughout the city. With *Bobolink* and *Oriole* already in the neighborhood, Wren was added in 1949.

WRIGHT STREET

2500 North, between 1300 East and 6100 West
Origin: *Harambee*

Timothy Wright named this street as part of Wright's Addition platted in 1856.

WYOMING PLACE

2200 North, between 2300 and 2500 East
Origin: *Northpoint*

While we associate Wyoming with a western state, the name comes from a valley in Pennsylvania where settlers were massacred during the Revolutionary War. English, Tories, and Iroquois Indians slaughtered the wives and children of rebels off fighting elsewhere. The name was kept alive throughout the 19th century in a poem by Scottish poet Thomas Campbell, called "Gertrude of Wyoming." Wyoming shows up on Wisconsin maps as the name of two towns and a valley, and as the name of many of its cities' streets and avenues.

Wyoming Place took the place of Seventh Street by ordinance in 1875. The word means "great plains" in the Delaware Indians' language.

YOUNG STREET

300 East and 100 North/South
Origin: *Historic Third Ward*

David Parker Young, born in Scotland in 1871, owned the land that this short street cut through to connect Milwaukee Street and Pittsburgh Avenue. Young, who settled in Milwaukee when he was twenty years old, was president of the Northwestern Transfer Company which had its headquarters and stables nearby.

Before coming to Milwaukee, Young was a cowboy near the Mexican border, and his first job in the city was caring for horses. An adventurous man, he was the first person to drive a car from Milwaukee to Green Bay. This street was named Young Street by ordinance in 1929.

YUBA STREET

7100 West and 6600 North
Origin: *Menomonee River Hills East*

Yuba, Wisconsin and Yuba, California are named for the Yuba Indians, who lived in north central California, where a county and a river are also named for them. When this street was named in 1958, the City Engineer's Office had responsibility for naming new streets. At that time the department was naming streets for cities in both the western United States and Wisconsin. Since most of the other streets in this subdivision are named for western cities, this street is probably the namesake of the California community rather than the Wisconsin city.

ZELLMAN COURT

6500 South, between 1300 and 1400 West
Origin: *College Heights*

Jewell Court was renamed Zellman Court in 1983. Jerry Zellman was the manager of the Burlington Coat Company, the business that this short street leads to, before his death.

Milwaukee Neighborhood Maps

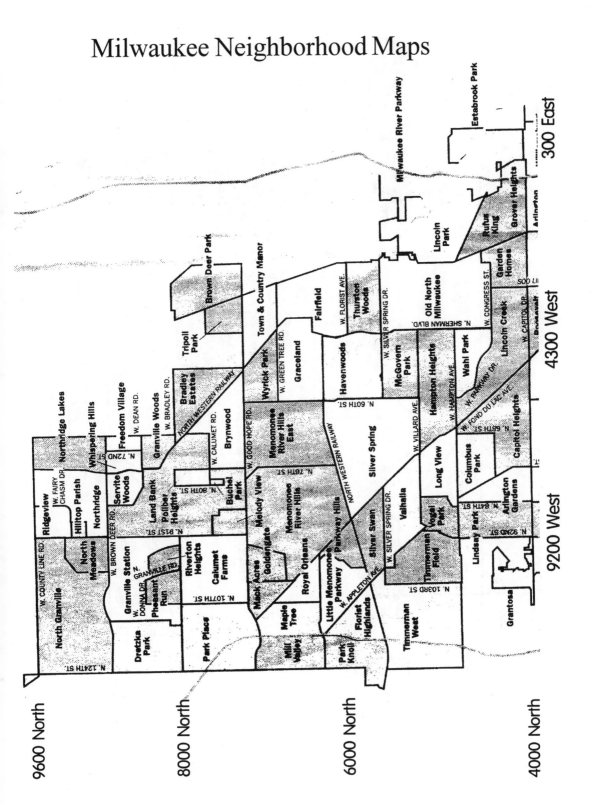

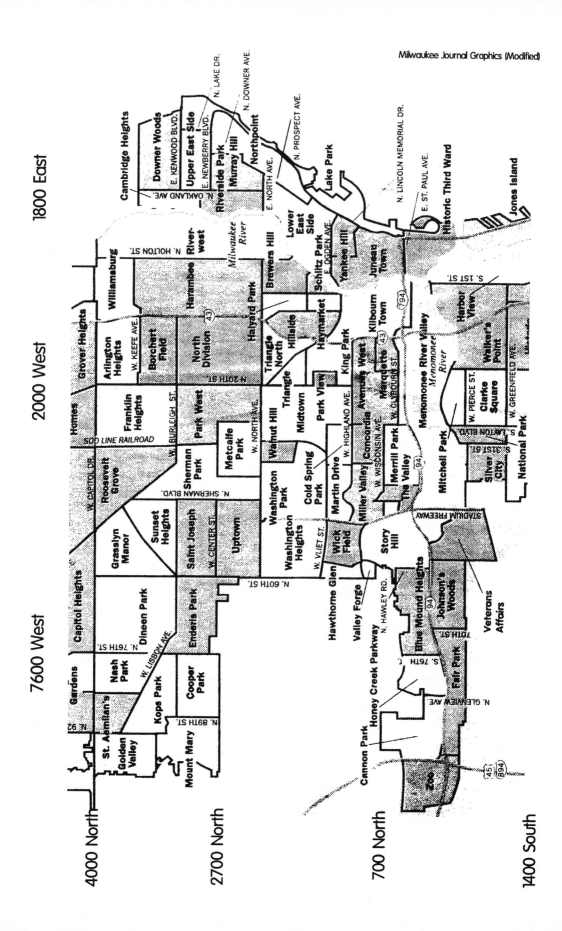

Milwaukee Journal Graphics (Modified)

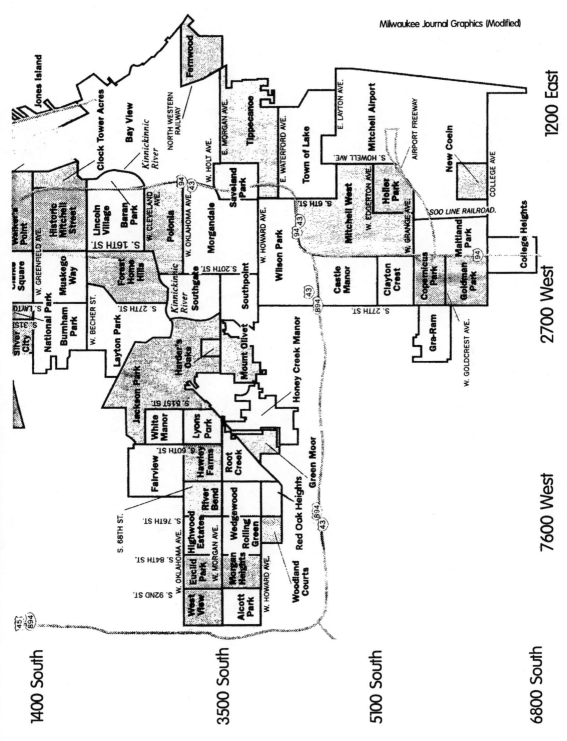

Milwaukee Journal Graphics (Modified)

1400 South

3500 South

5100 South

6800 South

7600 West

2700 West

1200 East

Jones Island

Walker's Point

Clarke Square

Silver City

National Park

Burnham Park

Muskego Way

Historic Mitchell Street

Lincoln Village

Baran Park

Clock Tower Acres

Bay View

Kinnickinnic River

NORTH WESTERN RAILWAY

Fernwood

Tippecanoe

E. MORGAN AVE.

W. HOLT AVE.

W. GREENFIELD AVE.

S. 16TH ST.

W. CLEVELAND AVE.

Pokonia

Morgandale

Saveland Park

W. OKLAHOMA AVE.

Town of Lake

E. WATERFORD AVE.

Mitchell Airport

E. LAYTON AVE.

S. HOWELL AVE.

AIRPORT FREEWAY

New Coeln

COLLEGE AVE

Forest Home Hills

W. BECHER ST.

Layton Park

S. 27TH ST.

Kinnickinnic River

Southgate

S. 20TH ST.

Southpoint

Wilson Park

W. HOWARD AVE.

Mitchell West

W. EDGERTON AVE.

Holler Park

W. GRANGE AVE.

SOO LINE RAILROAD.

Maitland Park

College Heights

Harder's Oaks

Mount Olivet

S. 51ST ST.

Jackson Park

White Manor

Lyons Park

Honey Creek Manor

Castle Manor

Clayton Crest

Copernicus Park

Gra-Ram

Goldman Park

W. GOLDCREST AVE.

S. 27TH ST.

Fairview

S. 60TH ST.

Hawley Farms

Root Creek

Green Moor

S. 68TH ST.

S. 76TH ST.

S. 84TH ST.

S. 92ND ST.

Highwood Estates

River Bend

Red Oak Heights

Euclid Park

Wedgewood

Rolling Green

Morgan Heights

W. MORGAN AVE.

W. OKLAHOMA AVE.

Woodland Courts

W. HOWARD AVE.

West View

Alcott Park

45; 894

S. LAYTO

S. 31ST E

293

SELECTED BIBLIOGRAPHY

Aderman, Ralph M., ed. *Trading Post to Metropolis: Milwaukee County's First 150 Years.* Milwaukee: Milwaukee County Historical Society, 1987.

Austin, H. Russell. *The Milwaukee Story: The Making of an American City.* Milwaukee: The Journal Company, 1946.

Baehr, Carl and Mary Frances Turk. *Bibliography of Milwaukee City Maps.* Milwaukee: 1989.

Baist, G.W. *Baist's Property Atlas of the City of Milwaukee and Vicinity.* Philadelphia: G. Wm. Baist Co., 1896.

Beldon, H. *Illustrated Historical Atlas of Milwaukee County, Wisconsin.* Chicago: H. Beldon and Co., 1876.

Bruce, William George. *History Of Milwaukee, City and County.* Chicago: S.J. Clarke, 1922.

Buck, James S. *Pioneer History of Milwaukee and Milwaukee Under the Charter.* Milwaukee: 1876-1886.

City of Milwaukee. *Uniform Street Numbering System.* Milwaukee: Legislative Reference Bureau, City of Milwaukee, 1929.

_____. *The Charter and Ordinances of the City of Milwaukee.* Milwaukee: Milwaukee Common Council, 1848-.

_____. *Milwaukee Code of Ordinances.* Milwaukee: Milwaukee Common Council, 1896.

_____. *Proceedings of the Common Council of the City of Milwaukee, for the Year Ending...* Milwaukee: The Council, 1847-.

_____. *Commission on House Numbering and Street Nomenclature - Report on Street Name Changes.* Milwaukee: Common Council, City of Milwaukee, May 7 and Dec 9, 1913; Oct 16, 1922.

_____. *Milwaukee Street Name File.* Milwaukee: Legislative Reference Bureau, City of Milwaukee, n.d.

_____. Schwada, J.R. *Installation of New House Numbers and Street Names in Milwaukee*. Milwaukee: City Engineer's Office, 1933.

_____, *Milwaukee Street Name File*. Milwaukee: City Engineer's Office, n.d.

Conard, Howard L., ed. *History of Milwaukee: From Its First Settlement to the Year 1895*. Chicago: American Biographical Publishing Co., n.d.

Corwin, Margaret A. *Street-Naming and Property-Numbering Systems*. New York: American Society of Planning Officials, 1978.

County of Milwaukee. *Plat Maps*. Milwaukee: Register of Deeds Office, 1835-.

Empson, Donald Lawrence. *The Street Where You Live: The Street Names of St.Paul*. St. Paul: Witsend Press, 1975.

Fleckner, John A. and Stanley Mallach, eds. *Guide to Historical Resources in Milwaukee Area Archives*. Milwaukee: Milwaukee Area Archives Group, 1976.

[Flower, Frank A.] *History of Milwaukee, Wisconsin, From Prehistoric Times to the Present Date*. Chicago: Western Historical Co., 1881.

Gard, Robert and L.G. Sorden. *The Romance of Wisconsin Placenames*. Minocqua, WI: Heartland Press, 1988.

Gauer, Paul. *The Gauer Story*. Milwaukee: Paul Gauer, 1956.

Gregory, John Goadby. *History of Milwaukee, Wisconsin*. Chicago: Clarke Publishing Co., 1931.

Harder, Kelsie B., ed. *Illustrated Dictionary of Place Names: United States and Canada*. New York: Facts on File, 1976.

Hayner, Don and Tom McNamee. *Streetwise Chicago: The History of Chicago Street Names*. Chicago: Loyola University Press, 1988.

Koss, Rudolph A. *Milwaukee*. Milwaukee: 1871 (English translation).

Loewenstein, Louis K. *Streets of San Francisco: The Origins of Streets and Place Names*. San Francisco: Lexikos, 1984.

296

Maps of the City of Milwaukee and Milwaukee County. Many street maps from 1835 to the present are available at the Milwaukee Public Library, the Milwaukee County Historical Society and The American Geographical Society Collection, Golda Meir Library.

Milwaukee Journal. Milwaukee. Began publication in 1882.

Milwaukee Sentinel. Milwaukee. Began publication in 1837.

Milwaukee Sentinel Newspaper Index. 1837-1890. At the Milwaukee Public Central Library.

Stennet, W.H. *The History of the Origin of the Place Names Connected with the Chicago and North Western and Chicago, St. Paul, Minneapolis, and Omaha Railways*. Chicago: n.p., 1908.

Still, Bayrd. *Milwaukee: The History of a City*. Madison: State Historical Society of Wisconsin, 1948.

Street Directory of Principal Cities of the United States. Post Office Department, 1908.

Vogel, Virgil J. *Indian Names on Wisconsin's Map*. Madison: University of Wisconsin Press, 1991.

Waterstreet, Darlene. *Biography Index to the Wisconsin Blue Books*. Milwaukee: Badger Infosearch, 1974.

Watrous, Jerome A., ed. *Memoirs of Milwaukee County*. Madison: Western Historical Association, 1909.

Wells, Robert W. *This is Milwaukee*. New York: Doubleday, 1970.

Wright Directory Company. *City of Milwaukee Directory*. Milwaukee: Wright Directory Company, 1880-.

Zimmermann, H. Russell. *The Heritage Guidebook: Landmarks and Historical Sites*. Milwaukee: Heritage Wisconsin Corp., 1976.

INDEX

300

302

Maxwell Place, 172
Mayfair Road, 160, 172
Mayfair (shopping center), 172
Mayflower (ship), 172, *172*
Mayflower Court, 172
McAuley, Raymond R., 173
McAuley Place, 173
McKinley, William, 173
McKinley Avenue, 173
McKinley Boulevard, 173
McKinley Court, 173
Medford (Mass.), 173
Medford (Wis.), 173
Medford Avenue, 78, 173
Meilahn, William O., 234
Meinecke, Adolph, 174
Meinecke, Ferdinand, 174
Meinecke Avenue, 174
Melinda Street, 174-175
Melody Acres Subdivision, 17
Melody View Subdivision, 71, 164, 258
Melvina (Wis.), 175
Melvina Avenue, 47
Melvina Place, 175
Melvina Street, 175
Memphis (Tenn.), 20
Menominee tribe, 175
Menomonee Drive, 261
Menomonee Hotel, 7
Menomonee Park Court, 175
Menomonee River, 176, 227, 250
Menomonee River Hills, 36, 44, 48, 61, 65, 69, 95,
    115, 118, 127, 207, 243, 251
Menomonee River Hills East, 32, 52, 129, 149, 153,
    239, 283, 287
Menomonee River Parkway, 176, 204
Menomonee River Valley, 41, 81
Menomonee Street, 175
Meredith, Eliza Swain, 249
Meredith, George, 165, 176, 249
Meredith, Horatio Samuel, 249
Meredith, John T., 86-87, 176, 249
Meredith, Sarah Ann Swain, 249
Meredith Street, 176
Merrill, Olive E., 198
Merrill, William P., *176*, 176-177
Merrill, Zachara, 168, 198
Merrill Park, 107, 186, 204, 245
Merrill Street, 176-177
Messmer, Sebastian Gebhard, 177
Messmer High School, 177, *177*
Messmer Street, 177
Metcalf, William, 177-178, 198
Metcalf Place, 177-178
Metcalfe Park, 206
Mexican War, 236, 252
Meyers, Sylvia *See* Haas, Sylvia Meyers
Michele Street, 178
Michigan Street, 140, 178
Michigan Territory, 45, 171
Middlemass, Archibald, 178-179
Middlemass Street, 178-179
Midland Drive, 179
Midtown, 266
Mill Court, 179
Mill Place, 179
Mill Road, 23, 179
Mill Valley, 179
Miller, Allyn, 7
Miller, Andrea, 9
Miller, Angela Ava, 9
Miller, Beatrice J. Prause, 20, *20*
Miller, Clarence, 7, 9, 20-21, 87, 133, 178
Miller, Ernest G., 179

Miller, Fred A., 179
Miller, Frederick, 179
Miller, Michele, 178
Miller Brewing Company, 179, *179*
Miller Lane, 179
Miller Valley, 155, 179, 183
Milwaukee (town) *See* Town of Milwaukee
Milwaukee Advertiser, 224
Milwaukee and Fond du Lac Plank Road, 254
Milwaukee and LaCrosse Railroad, 34
Milwaukee Auditorium, 35
Milwaukee Bay, *155*
Milwaukee Bucks, 192
Milwaukee Chess Club, 79
Milwaukee Community Development Corporation, 166
Milwaukee County Courthouse, 33, 59, *59*, 61
Milwaukee County Medical Society, 20
Milwaukee County Park Commission, 279
Milwaukee County Stadium, 246
Milwaukee Gas Company, 60
Milwaukee Iron Company, 51, *129*,153, 200, 280
Milwaukee Journal, 157
Milwaukee Lake (S.D.), 180
Milwaukee News, 136
Milwaukee Orphan Asylum, 239
Milwaukee Proper, 273
Milwaukee River, 180, 226, 274
Milwaukee River Parkway, 150, 180-181, 180
Milwaukee Road (railroad), 233
Milwaukee Sentinel, 140, 187, 235; quoted, 151,
    245
Milwaukee Street, 180, 287
Milwaukee Street Railway Company, 265
Milwaukee Turner Society, 254
Milwaukee Whist Club, 79
Milwaukee Willow Works, 174, *174*
Milwaukie (Ore.), 180
Miner Street, 181
Mineral Point (Wis.), 181, 267
Mineral Road, 181
Mineral Street, 181
Mitchell (S.D.), 182
Mitchell, Alexander, 121, 167, 181-182
Mitchell, Billy, 182
Mitchell, John, 182
Mitchell, Margaret *See* Johnston, Margaret Mitchell
Mitchell, William, 179
Mitchell Highlands Subdivision, 179
Mitchell International Airport, 69, 144, 182, 268
Mitchell Park, 182, 223
Mitchell Park Drive, 83
Mitchell Street, 7, 21, 37, 83, 158, 181-182, 196,
    198, 228
Mitchell West, 91
Mohawk Avenue, 182-183
Mohawk tribe, 130, 183
Moltke Avenue, 183
Monarch Park, 183
Monarch Place, 183
Monarch Stone Quarry Company, 183
Monroe, James, 183-184, 220
Monroe Street, 183-184
Monrovia (Liberia), 184
Monrovia Avenue, 184
Montana Street, 184
Montana Territory, 184
Montreal (Canada), 184
Montreal Street, 184
Montrose (Scotland), 185
Montrose Avenue, 184-185
Moran, Louis, 180
Morgan, Lynn, 162
Morgan, Winfield, 162, 185, *185*
Morgan Avenue, 185, 222

312

Providence Avenue, 218
Pryor, Elizabeth, 218
Pryor, William J., 218
Pryor Avenue, 218, 229
Pryor Avenue well, 218, *218*
Pulaski, Casimir, 218-219
Pulaski Avenue, 161
Pulaski Street, 161, 218-219
Purchas, Dorothy, 73
Purchas, Emma, 73
Purchas, John, 73
Purdue, John, 219
Purdue Street, 219
Purdue University, 219

Quarles, J. V., 275
Quarlles, Caroline, 34
Quincy Avenue, 3, 94, 220
Quincy Court, 220

Racine (Wis.), 144
Rae Avenue, 221
Railroad Avenue, 106
Railroad stations, *233*
Rainbow Ridge Subdivision, 225
Ramee, Marie Louise de la, 272
Ramsey, Thomas, 221
Ramsey Avenue, 221
Randolph Court, 222
Randolph Street, 222
Raskin, Melvin, 221
Raskin, Rae, 221
Ravenswood Subdivision, 116
Ravine Road, *222*, 222
Ray, James Earl, 142
Realty Syndicate of America, 57
Reichert, Conrad K., 222
Reichert, Joseph B., 222
Reichert Brothers Subdivision, 222
Reichert Place, 222
Reinertsen, Robert Christian, 227
Reliance Land Company, 271
Renaming program *See under* Names (origin)
Renee Street, 223
Reservoir Avenue, 100, 223
Reservoir Park, 223
Residences, *23, 55, 136, 268, See also under*
  Names (origin)
Revolutionary War, 261, 273, 286
Reynolds, Thomas, 223
Reynolds Place, 223
Rhode Island, 223
Rhode Island Avenue, 223
Richards, Daniel Hamilton, 224
Richards Street, 224, 233
Richardson, Ray, *224*, 224
Richardson Place, 224
Richmond Avenue, 225
Richter, August, Jr., 121
Ridge Court, 225
Ring, Hannah, 225
Ring Street, 93, 225
Rio (Wis.), 225
Rio Street, 225
Ripon (England), 226
Ripon (Wis.), 226
Ripon Place, 226
River Bend Drive, 226
River Bend Subdivision, 226
River Hills (Wis.), 29
River Street, 77
River Trail Drive, 227
Riverboat Cocktail Lounge and Restaurant, 226
Riverboat Road, 226

Riverside (Calif.), 108
Riverside High School, 100
Riverside Park, 20, 56, 97, 189, 190, 203, 225,
  277
Riverside Place, 226
Riverton Heights, 9
Riverwest, 15, 31, 38, 46, 74, 93, 100, 101, 110,
  122, 126, 138, 210, 227, 241, 244, 271
Roadsmeet Street, 227
Roberts Street, 227
Robinson, Chauncey Clark, 227-228, 272
Robinson, Mary Alexander, 228
Robinson Avenue, 227-228
Robinson Street, 32
Rochelle Avenue, 228
Roddis, Edward, 254
Roddis, Thomas, 254
Roddis, William H., 257
Roder Court, 228
Rogers, Daniel G., 37, 228
Rogers, George, 12
Rogers, Henry, 12
Rogers, James H., 217
Rogers Street, 228
Rohr, John H., 229
Rohr Avenue, 228-229
Rolling Green, 15
Ronalds, Hugh, 5
Roosevelt, Theodore, 173, 229, *229*
Roosevelt Drive, 229
Roosevelt Grove, 125, 225, 229, 237
Root Creek, 112, 166, 190
Rosedale Avenue, 229
Rosedale Subdivision, 72
Royal Orleans, 20, 28, 133
Royall Place, 229-230
Ruby Avenue, 230
Rufus King, 58, 88
Rusk, Jeremiah, *230*, 230-231
Rusk Avenue, 230-231
Ruskin, John, 231
Ruskin Court, 231
Ruskin Street, 231
Russell, Thomas, 231
Russell Avenue, 51, 231, 232

Sacred Heart Church, 35
St. Aemilian's, 258
St. Alban's Episcopal Church, *249*
St. Andrew's Society, 179, 186
St. Clair, Arthur, 232
St. Clair Street, 232
St. Clare, 232
St. Francis (Wis.), 4, 76, 153, 253, 257, 268
St. Francis Heights Subdivision, 4
St. Francis Seminary, 253, 268
St. Lawrence Seaway Council, 34
St. Lawrence Street, 232
St. Monica Catholic Church, 233
St. Paul Avenue, 232-233
St. Paul Road, 233
St. Paul's Episcopal Church, 91
Salem (Wis.), 233
Salem Street, 233
Sampson, B. J., 105, 167, 186
Sampson, Harold, 105, 167, 186
Sampson, Harry E., 115
Sanderson, James, 198
Santa Monica Boulevard, 233-234
Sarasota (Fla.), 234
Sarasota Place, 234
Sarnow, Christian, 234
Sarnow Street, 234
Saveland, John, 234-235, 280

314

315

Whitnall Avenue, 106, 279-280
Whitnall Park, 279
Whittaker, Francis, 279
Whittaker and Sons Meatpacking, 279
Wichman, Gerald, 133
Wichman, Margaret, 133
Wick, Paul, 280
Wick Field, 8, 194, 228
Wick Place, 280
Wiersum, John, 79, 205
Wilbur Avenue, 280
Wilbur Court, 280
Wild, Charles, 160, 208
Williams, Catherine, 102, 281
Williams, Joseph, 58, 123, 153, 156, 216, 280, 281, 285
Williams, Roger, 218
Williams, Sanford, 74, 102, 281
Williams Street, 280
Williamsburg, 175, 265
Williamsburg Heights Subdivision, 15, 89
Willis Place, 280
Willow Street, 157
Wilmann, Augustus, 259
Wilson, Thomas Woodrow, 281
Wilson, Woodrow, 32
Wilson Drive, 32, 281
Wilson Park, 138, 160, 253
Wilson Street, 102, 281
Winchester Street, 281-282
Wind Lake (Wis.), 159, 282
Windermere Court, 282
Windlake Avenue, 282
Windsor (England), 283
Windsor Place, 283
Wine Street, 8
Winfield Avenue, 61, 283
Winnebago Street, 283
Winnebago tribe, 283
"Winona", 283
Winona Lane, 283
Wisconsin Avenue, 140, 208, 284
Wisconsin Land and Realty Exchange, 81
Wisconsin Land Company, 162
Witte, R. S., 185
Woeher, Eugene L., 191
Woelky, Bernhard, 24
Wolf, William H., 66
Wolf and Davidson, 66
Wood (Wis.), 285
Wood Avenue, 284-285
Woodlawn Court, 285
Woodstock, 285
Woodstock Place, 276, 285
Woodward Street, 282, 285
Woolworth, F. W., 285
Woolworth Avenue, 285
Wootsch, Herman, 7
Wordsworth, William, 282
World War I, 11, 183, 277
Wren Avenue, 286
Wren Court, 286
Wright, Timothy, 286
Wright Street, 286
Wright's Addition, 286
Wyoming Place, 286
Wyrick Park, 26

Yankee Hill, 144, 196, 217, 275
York Street, 44
Young, David Parker, 287
Young Street, 287
Yuba (Calif.), 287
Yuba (Wis.), 287

Yuba Street, 149, 287-288

Zellman, Jerry, 289
Ziegler, George, 4, 257
Zimmermann, Lynne, 162
Zimmermann, Mary, 162
Zimmermann, Val, 162
Zingan and Braun's Fairfield Subdivision, 84

317